WITHDRAWN
WRIGHT STATE UNIVERSITY LIBRARIES

Ensuring Intellectual Freedom and Access to Information in the School Library Media Program

Helen R. Adams

Foreword by Dr. Dianne McAfee Hopkins

To ~~Marjorie~~

For all the memories.

Helen

D1501806

LIBRARIES
U N L I M I T E D
A Member of the Greenwood Publishing Group
Westport, Connecticut • London

EDUCATIONAL RESOURCE CENTER
COLLEGE OF EDUCATION & HUMAN SERVICES
WRIGHT STATE UNIVERSITY

Library of Congress Cataloging-in-Publication Data

Adams, Helen R., 1943-
  Ensuring intellectual freedom and access to information in the school library media program /
Helen R. Adams; foreword by Dianne McAfee Hopkins.
    p. cm.
  Includes bibliographical references and index.
  ISBN 978-1-59158-539-8 (alk. paper)
  1. School libraries—Censorship—United States. 2. Freedom of information—United
States. I. Title.
  Z675.S3A219   2008
  027.80973—dc22   2008016753

British Library Cataloguing in Publication Data is available.

Copyright © 2008 by Helen R. Adams
Chapter 2 Copyright © by Mary Minow and Helen R. Adams

All rights reserved. No portion of this book may be
reproduced, by any process or technique, without the
express written consent of the publisher.

Library of Congress Catalog Card Number: 2008016753
ISBN: 978-1-59158-539-8

First published in 2008

Libraries Unlimited, 88 Post Road West, Westport, CT 06881
A Member of the Greenwood Publishing Group, Inc.
www.lu.com

Printed in the United States of America

The paper used in this book complies with the
Permanent Paper Standard issued by the National
Information Standards Organization (Z39.48–1984).

10 9 8 7 6 5 4 3 2 1

At the time of publication, the American Library Association website is being redesigned, and
URL's in this book may change as a result. The author and publisher regret any inconven-
ience to readers. A list of updated Web addresses for resources will appear on the Libraries
Unlimited website on a periodic basis.

To my husband Ed, who has always supported my projects, and to Jake, the German shepherd who faithfully stayed with me throughout hours of writing.

To all who protect students' First Amendment right to receive information in libraries.

Contents

Foreword

School librarianship is one of the most rewarding professions, in part because it provides the unique opportunity to work with all of the faculty and students in a school. What our youth learn at school is very important for their lives as adults and the societal contributions that they will make. Who decides what learning resources are available to students in school? What leadership should the school library media specialist provide? What is the school principal's authority? What role do teachers have? What can school boards mandate? What role do parents have? What decisions can youth make for themselves?

These important questions are among those that form the basis of Helen Adams' examination of intellectual freedom issues from a school library media perspective. The term "intellectual freedom" implies the freedom of intellect or the ability to think as one chooses. From the library media standpoint, the word "access" is an appropriate synonym. One of the most important responsibilities of library media professionals is to promote access to information for students in the school. It's easy to say, but it can be hard to implement.

Ensuring Intellectual Freedom and Access to Information in the School Library Media Program focuses on access concerns, including challenges to materials. But Adams understands that access is about much more than challenges. Access is also about staffing, location of materials, library budgets, overdue fines, resource format, Internet filters, language barriers, and treatment of students with disabilities. Student access is impacted by all of these areas and more. In this book, intellectual freedom is considered in its broadest sense.

Because a library media specialist is likely to be the single library media professional in the school, the library media specialist's leadership in intellectual freedom is especially important. Material selection, privacy, censorship, the Internet, advocacy, and the First Amendment rights of all students, including those with disabilities, are areas about which the school library media specialist must be articulate. *Ensuring Intellectual Freedom and Access to Information in the School Library Media Program* will provide library media specialists with essential core knowledge to advocate on behalf of all students in their schools.

There will be times when a library media specialist will need to defend students' intellectual freedom rights. At these times, s/he needs to seek and receive support. Support enables the library media specialist to provide important leadership in ensuring the rights of all students, regardless of school level. Library media specialists will find support in many ways. They find support in official statements, interpretations, and guidelines from professional associations at local, state, and national levels. They find support from professional colleagues, especially those with practical suggestions and experience. They will find support in professional development opportunities and college classes. They also find support through their knowledge and application of state and national laws as well as litigation outcomes.

Ensuring Intellectual Freedom and Access to Information in the School Library Media Program will be another vital source of information and support. While school library media specialists will find this book to be especially valuable, it will also be an eye-opener for the teacher, the school principal, the school board member, and even the parent who seeks to understand more about intellectual freedom and schools. And because of the book's emphasis on the Internet, the technology coordinator will find value in seeing how Internet resources fit within the intellectual freedom scope of the school library media center. College and university library media educators will find this book a valuable tool in teaching. It offers many opportunities to ponder important questions through discussions, role plays, and professional development opportunities.

Adams places a special emphasis on the school principal. As my research has shown, as the school's administrator, the principal sets the tone for how a challenge to material is dealt with and determines whether the established policy is followed. The school principal may also be the person who challenges the appropriateness of materials, and because of his/her authority, may be most likely to expect that challenged material will be removed.

In addition to the principal focus, the voices of experienced professionals are clearly evident throughout the book. Adams understands that library media specialists find experiences shared by other professionals to be invaluable. Whether they are speaking of practical options to achieve objectives or of their own soul-searching in making the right decision in a challenging time, these professionals bring a welcome sense of understanding and support.

Finally, Helen Adams brings her own reflections, grounded in professional literature and research, as a school library media specialist in a rural Wisconsin community. She brings insights as a district-level library media and technology coordinator as well as intellectual freedom workshop leader. She brings insights from other books and articles that she has written on policy development, privacy, and the Internet. She draws upon more than 25 years of professional leadership as president of two state associations, as well as the national president of the American Association of School Librarians. Adams draws upon her numerous interactions with other librarians as well as students that she teaches in university distance-education classes. For all of these reasons, Helen Adams demonstrates clearly the importance of intellectual freedom in school library media centers.

Whether you are in a public school, a parochial school, or an independent school, this book will be of value. Whether you are at the elementary level, middle school level, high school level, or a combination thereof, this book is important. Whether you are in an urban, suburban, or rural community, or whether you are a novice or a seasoned professional, there will be important information within these covers. You will also turn to this book for additional sources of information and relevant court litigation results.

Regardless of your background, you will be informed, updated, and challenged by this book. You will be inspired to articulate the value of intellectual freedom for us all, but especially for youth. You will know where support and allies are. You will find examples that are applicable to your circumstances, and you will learn how others handled similar situations. You will marvel, as I did, that Helen Adams understands the questions and issues so well, and the gray areas that complicate them. Adams gives a caring, human face to the importance of intellectual freedom, and she has made us want to persevere for youth, even in this complex world.

Dr. Dianne McAfee Hopkins
Professor Emerita
School of Library and Information Studies
University of Wisconsin–Madison

Acknowledgments

No one enters a substantial writing project without the assistance and support of many individuals. I want to acknowledge the consultation and expertise offered by:

- Public and private school library media specialists and technology coordinators, administrators, parents, and school board members both named and anonymous who contributed/told their stories
- Dr. Dianne McAfee Hopkins, professor emerita, School of Library and Information Studies, University of Wisconsin–Madison for providing the Foreword
- Mary Minow, attorney, consultant, and author for her legal expertise
- Award-winning authors Katherine Paterson and Suzanne Fisher Staples
- Megan Schliesman, a librarian, at the Cooperative Children's Book Center, School of Education, University of Wisconsin–Madison
- Ginny Moore Kruse, director emerita of the Cooperative Children's Book Center, School of Education, University of Wisconsin–Madison
- Debbie Abilock, longtime independent school library media specialist, consultant, and author
- Carin Bringelson, information manager at TeachingBooks
- Jolen Neuman, school library media specialist and online instructor, Mansfield University
- Catherine Beyers, Southern Bluffs Elementary School, Lacrosse, Wisconsin, and online instructor, Mansfield University
- Neah Lohr, former director of the Instructional Media and Technology Team, Wisconsin Department of Public Instruction
- Marie Kelsey, professor and program director of the Educational Media and Technology Program at The College of St. Scholastica, Duluth, Minnesota

- Robert Bocher, technology consultant with the Wisconsin Department of Public Instruction's Division for Libraries, Technology, and Community Learning

- Cheryl A. Adams, Dr. Eric P. Hartvig, and Kathi Schultz, Marathon County Special Education, Wausau, Wisconsin

- Kate Bugher, education consultant, Instructional Media and Technology Team, Wisconsin Department of Public Instruction

- Staff of the New London Public Library, New London, Wisconsin

- Sharon Coatney, acquisitions editor for Libraries Unlimited

Introduction

This book presents the fundamental ideas that symbolize intellectual freedom in school library media programs. In these pages, *candid voices* articulate intellectual freedom principles and concerns from the public and private school library communities. Their stories range from inspiring to realistic to humorous to sad. The majority of the library media specialists and technology staff who share their anecdotes and observations are identified by their first names and geographic region only, allowing them the freedom to be as open as possible without fear of retaliation. Unless otherwise identified, the individual being quoted is employed in a public school.

The chapters that follow will take readers from principles and professional association policy statements to realistic strategies and recommendations. Whether a library media specialist in the field or a student in a graduate or undergraduate library and information studies program, readers will find both practical information and advice to *complement* the concepts found in the American Library Association's *Intellectual Freedom Manual.*

Mary Minow, an attorney, consultant, and former librarian and library trustee in California, brings vital legal knowledge to this work. She is the coauthor with Tomas Lipinski of *The Library's Legal Answer Book* (ALA Editions 2003) and writes a blog on library law (http://blog.librarylaw.com). Mary coauthored Chapter 2, "The First Amendment in School Library Media Programs," and provided detailed information on important First Amendment court decisions impacting minors using school library media centers.

This book does not dispense legal advice. Instead, it seeks to educate library media professionals about the impact of the First Amendment, federal and state law, and court decisions on minors using libraries in schools. As the courts and legislatures work, laws and their interpretations are constantly changing. Readers with specific legal questions about local situations should seek the services of a qualified, licensed attorney.

Each chapter can stand on its own within the field of intellectual freedom, but together the nine chapters present a comprehensive resource for those working with youth in public and private schools.

Chapter 1 defines intellectual freedom, its relationship to the school library media program, and the role of the school library media specialist as guardian. It emphasizes that applying intellectual freedom concepts to real-life situations may not be easy and explores the idea that support for intellectual freedom is seldom black and white but rather nuanced in shades of gray.

Chapter 2 discusses how minors' First Amendment rights may be different or limited, depending on where the individual is exercising the right of free speech—a public or private school classroom, a public or private school library, or a public library. It emphasizes that school library media specialists and other educators use case law to learn how courts have ruled in cases involving minors' First Amendment rights and to interpret local school and school library situations. The text concludes with a table of court cases illustrating the progression of minors' First Amendment rights in school and public libraries.

Chapter 3 supplies information on creating a materials selection policy and its importance in maintaining a collection that meets the information and recreation needs of its patrons. It explores self-censorship, administrative intervention, and purchase of books to support computerized reading management programs. It briefly examines providing resources to meet the needs of multilingual students for whom English is a second language, stocking multicultural resources that reflect a community's ethnic minorities, and the addition of graphic novels.

Chapter 4 describes restrictions minors face in using school library media program materials based on age, grade level, or reading level; economic barriers such as late book fines, damaged or lost book fees, or other library fees; and parental limitations on children's reading choices. Students' First Amendment right to read is also affected by the lack of access to the services of a school library media specialist, up-to-date library resources, and an accessible facility.

Chapter 5 examines privacy and confidentiality in the school library media program in the context of minors' rights under state library records laws and the applicability of the Family Educational Rights and Privacy Act (FERPA) to school library records. Other topics include student expectations of privacy, the impact of technology, age and privacy rights, when violating a student's privacy may be necessary, records retention, and privacy-related policies.

Chapter 6 considers challenges to school library media program resources and the role of the school library professional. "Challenging" topics include considering the rationale for internal and external attempts to remove or restrict school library media program resources, preparing for a challenge, handling an oral or written complaint, managing the reconsideration process, working with the media, acknowledging that some challenges do succeed, and exploring the "gray areas" of censorship.

Chapter 7 discusses federal and state filtering legislation and the effect of filtering on access to information. It lays out more than a dozen strategies not involving filtering that a school library media specialist may employ to advocate for use of the Internet in an educationally sound manner and to ensure students' access to legal information. Blogs, wikis, and other social technologies are portrayed as *another format in which to access and receive information,* and as such, library staff and other educators must protect students' First Amendment right to use them.

Chapter 8 explores access to the library media center facility, its resources, and services for students with physical, cognitive, and learning disabilities. The chapter introduces provisions of three key federal laws—the Rehabilitation Act, the Individuals with Disabilities Education Act, and the Americans with Disabilities Act—that support students with disabilities. It examines common barriers to access, such as insufficient staff knowledge, physical impediments, incomplete collections, inaccessible library website and electronic resources, and inadequate technology. The importance of collaboration between special education staff and the library media specialist is emphasized.

Chapter 9 urges library media specialists to advocate for intellectual freedom on the basis of its being essential to democracy and suggests ways to educate and build common ground with administrators, teachers, school board members, students, parents, and the local community. It provides ideas for promoting school and public library collaboration to increase access to information and develop lifelong learners. It also describes the assistance and support available from the ALA Office for Intellectual Freedom, AASL, and the Freedom to Read Foundation.

The Appendices include the text of the *Library Bill of Rights* and the *Code of Ethics for the American Library Association* (Appendix A), an annotated list of Pro-First Amendment Organizations (Appendix B), compelling statements about censorship by authors Harry Mazer, Suzanne Fisher Staples, and Katherine Paterson (Appendix C), and lesson plans emphasizing the right to read (Appendix D).

At the time of publication, the American Library Association website is being redesigned, and URL's in this book may change as a result. The author and publisher regret any inconvenience to readers. A list of updated Web addresses for resources will appear on the Libraries Unlimited website on a periodic basis. The ALA's interpretations of the *Library Bill of Rights* and other statements supporting intellectual freedom are reviewed periodically for possible revision, and new interpretations are added as needed. Revisions of these documents will also be posted on the Libraries Unlimited website as they occur.

What Is Intellectual Freedom in a School Library Media Program?

A democratic society depends upon an informed and educated citizenry.[1]

—Thomas Jefferson

Defining Intellectual Freedom

"Intellectual freedom" is a term encompassing the core beliefs of librarians relating to intellectual and physical access to information, First Amendment liberties, and the right to privacy in using library facilities, resources, and services. According to the American Library Association (ALA), "Intellectual freedom is the right of every individual to both seek and receive information from all points of view without restriction."[2] In fact, intellectual freedom is one of the 11 core values of the profession articulated by the ALA.

U.S. Supreme Court Justice Potter Steward said he could not define pornography but knew it when he it saw it. Similarly, school library media specialists *know* intellectual freedom when they see it. The spirit of intellectual freedom pervades the library media center when students:

- enjoy the right to read and borrow resources free from scrutiny
- select books and other materials, without constraints based on age, grade level, or reading level
- find materials and information representing diverse points of view
- are <u>not</u> required to request materials on "controversial topics" from a restricted area
- ask reference questions without being cross-examined about why the information is needed

- search Internet sites without encountering over-blocking of legal information
- utilize social technologies [blogs, wikis, and others] to complete assignments and share creative expression
- obtain materials through interlibrary loan services
- find the facility, materials, and services meet the needs of *all students* including those with physical, cognitive, and learning disabilities
- are <u>not</u> barred from borrowing or using library materials because of overdue book fines, assessments for damaged materials, or replacement costs for lost materials
- trust their library use and records are kept confidential by staff
- possess the information and technology literacy skills needed to be effective users of information
- learn about their First Amendment rights in the school library media center

The ALA *Intellectual Freedom Manual* states that intellectual freedom exists when there is "an equal commitment to the right of unrestricted access to information and ideas regardless of the communication medium used."[3] Unfortunately, as a result of the Children's Internet Protection Act (CIPA), students and staff in many schools are not afforded free access to legal information on the Internet. CIPA requires "technology protection measures" to be used, and it is difficult to fulfill the promise of intellectual freedom when filtering software arbitrarily blocks educationally useful websites and legal information without explanation.

The Library Bill of Rights *and School Library Media Programs*

After the First Amendment, the ALA *Library Bill of Rights* is the foremost document for school library media specialists. Reprinted in Appendix A, the policy statement makes a forceful case for intellectual freedom in *all* libraries. It offers special protections to minors using libraries when it affirms that "A person's right to use a library should not be denied or abridged because of origin, *age*, background, or views."[4] The word "age" was added in 1967 and reaffirmed in 1996 to assert the rights of children and young adults while using libraries and their collections.[5]

The *Library Bill of Rights* offers uncompromising guidance to school library professionals. For example, Article II directs library staff to provide "materials and information presenting all points of view."[6] For school library professionals this means selecting materials not only to support the curriculum but also in many libraries, to meet the recreational reading and interests of student patrons. Article III charges librarians to "challenge censorship." This statement is particularly relevant to school library media specialists because the majority of challenges reported to the ALA Office for Intellectual Freedom occur in schools and school libraries.

Beyond the original document, the interpretations of the *Library Bill of Rights* embody concepts related to school libraries. Two of the interpretations, "Access to Resources and Services in the School Library Media Program" and "Free Access to Libraries for Minors," articulate the responsibilities of school library media specialists in protecting and affirming students' intellectual freedom. Interpretation of the *Library Bill of Rights* are received periodically, and new interpretations are added as needed.

The Code of Ethics *and Intellectual Freedom*

The *Code of Ethics of the American Library Association* provides direction and can be used to clarify decision making, especially in situations that are complex or uncomfortable. Perhaps a principal or administrator is applying pressure to have a book removed without using the district's reconsideration process. Maybe a teacher is asking for a list of books checked out by a specific student. Or a library media specialist may be struggling with his or her own biases when it comes to collecting books on a certain subject, such as homosexuality. In the *Code of Ethics*, statements, such as "We uphold the principles of intellectual freedom and resist all efforts to censor library resources." (Article II),[7] "We protect each library user's right to privacy and confidentiality with respect to information sought or received and resources consulted, borrowed, acquired or transmitted." (Article III),[8] "We distinguish between our personal convictions and professional duties and do not allow our personal beliefs to interfere...." (Article VII),[9] offer a moral framework for school library media specialists in their daily practice. The *Code of Ethics* is reprinted in Appendix A.

Intellectual Freedom and Democracy

Democracy rests on the intellectual freedom of its citizens, young and old. Therefore, every school library media specialist must understand why intellectual freedom is essential to democratic government. Most school library media specialists do not think of themselves as protectors of democracy. However, they are often the only ones who advocate for keeping a book or magazine in the collection when a parent, administrator, or fellow staff member objects to the ideas or images expressed. Most often, they are the sole member of the faculty who understands the unique connections between the First Amendment and minors' rights to seek information freely in a school library media center. In its opening words, *The Freedom to Read*, a joint statement by the ALA and the Association of American Publishers, warns of the constant danger to democracy from those who would censor:

The freedom to read is essential to our democracy. It is continuously under attack. Private groups and public authorities in various parts of the country are working to remove or limit access to reading materials, to censor content in schools, to label "controversial" views, to distribute lists of "objectionable" books or authors, and to purge libraries. These actions apparently rise from a view that our national tradition of free expression is no longer valid; that censorship and suppression are needed to counter threats to safety or national security, as well as to avoid the subversion of politics and the corruption of morals.[10]

Teaching about Intellectual Freedom

According to the 2003 report "Civic Mission of Schools," Americans are disengaging from civil and political institutions, appear less informed about public issues, and are voting in smaller numbers. Voter participation for those ages 18–24 declined substantially since 1972, and only 5 percent of those ages 18–25 say they regularly "follow public affairs."[11] Assessments and surveys show young adults lack knowledge about how the U.S. government operates and the principles of democracy.[12] Because young Americans do not automatically become knowledgeable about citizenship when they reach the age of 18, schools must teach students about their rights and responsibilities as citizens. This is not a new role because 40 state constitutions highlight "civic literacy" and 13 declare "the central purpose of their educational system is to promote good citizenship, democracy, and free government."[13]

In fall 2007 the American Association of School Librarians (AASL) introduced its "Standards for the 21st Century Learner." The latest Standards state: "Learners use skills, resources, and tools to:

- Inquire, think critically, and gain knowledge.
- Draw conclusions, make informed decisions, apply knowledge to new situations, and create new knowledge.
- Share knowledge and participate ethically and productively as members of our democratic society."[14]

The new learning standards from AASL are ideal for integration with academic subjects. They can be used by library media specialists and educators providing instruction in U.S. history, government, and law to teach students the critical thinking, evaluation, and decision-making skills needed by tomorrow's citizens.

Jerome, a library media specialist in Ohio, has made the connection between intellectual freedom and democracy. He states, "I believe that it is imperative to maintain intellectual freedom in school media centers. Schools are training grounds. They help prepare students to assume the roles and responsibilities of citizens that are essential if our democracy is to continue. To deny students the freedom to explore ideas that are of interest to them or to express ideas which hold importance to them, is to deny students the opportunity to become informed and knowledgeable participants in a global society. Students must be prepared to grapple with many complex issues if we are to successfully build a world that is inclusive, harmonious, and tolerant of differences."[15]

Broader Support for Intellectual Freedom

Beyond the *Library Bill of Rights*, the *Code of Ethics*, and *The Freedom to Read*, other associations have taken bold stands for intellectual freedom and against censorship of classroom and library resources and ideas. In 1981 the National Council of Teachers of English (NCTE) published "The Students' Right to Read." In its current version, it states:

> The right to read, like all rights guaranteed or implied within our constitutional tradition, can be used wisely or foolishly.... The right of any individual not just to read but to read whatever he or she wants to read is basic to a democratic society. This right is based on an assumption that the educated possess judgment and understanding and can be trusted with the determination of their own actions.[16]

The International Reading Association (IRA) and the National Council for Social Studies (NCSC) also have unyielding position statements on the selection of reading materials, academic freedom, and the connection between democracy and free access to materials, including those on controversial topics.

The humanities are not the only curricular areas in which censorship is challenged and intellectual freedom supported. For decades the National Science Teachers Association (NSTA) opposed the teaching of "creation science" in science classrooms. In its position statement, "The Freedom to Teach and the Freedom to Learn," the NSTA states:

> As professionals, teachers must be free to examine controversial issues openly in the classroom. The right to examine controversial issues is based on the democratic commitment to open inquiry and on the importance of decision-making involving opposing points of view and the free examination of ideas. The teacher is professionally obligated to maintain a spirit of free inquiry, open-mindedness and impartiality in the classroom. *Informed diversity is a hallmark of democracy to be protected, defended, and valued.*[17] [emphasis added]

Across the core curricula, library media specialists can reach out and base their practice not only on position statements from the library world but also on a solid framework from other professional associations.

The School Library Media Specialist and Intellectual Freedom

What is the role of the school library media specialist in promoting and maintaining a climate of intellectual freedom? According to "Access to Resources and Services in the School Library Program: An Interpretation of the *Library Bill of Rights*," "School library media professionals assume a leadership role in promoting the principles of intellectual freedom within the school by free inquiry."[18] The school library media specialist is the school's *resident expert* on intellectual freedom as it relates to the school library media program—the person with the most knowledge about the uncompromising link between students' free speech rights under the First Amendment and patron use of the library's collection, electronic reference resources, and the Internet. It is the school library media specialist who selects resources reflecting diverse viewpoints and ensures access to them and to materials from other libraries' collections through interlibrary loan. The library professional defends minors' rights to receive ideas and information when a concern is expressed about specific library resources. After a complaint is received, the library media specialist serves as an advisor to the principal during the reconsideration process. S/he provides information to the reconsideration committee, a group formally appointed by an administrator to review a challenged resource. To promote education of students rather than filtering, the library media professional collaborates with teachers to instruct students about evaluation of information on websites and being responsible searchers. In addition, s/he proactively informs the entire school community about minors' rights under the law and the connection between intellectual freedom and democracy.

School library media specialists take responsibility for the intellectual freedom of their students seriously. Candice, a first year school library professional and former journalism teacher in a high school in central Pennsylvania, states, "It is my responsibility to encourage intellectual freedom by providing students with materials that express different viewpoints and ideologies, even when they may not be the popular opinion. The media center must be a place where students feel comfortable to choose what they want to read."[19]

Intellectual Freedom—Shades of Gray

"Intellectual freedom is an ideal that is basic to librarianship. It seems black and white when you are discussing the concept in a classroom setting or reading about it in an article or textbook. Librarians are all champions of the idea in theory. But, the reality of it has so many shades of gray."[20]

Lea, Director of Learning Resources, Texas

Applying intellectual freedom principles to real-life situations in schools and school library media programs is not a simple task. Black-and-white principles do not always translate neatly into clear-cut practices. Unsettling gray areas can emerge on the basis of personal interpretation, experience, and many other factors, from what is stated in policies to the understanding (or lack thereof) and influence of administrators. Here are three examples:

- *Self-censorship or Pre-censorship*: If honest, every school library media specialist will acknowledge struggling with self-censorship, or not selecting for purchase a library resource based on a conscious or unconscious bias. This internal conflict may be rooted in a failure to examine one's personal preferences or prejudices. Or it may be based on fear of selecting a resource on an unsettling topic and anticipating pressures and possible objections from the administration or community. Yet, the *Code of Ethics* asks librarians to "uphold the principles of intellectual freedom," and the *Library Bill of Rights* directs librarians to provide materials on all points of view. Strategies for combating self-censorship are discussed in Chapter 3.

- *Parents' rights*: ALA acknowledges that parents have the right to direct the reading of their child(ren). On the other hand, the First Amendment gives minors the right to read and receive information in a school library media center, and this is a fundamental belief of the library profession. If a parent asks the school library professional to monitor his/her child's reading choices and not allow checkout of books on specific topics, such as holidays or witchcraft, the school library professional faces a conflict between the parent's request and intellectual freedom principles. Chapter 5 discusses strategies the library media specialist can use to inform and work with parents.

- *Personal versus professional beliefs*: In a school climate where protecting the young is emphasized through policies and rules, library media professionals may hold personal beliefs about what is "age appropriate" for children and young adults to read from among materials within the collection. Under their individual belief systems, they want to shield students from making reading choices about anything that is unpleasant and restrict access to resources they perceive to be too mature or controversial for their age. In contrast, Article VII of the *Code of Ethics* instructs the library media specialist not to let personal beliefs interfere with professional duties. Students also have First Amendment rights to receive information and ideas in the media center. The topic of what "is appropriate" for children and young adults to read is discussed in Chapters 4 and 6.

As the quotation from Lea stated, the concepts of intellectual freedom are black and white in a hypothetical discussion but can become gray when applied to day-to-day situations involving the lives of students. School library professionals must realize that there are ranges of solutions that can be considered when they find it impossible to fully uphold the principles of intellectual freedom. Some solutions are closer to and some farther from the ideal. What remains essential is continuing to strive to fulfill professional principles and being aware of each time—and how much—they have been compromised. Otherwise, library media specialists risk losing sight of the principles that should be their guide; ultimately, finding the best course of action when trying to apply the principles of intellectual freedom is among the many challenges a school library professional faces. It is also a fact of life in the media center.

Is Intellectual Freedom Universally Accepted?

Not everyone agrees with the principles of intellectual freedom and the policy statements adopted by the American Library Association and other professional associations. The idea of protecting children from harmful or controversial ideas is seen across our culture. It can be found among individuals acting on their own as well as within established groups.

Based on the tenet that parents should guide the education of their children, organizations on the local, regional, and national level urge parents to scrutinize school library media program collections. For example, Parents Against Bad Books in Schools (PABBIS) welcomes visitors to its website with this message: "You might be shocked at the sensitive, controversial and inappropriate material that can be found in books in K-12 schools. Both in the classroom and library."[21] The group's statement illuminates its purpose, "... to identify some books that might be considered bad and why someone might consider them bad ... [and] ... to provide information related to bad books in schools."[22] Universally labeling specific books as "bad" and seeking to remove them from libraries takes away the individual choice of student patrons and their families.

PABBIS is not the only group targeting resources in school libraries. Focus on the Family, Concerned Women for America, the Traditional Values Coalition, the American Family Association, and others have spoken out against the themes of witchcraft and the occult found in the *Harry Potter* books and tried to have the books removed from school libraries.[23] In December 2001, Pat Robertson, founder of the Christian Coalition, lashed out against "teaching witchcraft in the schools," a reference to *Harry Potter* books.[24] Family Friendly Libraries (FFL) was formed in "response to a proliferation of internet pornography and age-inappropriate materials in local school and public libraries."[25] FFL supports a "rating system," such as those used by the film, television, music, and video gaming industries to assist library users to learn more about printed material in library collections.[26]

Other Voices of Dissent

In *The Language Police,* author Diane Ravitch gives numerous examples of those across political and ideological spectrums who do not support intellectual freedom and would attempt to censor words, ideas, and topics from textbooks and tests. Individuals and groups often pressure school administrators and library staff to remove certain books or magazines from school curricula and library media centers. There are also internal constraints among some publishers to pre-censor textbooks and children's and young adult fiction before publication to lessen controversy and ensure wide sales across the nation.[27]

Branches of the National Association for the Advancement of Colored People (NAACP) have been vocal in opposing books that they consider either offensive to African American students or erosive of their self-esteem. Published in 1885, Mark Twain's classic novel *The Adventures of Huckleberry Finn* has been a lightning rod. In 1995 a complaint was filed by a local chapter of the NAACP in Kenosha, Wisconsin, citing the book as offensive to African American students. In 1998 the Pennsylvania NAACP called for its removal from reading lists in all Pennsylvania school districts based on racially offensive language.[28] Amid protests from black parents and the NAACP, Harper Lee's *To Kill a Mockingbird* has also been cited as unfit for use in junior high school in Arizona.[29]

Sometimes opposition to specific materials used in schools has a political slant. A science teacher in Washington sparked a district-wide controversy when she planned to show the film "An Inconvenient Truth" to her seventh grade class. Parent complaints against the film as propaganda and showing a single side to the global warming issue caused a moratorium on its showing. Proponents of the film expressed their opinions that the film was scientifically true. Eventually, the school board decided the film could only be shown with written permission from a principal and only when it is "balanced" by alternative views that are approved by a principal and the superintendent.[30]

Attempted censorship can represent opposition to perspectives on historical and cultural events, such as the intense feelings in the Korean community in the United States about *So Far from the Bamboo Grove* by Yoko Kawashima Watkins. The fictional autobiography of an 11-year-old girl who escapes from Korea with her family at the end of World War II has been objected to by some Korean families. Opposition appears to center on two concerns: the book includes subject matter (i.e., rape and violence) not appropriate, in their judgment, for middle school students, and the autobiographical novel only portrays violence perpetrated by Korean soldiers, while not including violence perpetrated by Japanese soldiers against Koreans.[31]

Censorship can also have a cultural and religious basis. Suzanne Fisher Staples' book *Shabanu, Daughter of the Wind* has received criticism from some in the Muslim community both inside and outside the United States. The Islamic Networks Group purports to inform the American public about misconceptions and the beliefs of Islam. This group disagrees with the book's portrayal of an 11-year-old Pakistani girl who is pledged to an older man and will be forced to marry him. They complain that the book "presents an extremely narrow view of a subculture in Pakistan, and reinforces common stereotypes and misconceptions about Islam and Muslims."[32] In addition, complaints of "teaching pornography" because of sexual references have led some schools to either remove this book or add other books as alternatives. Indiana social studies teacher Tim Lax defended the book, intended for children ages 9–12, stating, "I feel the book presents an educational value in giving the maturing adolescent reader a greater understanding of the challenges faced by youth in other cultures, as well as insight to the culture itself."[33]

Staples has responded to criticism from the Islamic Networks Group stating, "I have received much encouragement and praise from Muslims in America and other parts of the world for my sympathetic portrayal of a people and place that is much misunderstood, even in Pakistan. I have asked people who have objected to *Shabanu* and *Haveli* [sequel to *Shabanu*] what they find inaccurate or misleading in the novels. One man (the director of an Islamic academy in Florida) said it wasn't inaccuracy that bothered him, but that 'if people read this book they'll think all Muslims are backward camel herders.' I think what this man says accurately reflects the real problem that 'modern' Muslims have with these novels."[34]

From American literature classics to a contemporary film to fiction reflecting other cultures, there is no shortage of dissenting voices or targets for those who oppose the use of *this* book or *that* film in schools. Each group has its own reasons for objecting to the use of the resource with children or young adults. If each group's "bad" book or film is removed from the school library collection or classroom use, what will students learn about democracy and the ability to accept the different perspectives of others? Article II of the *Library Bill of Rights* states, "Libraries should provide materials and information presenting all points of view on current and historical issues. Materials should not be proscribed or removed because of partisan or doctrinal disapproval."[35] It is the responsibility of the library media professional to oppose the actions of those who do not support intellectual freedom in schools and ensure that the collection contains the "slices of life" critics attempt to censor.

There are also dissenting voices within the library community. These concerns relate to some of ALA's intellectual freedom policy statements and stances. For example, not all librarians support an antifiltering philosophy, nor do all recognize the rights of minors to freely use libraries without restrictions and scrutiny. Some struggle with the selection of materials that are counter to their personal beliefs. Others find it difficult to balance the day-to-day realities of working in a conservative district or community with the strict professional policy statements made by an organization they consider to be distant from these realities and therefore unrealistic about practical application of the First Amendment rights within their own communities.

Intellectual Freedom Supporters

Fortunately, there are national groups that oppose censorship and support intellectual freedom in libraries. They include People for the American Way, the National Coalition Against Censorship, the American Civil Liberties Union (ACLU), and the American Booksellers Foundation for Freedom of Expression (ABFF), to name a few. The ACLU frequently joins with the ALA in efforts to protect First Amendment rights. Emilio de Torre, youth program director for the ACLU of Wisconsin, stated, "There are many threats to liberty that face our nation and the ACLU and similar organizations continue to fight to allow young people to receive a first rate education and so that books and information are not denied students solely on content or the suspected influences the information will have on the readers."[36] An annotated list of national pro–First Amendment organizations is located in Appendix B.

✍ Key Ideas Summary

This chapter defined intellectual freedom, its relationship to school libraries, and the role of the school library media specialist in maintaining it. To review some of the major ideas:

- ALA's definition of intellectual freedom is "the right of every individual to both seek and receive information from all points of view without restriction."

- The *Library Bill of Rights* and its interpretations provide uncompromising support for intellectual freedom in all types of libraries.

- Minors should not be denied use of a library and its resources because of their age.

- Library media specialists protect minors' rights to receive ideas and information under the First Amendment.

- The *Code of Ethics of the ALA* provides guidance to library media specialists when faced with ethical dilemmas related to access to information for minors.

- The concepts of intellectual freedom are black and white in a hypothetical discussion but can become gray when applied to day-to-day situations involving the lives of students.

- Not everyone supports the concepts of intellectual freedom.

Basic Intellectual Freedom Resources

- **American Library Association, Office for Intellectual Freedom website,**
  http://www.ala.org/oif
  The website includes a broad range of intellectual freedom resources, including the *Library Bill of Rights* and its many interpretations, the *Code of Ethics of the ALA*, and resources to fight censorship. It is the best online starting point on the topic of intellectual freedom.

- **American Library Association, Office for Intellectual Freedom,** *Intellectual Freedom Manual.* **Chicago: American Library Association.**
  The entire volume is the "Bible of Intellectual Freedom," for all types of libraries. It includes an overview of issues, interpretations of the *Library Bill of Rights*, ALA policy statements related to access to information and privacy and confidentiality, the *Code of Ethics of the ALA*, how the law affects intellectual freedom, preparing for challenges, and advocacy. It is revised on a continuing basis.

- **Hopkins, Dianne McAfee, "School Library Media Centers and Intellectual Freedom" chapter from the American Library Association Office for Intellectual Freedom,** *Intellectual Freedom Manual,* **5th ed., 1996.**
  http://www.ala.org/ala/oif/iftoolkits/ifmanual/fifthedition/schoollibrary.htm

Hopkins' classic essay defines intellectual freedom in school libraries and touches on access, policies and procedures, challenges, promotion of intellectual freedom, and the role of the school library professional in maintaining intellectual freedom.

- **International Reading Association, "Resolution on the Selection of Reading Materials," (1994, reaffirmed 1997)**
  http://www.reading.org/downloads/resolutions/resolution97_selection_reading_materials.pdf
  The IRA Resolution recommends every district have a selection policy that includes a set of procedures for dealing with complaints.

- **National Council of Social Studies, "Academic Freedom and the Social Studies Teacher," (1969)**
  http://www.socialstudies.org/positions/freedom
  Approved by the NCSS board, the lengthy statement lays out why academic freedom is important, the need for schools to help students prepare to become citizens in a democratic society, the importance of studying controversial issues, and strategies for preserving academic freedom.

- **National Council of Teachers of English**
  http://www.ncte.org/about/over/positions/category/cens/107616.htm
  At its website, the NCTE has numerous documents that emphasize intellectual freedom and resistance to censorship. These include the "Students Right to Read," "Common Ground: Speak with One Voice on Intellectual Freedom and the Defense of It," and others.

- **Carol Simpson, ed. *Ethics in School Librarianship: A Reader.* Worthington, Ohio: Linworth Publishing, 2003.**
  This series of essays addresses common ethical issues in collection development, access, use of technology, confidentiality, Internet use, intellectual property, and intellectual freedom.

Notes

1. Doyle, Robert P., *Banned Books: 2007 Resource Book* (Chicago: American Library Association, 2007), 200.
2. American Library Association, Office for Intellectual Freedom, "Intellectual Freedom and Censorship Q & A," http://www.ala.org/ala/oif/basics/intellectual.htm.
3. American Library Association, Office for Intellectual Freedom. *Intellectual Freedom Manual,* 7th ed. (Chicago: American Library Association, 2006), xv.
4. American Library Association, Article V, *Library Bill of Rights,* http://www.ala.org/ala/oif/statementspols/statementsif/librarybillrights.htm.
5. *Intellectual Freedom Manual,* 65, 70.
6. Article II, *Library Bill of Rights.*
7. American Library Association, Article II, *Code of Ethics of the American Library Association,* http://www.ala.org/ala/oif/statementspols/codeofethics/codeethics.htm.
8. Ibid, Statement III.
9. Ibid, Statement VII.
10. American Library Association and the Association of American Publishers. *The Right to Read,* http://www.ala.org/ala/oif/statementspols/ftrstatement/freedomreadstatement.htm.

11. "The Civic Mission of Schools: A Report from Carnegie Corporation of New York and CIRCLE: The Center for Information and Research on Civic Learning and Engagement," 2003, 19, http://civicmissionofschools.org/site/campaign/cms_report.html.

12. Ibid.

13. Ibid, 5.

14. American Association of School Librarians, "Standards for the 21st-Century Learner, Learners Use Skills" (Chicago: American Library Association, 2007) 3.

15. Jerome, email to author, April 28, 2007.

16. National Council of Teachers of English, "The Students' Right to Read," http://www.ncte.org/about/over/positions/category/cens/107616.htm.

17. NSTA Position Statement, "The Freedom to Teach and the Freedom to Learn," July 1985, http://www.nsta.org/about/positions/freedom.aspx.

18. "Access to Resources and Services in the School Library Media Program: An Interpretation of the *Library Bill of Rights*," http://www.ala.org/Template.cfm?Section=interpretations&Template=/ContentManagement/ContentDisplay.cfm&ContentID=103206.

19. Candice, email to author, March 1, 2007.

20. Lea, email to author, March 1, 2007.

21. "Welcome," Parents Against Bad Books in Schools, http://www.pabbis.org.

22. Ibid.

23. "Back to School with the Religious Right," People for the American Way Report, http://www.pfaw.org/pfaw/general/default.aspx?oid=3655.

24. "Harry Potter and the Censor's Menace," People for the American Way Press Release, 3-3-2003, http://www.pfaw.org/pfaw/general/default.aspx?oid=8997.

25. "About Us," Family Friendly Libraries, http://www.fflibraries.org/About_Us_1.html.

26. "What FFL Truly Is and Is Not," Family Friendly Libraries, http://www.fflibraries.org.

27. Ravitch, Diane, *The Language Police* (New York: Alfred A. Knopf, 2003), 62–63.

28. Doyle, *Banned Books*, 166–167.

29. Ibid, 100.

30. Harden, Blaine, "Gore Film Sparks Anger in Wash. School District," *Washington Post*, January 26, 2007, reposted online by the *Boston Globe*, http://www.boston.com/news/nation/articles/2007/01/26/gore_film_sparks_anger_in_wash_school_district.

31. Barbara, email to author, July 23, 2007.

32. "Shabanu, Daughter of the Wind, Book Review as it Relates to the Books' Use in Humanities for Complementing Studies About Islam and the Muslim World in the Context of World History & Social Studies," Islamic Networks Group, http://www.ing.org/speakers/subpage.asp?num=3&pagenum=1.

33. "Parents Object to Sexual References in Novel for 7th Graders," NWI.com, January 26, 2005, http://www.thetimesonline.com/articles/2005/01/26/updates/region_and_state/153dc902fbe33c9286256f9500639901.txt.

34. Staples, Suzanne Fisher, email interview with author, August 17, 2007.

35. Article II, *Library Bill of Rights*.

36. De Torre, Emilio, email to author, March 8, 2007.

CHAPTER 2

The First Amendment in School Library Media Programs

> It can hardly be argued that either students or teachers shed their constitutional rights to freedom of speech or expression at the schoolhouse gate.
> —*Tinker v. Des Moines Independent Community School District,*
> U.S. Supreme Court, 393 U.S. 503, (1969).

The First Amendment, Minors, and Free Speech

When does a student who is a minor have the right to read a book, watch a video, or access an Internet site without being forbidden from doing so? The answer depends in large part on the First Amendment, court decisions, and who is making the restriction. It also depends on whether the child or young adult is in a public or private school library media center, a classroom in a public or private school, or a public library. While the focus of this book is on school library media centers, information about minors' rights in classrooms and the public library is included to provide contrast and clarification about the differences.

The First Amendment of the United States Constitution, along with state constitutions, forbids *the government* from abridging free speech:

Congress shall make no law respecting an establishment of religion, or prohibiting the free exercise thereof; or *abridging the freedom of speech*, or of the press; or the right of the people peaceably to assemble, and to petition the government for a redress of grievances.

U.S. Constitution, First Amendment

Copyright © 2008 by Mary Minow, Library Law Consultant, LibraryLaw.com and Helen R. Adams

Courts have interpreted "freedom of speech" more broadly than solely verbal communication. The Supreme Court is the interpreter of the First Amendment, and its decisions, along with those by lower courts, frame the parameters of minors' free speech rights. For example, in 1965, three public school pupils in Des Moines, Iowa, were suspended from school for wearing black armbands to protest the Vietnam War. The students challenged the suspension, and the Supreme Court ruled in *Tinker v. Des Moines Independent Community School District* (1969) in favor of the students. It said in this case that wearing armbands was not disruptive conduct and was closely akin to "pure speech." While not a case directly related to school libraries, the *Tinker* decision is frequently cited in First Amendment references and is important in the context of minors' rights in school settings.

Under the umbrella of First Amendment "free speech," court decisions have also recognized a minor's right to *receive information*. In *Board of Education v. Pico*, the only case of school library censorship to reach the U.S. Supreme Court, a plurality of the justices (defined as "a large number that does not constitute a majority"[1]) recognized that minors have a "right to receive information." Although the decision was issued without a majority opinion, which means it is not binding, this concept is frequently cited in other court decisions and has continued to play a critical role in subsequent library-related cases.

Does the Supreme Court's recognition of a minor's right to "receive information" mean that a student in early elementary grades may legally claim access to the same print or electronic resources selected for middle and senior high school students? The answer is generally no. In practical terms, the school's role as an educator confers authority to the library media specialist to apply materials selection criteria including *appropriate for the age, interests, emotional development, ability levels, learning styles, and social development of the students for whom the resources are intended.* Reviews and selection tools provide guidance on the reading level and interest level of the work being considered.

Private versus Public Schools

The First Amendment only forbids *government* restrictions on speech. It does not forbid *private institutions'* restrictions on speech. Private schools generally can legally restrict children's viewing or reading materials without violating the federal Constitution. Administrators and teachers should be aware, however, that there may be state, local, or institutional rules that give children free speech rights, even in a private school environment. For example, California state laws guarantee a large measure of free speech, even to students in private schools. California Education Code § 48950 states that private secondary schools may not "make or enforce any rule subjecting any high school pupil to disciplinary sanctions solely on the basis of conduct that is speech or other communication that, when engaged in outside of the campus, is protected from governmental restriction by the First Amendment to the United States Constitution or Section 2 of Article 1 of the California Constitution."[2]

 Defining the Term "Government"

In the First Amendment, the term "government" has a broad definition and includes all government officials such as legislators, governors, and mayors. In the world of public education, it may include the board of education and the principal, who set policy for how schools will operate.[3]

 What is a Private [Nonpublic] School?

By Laura Pearle, Head Librarian, Hackley School, Tarrytown, New York

Chapter 2 discusses minors' rights in public and private schools. Nonpublic or private schools come in many "flavors" including parochial, independent, charter, and others simply designated as private. Independent school librarian Laura Pearle introduces readers to nonpublic schools and sorts out some of the differences among the various types.

In the minds of many, the phrase "private school" refers to wealthy college-preparatory schools. More accurately, this term denotes a school not directly under the supervision of state, city, or other public boards of education, nor funded by public money (although they may derive limited monetary benefit from participating in government grants or programs). Charter schools are a hybrid—independent, but are under the supervision, accreditation, and funding of the state/city. One subset of private schools, called "parochial schools," is under "parish" or congregational jurisdiction (e.g., a Jewish *yeshiva* or a Catholic school). In contrast, schools supported by religious orders, such as the Jesuits or Sisters of the Sacred Heart, and Quaker schools are considered independent schools, in the same category as schools like Dalton, Hockaday, Phillips Andover, and Chadwick. Independent schools vary widely in their mission, pedagogy and goals. They may offer specialized programs in the arts or environmental education, serve specific populations like the intellectually gifted or learning disabled, or belong to international educational alliances (e.g., International Baccalaureate, Waldorf, Reggio Emilia) with a specific mission or philosophy.

Since their operating expenses are not funded by public money, private schools rely on tuition (or, in some cases for charter schools, vouchers), supplemented with fundraising, gifts, grants and, in some cases, interest from an endowment fund. Without governmental supervision or federal legislation like No Child Left Behind (NCLB), private schools are able to decide what and how they teach, and to set entrance requirements. Applicants may be asked to take the Secondary School Aptitude Test, demonstrate achievement in some subject or sport, or even present a portfolio as part of the admissions process.

Continued

Private schools serve students from preschool through grade 12 under diverse structures. Students may be grouped by age, gender, or even "families" of mixed grades. Some schools board students (either seven or five days a week) while others are day schools. As with public schools, terminology for the different levels of students is not standard. Most (but not all) K-12 independent schools refer to K-Grades 4/5 as Lower School; Grades 5/6-8 as Middle School; and Grades 9–12 as Upper (or High) School. Schools that are not K-12 may use similar terminology but apply it to different grades. For example, a school that only goes through Grade 8 may use the term "Upper School" to refer to the students in grades 7/8. Some schools may use the term "form" instead of "grade" (e.g., Sixth Form). "Preschool" may be designated as "Pre-K" or "N," depending on the school.

Independent schools usually belong to the National Association of Independent Schools (NAIS) and receive accreditation via one of the NAIS divisions. One requirement for accreditation is some form of library services, although the standards for evaluating independent school libraries is not uniform. The Independent Schools Section of the American Association of School Librarians (AASL) has been working with regional associations, such as the New York State Association of Independent Schools and the Western Association of Schools and Colleges, to establish a standard set of best practices and principles for evaluating the library space, staffing and program. (Note: Most independent schools retain the terms "library"/"librarian" and have deliberately not changed to "library media center"/"library media specialist"). One thing that surprises public school library media specialists is the fact that NAIS (and the state/regional accrediting bodies) does not require state certification for either teachers or librarians in nonpublic schools. However, faculty is expected to be expert in their field. For a librarian, this means having an MLS; for a teachers, it often means having a master's degree in the subject area taught. Most charter schools, however, do require state certification (although many do not mandate that there be a library in their facility!).

The library and the library program in a private school share many similarities with those in a public school. Intellectual freedom and information literacy are valued, research skills are taught, and reading for pleasure is stressed. Parochial, independent, charter, and other private school librarians struggle with many of the same issues as their public school counterparts: flexible versus fixed scheduling, shrinking budgets, and the negotiation of student time among various subject specialists. Like their public school colleagues, they also strive to support students' right to read while allaying parental fears about inappropriate materials.

There are also areas where private and public school libraries differ, most notably in Internet access. Because nonpublic schools are not government-funded and carry out their educational philosophy unhampered by state and federal requirements, many do not filter. However, if these schools participate in the federal E-rate program, they are required to use some filtering program. Many private school faculty and librarians strongly support teaching students about safe and effective searching rather than imposing filtering and limiting real-world experience. Students generally sign an Acceptable Use Policy for the Internet, and infractions are dealt with by the school (remember—a student can be expelled from a private school for repeated violations of school code, a remedy rarely used in public schools).

In brief, while the nature of the student body may be self-selected and the funding may differ, school libraries and librarians in the various types of private schools are very similar to public school library media programs and library media specialists in respect to intellectual freedom. *The principles of intellectual freedom are shared by us all.*[4]

Public schools present a complicated setting for minors' First Amendment rights. They must be careful when restricting children's speech, which includes their right to *receive information* via books, video presentations, the Internet, and other means. As part of local government responsibilities, school boards are *charged with guiding children's education* and necessarily must make choices to purchase materials that students receive. The school board has broad discretion in choosing the material it allows teachers to use *in the classroom.* Courts have consistently cited the purpose of the school as "inculcating fundamental values necessary to the maintenance of a democratic political system."[5]

School administrators and the board may also remove books *from the curriculum* as long as they have a reasonable educational basis for doing so. Case law on student First Amendment rights such as *Virgil v. School Board of Columbia County,* 862 F.2d 1517 (11th Cir. 1989) and the *Right to Read Defense Committee v. School Committee of the City of Chelsea,* 454 F. Supp. 703 (D. Mass. 1978) differentiates between the broad administrative control administrators and boards of education have on the removal of curricular materials required in courses and the narrow control administrators have when it comes to removing library resources intended for free inquiry by students.[6] For more information, refer to Figure 2.3, "Court Cases on Intellectual Freedom Involving Minors' First Amendment Rights," located later in Chapter 2.

When the restriction on the right to receive information takes place in a *school library,* on the other hand, the courts are more reluctant to give the school board such broad discretion. In the Supreme Court case *Board of Education v. Pico,* Justice Brennan wrote that although local school boards must be permitted to establish and apply their curriculum with broad discretion to transmit community values, at the same time, school boards are bound to uphold the First Amendment.

The Justices in the *Pico* case were divided in their opinion. There was no majority vote on the key issues of the case, and the case was later settled. Although this means that the opinion has little value as a binding precedent-setting opinion on school library censorship, lower courts have cited *Pico* for the principles expressed in Justice Brennan's opinion. These include

- School boards may remove materials from a school library if they find the books "pervasively vulgar" and "educationally unsuitable."

- School boards may *not* remove books from school library shelves simply because they dislike the ideas contained in those books.

- School boards may not remove school library books to try to proscribe what they deem to be orthodox in politics, nationalism, religion, or other matters of opinion.[7]

The *Pico* opinion emphasized that book *removal* from the school library was the issue. There is no First Amendment requirement for a library to *purchase* a particular item. However, once that item has been acquired, a school board may not remove it based merely on the ideas contained therein.

In a more recent case the Miami-Dade County School District Board voted to remove the Spanish and English language editions of *Vamos a Cuba* (or *A Visit to Cuba*) from its school library media centers based largely on the concerns of a parent who had been a political prisoner in Cuba. The parent believed the book failed to accurately depict life under a dictatorship. The board disagreed with two reconsideration committees' recommendations and the opinion of the district's superintendent to retain the title and voted to remove the book, citing it as biased and inaccurate. The removal was challenged in the U.S. District Court for the Southern District of Florida by another parent, the American Civil Liberties Union of Florida, and the Miami-Dade Student Government Association.[8]

In June 2006 a federal judge issued a preliminary injunction against the removal of the books from the district's elementary school libraries and required the book be returned to library media center shelves. Judge Alan S. Gold stated when issuing the injunction, "the School Board's claim of 'inaccuracies' is a guise and pretext for 'political orthodoxy.'"[9] Currently, the case is with the U.S. Circuit Court of Appeals awaiting a decision based on the board's rationale that the book should be removed because it did not mention "Cuba's lack of civil liberties, the political indoctrination of public school children, or food rationing, among other issues."[10] Florida ACLU director Howard Simon disagreed stating, "Access to information in libraries with all points of view—libraries serving as a marketplace of ideas—that is the heart and soul of what the First Amendment is all about. This is very dangerous ground the Miami-Dade School Board is treading on."[11]

Minors' Off-Campus Rights

In the off-campus world, such as a public library, very few restrictions by government officials, such as a library board, are legally permissible even when minors are involved. An interesting point related to public libraries was made in a *dissenting* opinion written by Justice Rehnquist in the *Board of Education v. Pico* case. He noted that the contents of the books that had been removed from the high school library were still fully accessible to any inquisitive student, because the local public library had put all nine books on display.[12]

In fact, minors have greater First Amendment rights when they leave the school setting and venture into the public library, bookstores, or access the Internet in public commercial settings such as Internet cafes. However, it is worth noting that whether in an off-campus or school setting, the chief difference between minors' and adults' First Amendment rights is that children and young adults do not have a right to materials considered *"harmful to minors."* Such materials are defined by state law and focus on sexual content.

The Internet and Minors' Rights

The Internet has brought much unwanted material to school library media centers. The *Pico* distinction between acquiring and removing unwanted materials can no longer be neatly applied. In 2000 Congress passed the Children's Internet Protection Act (CIPA), which requires schools and public libraries that receive certain federal funds to use "technology protection measures" or filters to block the following:

- *visual depictions* of "child pornography" as defined under Section 22 of Title 18 of U.S. Code,

- "obscenity" as defined under Section 1460 of Title 18 U.S. Code, and

- material "harmful to minors" as defined in Section 1703 of Title 17 of U.S. Code.[13]

Schools and school libraries did not challenge CIPA in the courts. School libraries could not join the American Library Association (ALA) in its legal action against CIPA, because school libraries are not legal entities unto themselves, but rather are indirect recipients of the federal discounts that are directed by law to the schools as elementary and secondary educational institutions. Although ALA offered support to any legal effort by schools to challenge CIPA in the courts, no school entity chose to do so.[14]

On the other hand, the ALA did challenge CIPA as unconstitutional on behalf of *public libraries,* saying that the filters used to block these images are not precise and block many websites that are protected under the First Amendment, such as the site for Super Bowl XXX. The Supreme Court ruled in *United States v. American Library Association* that the law requiring filters *did not* violate the First Amendment rights of library users. However, the Court noted that only speech *unprotected* by the First Amendment—obscenity, child pornography, and material "harmful to minors"—was restricted. It added that public libraries may disable the filters *if* material that falls outside the definition of restricted speech is blocked beyond the requirements of CIPA.

Although the decision applies to public libraries, the reasoning based on the text of the law applies to schools as well. That is, CIPA only requires schools to block *images* or *visual depictions* of child pornography, obscenity, and material legally defined as "harmful to minors."

 Defining and Interpreting "Harmful to Minors"

The federal definition of "harmful to minors" under CIPA is: "any picture, image, graphic image file, or other visual depiction that—(A) taken as a whole and with respect to minors, appeals to a prurient interest in nudity, sex, or excretion; (B) depicts, describes, or represents, in a patently offensive way with respect to what is suitable for minors, an actual or simulated sexual act or sexual contact, actual or simulated normal or perverted sexual acts, or a lewd exhibition of the genitals; and (C) taken as a whole, lacks serious literary, artistic, political, or scientific value as to minors."[15]

In other words, the materials must depict *sexual content* and must meet *all three* criteria: They must appeal to a prurient interest, they must depict sexual contact in a patently offensive way, and they must, taken as a whole, lack serious value, in order to be "harmful to minors."

However, in 2000 Congress also passed the Neighborhood Children's Internet Protection Act (NCIPA) as a companion measure to CIPA. NCIPA applies only to schools (and libraries) receiving E-rate discounted services and specifies that schools must create and implement an Internet safety policy that addresses access by minors to "inappropriate matter" on the Internet and World Wide Web as well as other provisions related to the safety and security of minors online, unlawful activities by minors while online, and protection of the personal information of minors.[16]

Under NCIPA, the school board or local educational agency still enjoys its broad discretion as an educator of youth to try to determine what gets blocked on the Internet. While CIPA defines the term "harmful to minors," NCIPA does not provide a definition for "*matter inappropriate for minors,*" instead allowing the local school board or governing body to determine what is and is not inappropriate for minors to access under its Internet safety policy, often referred to as an acceptable use policy or AUP. NCIPA states that the federal government is *not* to define "inappropriate matter" for minors:

> (2) **LOCAL DETERMINATION OF CONTENT**—A determination regarding what matter is inappropriate for minors shall be made by the school board, local educational agency, library, or other authority responsible for making the determination. No agency or instrumentality of the United States Government may;
>
> (A) establish criteria for making such determination;
>
> (B) review the determination made by the certifying school, school board, local educational agency, library, or other authority; or
>
> (C) consider the criteria employed by the certifying school, school board, local educational agency, library, or other authority in the administration of subsection (h)(1)(B).[17]

On the question of whether schools may disable filters when requested by students and staff, the answer depends on the *type of federal funding* the school or district is receiving. Currently, recipients of the Elementary and Secondary Education Act (ESEA) federal funding, under 20 USC 6777(c), may allow

> An administrator, supervisor, or person authorized by the responsible authority under subsection (a) of this section to disable the technology protection measure concerned to enable access for bona fide research or other lawful purposes.[18]

Therefore, those school staff authorized by district administration may disable the filter if the request by the minor student (under 17) is to view materials that are not child pornography, obscenity, nor "harmful to minors."

On the other hand, recipients of E-rate program funding, according to 47 USC 254(H), may disable filters *only for adults for bona fide research*.[19] However, if a district over-blocks beyond the requirements of CIPA, district staff may unblock for minor students engaged in legitimate research on an over-blocked site that does not include visual depictions of child pornography, obscenity, or material legally defined as "harmful to minors." To be safe, school personnel should check if their state laws or local school policies are more restrictive, although such limitations may not be constitutional. It would take a court challenge to determine this for certain. Summaries and links relating to state laws on filtering in libraries are located at the National Conference of State Legislatures website [http://www.ncsl.org/programs/lis/cip/filterlaws.htm].

Minors' Rights and Violence

In recent years as the dimension of violence in video games has escalated, there have been repeated attempts by local and state governments to restrict minors' access to depictions of decapitations, serial killings, and other violent acts. Each time these laws are challenged, and each time they have been overturned by the courts. Courts have not upheld restrictions on minors' access to materials that are violent, hateful, inappropriate, or disgusting *outside the classroom*. For specific cases related to violent video games, such as *American Amusement Machine Association v. Kendrick* (2001), see Figure 2.3, the "Court Cases on Intellectual Freedom Involving Minors' First Amendment Rights," at the end of this chapter.

Inside the classroom, however, and to an extent, inside the school library, school boards and staff can restrict materials based on "educational suitability," even if those resources are not within the legal definition of "harmful to minors." For example, if a school's Internet Acceptable Use Policy states that students may access only those sites related to district educational goals, it would be difficult for a student to argue that viewing a site dedicated to photos that oppose those goals is within his or her First Amendment rights to receive information.

Understanding the U.S. Court System

Knowledge of the federal and state judicial system is important to comprehend how the courts affect minors' First Amendment rights in school libraries and where their rulings apply. The U.S. judiciary consists of the U.S. Supreme Court, 13 Federal Appellate Circuits (court regions), 94 Federal District Courts, and 50 state court systems.[20] First Amendment cases are usually heard in federal courts, but they may also be heard in state courts.

The decisions by the **U.S. Supreme Court** are binding everywhere in the United States. **Federal Appellate Circuit** decisions are binding only in their own geographic regions. For example, First Appellate Circuit decisions are binding *only* in Maine, New Hampshire, Massachusetts, Rhode Island, and Puerto Rico, the geographic area for the First Appellate Circuit. Each circuit's decisions can be *persuasive,* or considered by a court in another circuit, even though they are not binding outside their jurisdictions. Figure 2.1 depicts 11 of the 13 Federal Appellate Circuits.

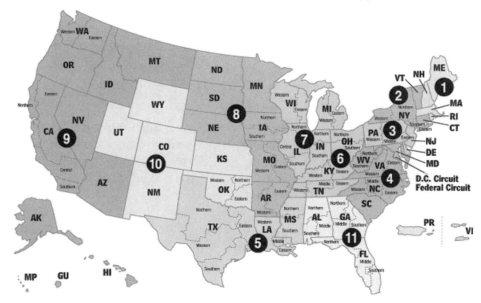

Figure 2.1: Federal Appellate Circuits.
Source: http://www.uscourst.gov/courtlinks

Federal District Courts are lower courts, and their decisions are also binding *only* within that specific jurisdiction. For example, *Counts v. Cedarville School District,* 295 F.Supp.2d 996 (W.D. Ark. 2003), described later in the chapter, was heard in the [Federal] Western District Court of Arkansas and is binding only in the western region of Arkansas. Figure 2.2 shows the hierarchical nature of the federal court system.

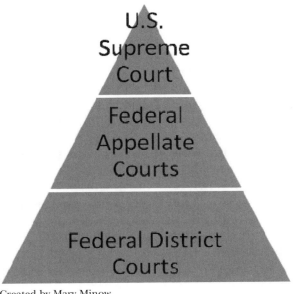

Created by Mary Minow.

Figure 2.2: Hierarchy of Federal Courts and Their Decisions.

The Effect of Case Law on Intellectual Freedom in Schools

Legislatures write and pass laws, but the interpretation of law in specific circumstances is left to state and federal courts. Court decisions result in "case law." Case law is "law based on judicial decision and precedent rather than on statutes."[21] School library media specialists and other educators use case law to learn how courts have ruled in cases involving minors' First Amendment rights and to interpret local school and school library situations.

Counts v. Cedarville School District (2003) is an example of a legal battle that resulted in case law. In this lawsuit, the school board voted to limit access to the *Harry Potter* books in the school library collection because it perceived that the books encouraged disobedience and included characters engaging in witchcraft and the occult. The board required students to have signed permission slips from their parents or guardians before checking out the books. The Court reversed the board's decision, citing *Tinker V. Des Moines Independent Community School District* (1969) and ruling that there was no evidence that showed substantial disruption with school activities if students were allowed unfettered access to the books. Schools may not restrict access to the books based on the ideas expressed and that even a minimal loss of First Amendment rights is injurious.[22] As a result, the *Harry Potter* books were returned to unrestricted circulation in the school library. As noted earlier, this decision is binding only in the Western District of Arkansas, but it may be persuasive or considered by other federal courts in future cases.

Library media specialists must know about recent court cases affecting minors' First Amendment rights in school libraries and be cognizant of the jurisdiction of the court making the ruling. The ALA's *American Libraries Online* reports on significant court decisions affecting libraries [http://www.ala.org/ala/alonline/index.cfm]. Findlaw [http://lp.findlaw.com] maintains a searchable summaries archive for opinions issued since September 2000 by the U.S. Supreme Court, the Federal Circuit Courts, the California Supreme Court and Court of Appeal, the Texas Supreme Court and Criminal Court of Appeal, and the New York Court of Appeals.[23] For questions relating to local ordinances, state and federal laws, and case law and how they may apply to district policy or local situations relating to minors' First Amendment rights, check with your institution's legal counsel. For additional information on how the courts view minors' First Amendment rights, see Figure 2.3, "Court Cases on Intellectual Freedom Involving Minors' First Amendment Rights" at the end of this chapter. The table shows the development of case law relevant to school library censorship from the present day to 1969. While not all cases are directly related to school libraries, the progression of minors' rights in schools and libraries is evident.

✍ Key Ideas Summary

This chapter covered a broad range of issues related to minors' First Amendment rights. To review, here are the major ideas:

- The First Amendment of the United States Constitution protects minors' free speech rights including the right to receive ideas.

- The Supreme Court, along with lower federal and state courts, interpret how the First Amendment applies to minors.

- Minors' First Amendment rights may be different or limited, depending on where the individual is exercising the right of free speech—a public or private school classroom, a school library, or a public library. Minors' free speech rights are substantial but do not equal those of an adult citizen.

- School library media specialists and other educators use case law to learn how courts have ruled in cases involving minors' First Amendment rights and to interpret local school and school library situations.

First Amendment Resources

- **American Library Association, Office for Intellectual Freedom. "First Amendment Resources, Advocates, and Notables First Amendment Court Cases,"** http://www.ala.org/ala/oif/firstamendment/firstamendment.htm
  This extensive listing of online resources on the First Amendment and its relationship to libraries is a good beginning point for library professionals.

- **Chmara, Theresa. "Minors' First Amendment Rights to Access Information," In** *Intellectual Freedom Manual,* **7th ed. Office for Intellectual Freedom, American Library Association, 384-393. Chicago: American Library Association, 2006.**
  The short essay reviews the rights of minors to receive information centering on court cases and their impact on student patrons' rights to use materials in the library as well to access information via the Internet.

- **Doyle, Robert P.** *Banned Books: 2007 Resource Guide.* **Chicago: American Library Association, 2007.**
  The resource guide is published every three years to promote Banned Books Week and contains information on notable First Amendment court cases and quotations about the First Amendment.

- **First Amendment First Aid Kit,** http://www.randomhouse.com/teens/first amendment
  Maintained by Random House Children's Books, the site includes short essays by authors whose books have been challenged, strategies for school library media specialists to combat censorship, and a list of organizations that will assist in the event of a challenge.

- **Haynes, Charles C., Sam Chaltain, John E. Ferguson Jr., David L. Hudson Jr., and Oliver Thomas.** *The First Amendment in Schools.* **Alexandria, Virginia: Association for Supervision and Curriculum Development and the First Amendment Center, 2003.**
  This concise but very informative book answers questions about applying the First Amendment to issues in schools. Particularly of interest are the chapters on use of the Internet and book removal from school library media centers.

- **LibraryLaw.com,** http://www.LibraryLaw.com
  Lawyer, author, and library consultant Mary Minow devotes a section of her website to Intellectual Freedom and the First Amendment and libraries. Her site is also linked to her blog where current intellectual freedom and First Amendment issues are posted.

- **Mart, Susan Nevelow. The Right to Receive Information. (2003, Spring).** *Law Library Journal,* **95, 175-189,** http://www.aallnet.org/products/pub_llj_v95n02/2003-11.pdf
  The author discusses the "legal evolution of the right to receive information" beginning with the Supreme Court's plurality decision in *Board of Education v. Pico.*

- **"Minors' Rights to Receive Information Under the First Amendment," Memorandum, Jenner & Block, prepared by Theresa Chmara and Daniel Mach, February 2, 2004,** http://www.ala.org/ala/oif/ifissues/issuesrelatedlinks/minorsrights.htm
  A legal memorandum from Jenner & Block lawyers to the Freedom to Read Foundation on minors' First Amendment rights to receive information which includes a discussion of the use of Internet filtering software.

Notes

1. Garner, Bryan A., ed., *Black's Law Dictionary*, 7th ed. (St. Paul, Minnesota: West Group, 1999), 1176.

2. Cal. Educ. Code § 48950. (a) School districts operating one or more high schools and private secondary schools shall not make or enforce any rule subjecting any high school pupil to disciplinary sanctions solely on the basis of conduct that is speech or other communication that, when engaged in outside of the campus, is protected from governmental restriction by the First Amendment to the United States Constitution or Section 2 of Article 1 of the California Constitution.

3. Intellectual Freedom Committee 2005–2007, The Association for Library Service to Children (ALSC), "Kids, Know Your Rights! A Young Person's Guide to Intellectual Freedom," p. 2, http://www.ala.org/ala/alsc/alscpubs/KidsKnowYour-Rights.pdf.

4. Pearle, Laura, "What is a Private School?," email to author, November 11, 2007 and June 12, 2008.

5. *Ambach v. Norwick*, 441 U.S. 68, 76-77, (1979), cited in *Bd. of Education, Island Trees Union Free School District v. Pico*, 457 U.S. 853, 864 (1982).

6. Doyle, Robert P., *Banned Books: 2007 Resource Guide* (Chicago: American Library Association, 2007), 182–186.

7. *Bd. of Education, Island Trees Union Free School District v. Pico*, 457 U.S. 853 (1982). http://caselaw.lp.findlaw.com/scripts/getcase.pl?court=US&vol=457&invol=853. See also *Pico*, 457 U.S. at 871.

8. *ACLU of Fla., Inc. v. Miami-Dade County Sch. Bd.*, 439 F. Supp. 2d 1242, 2006 U.S. Dist. LEXIS 50502; see also Laura Wides-Munoz, "Children's Book about Cuba at the Center of an Emotional Court Battle," Miami-Herald.com June 5, 2007, http://www.miamiherald.com:80/775/story/129207.html.

9. "It's Back to School Libraries for a Visit to Cuba," *American Libraries Online*, July 28, 2006, http://www.ala.org/ala/alonline/currentnews/newsarchive/2006abc/july2006a/vamosagain.cfm.

10. Wides-Munoz, Laura, "Children's Book about Cuba ..."

11. Ibid.

12. *Bd. of Education, Island Trees Union Free School District v. Pico*, 457 U.S. 853, 915 (1982) (J. Rehnquist, dissenting).

13. Children's Internet Protection Act, PL 106-554, 2000, http://www.cdt.org/legislation/106th/speech/001218cipa.pdf.

14. PL No. 106-554 Section 1711 of the Act amends the Elementary and Secondary Education Act of 1965, 20 U.S.C. §§ 6801 et seq. Section 1721 amends section 254 (h) of the Communications Act of 1934, as amended, 47 U.S.C. §§ 151 et seq. See also Texas Library Association TLA TEXLINE NO. 130, Legislative Issues Network, Posted: June 1, 2002, http://www.txla.org/pubs/texline/020601.html.

15. 20 U.S.C. § 9134(f)(7)(B).

16. Public Law 106-554, Subsection C. Neighborhood Children's Internet Protection Act, Sections 1731-1733, http://ifea.net/cipa.html.

17. Public Law 106-554, Subsection C. Neighborhood Children's Internet Protection Act, Sec. B (2), http://www.ifea.net/cipa.html.

18. 20 USC § 6777 (c).

19. 47 USC § 254(H) (D) (A) (i).

20. U.S. Courts, the Federal Judiciary, http://www.uscourts.gov/faq.html.

21. "Case Law" definition, Answers.com, http://www.answers.com/topic/case-law.
22. *Counts v. Cedarville School District*, 295 F.Supp.2nd 996 (W.D. Ark.2003).
23. Findlaw, "Opinion Summaries Archive," http://lp.findlaw.com.

Figure 2.3: Court Cases on Intellectual Freedom Involving Minors' First Amendment Rights

Created by Mary Minow

Year	Court Cases/Decisions Note: U.S. Supreme Court cases in **BOLD** type	Summary of Case/Outcome
2007	***Morse v. Frederick***, 127 S. Ct. 2618, 2007 U.S. LEXIS 8514, (U.S. 2007).	Student (Frederick) sued his principal (Morse) stating she had violated his free speech when, as an 18-year-old senior in 2002, he held up a banner across the street from Juneau-Douglas High School during the Olympic Torch Relay in Juneau, Alaska, reading "Bong Hits 4 Jesus," and she removed it from his hands. She claimed that the drug reference on the banner was in violation of the school's anti-drug policy. The Supreme Court ruled that the "substantial disruption" rule of ***Tinker v. Des Moines Independent Community School District*** (see below, 1969) was not the only basis for restricting student speech. A school may also restrict speech that can reasonably be regarded as encouraging illegal drug use.
2006	*ACLU of Florida v. Miami-Dade School Board,* 439 F. Supp. 2d 1242, (S.D. Fla. 2006).	ACLU sued after parent complaints about introductory book on Cuba for 4 to 8 year olds led the school board to ban the entire series, saying that the viewpoint of the book on Cuba was too favorable to Communist Cuba. Court cited the ***Board of Education v. Pico*** case (see below, 1982), saying that the removal was motivated by the board's disapproval of the content. Further, the district did not comply with its own book removal procedures. *Vamos a Cuba* and other books in the series were returned to elementary school library shelves. Currently on appeal.
2005–2001	Violent video game court cases *Video Software Dealers Ass'n v. Schwarzenegger,* No. C-05-04188 RMW (N.D. Cal., Dec. 21, 2005); *Entertainment Software Ass'n v. Blagojevich,* No. 05 C 4265 (N.D. Ill., Dec. 2, 2005); *Entertainment Software Ass'n v.*	Series of cases in Illinois, California, Michigan, Washington and Missouri in which video game associations brought cases against similar laws restricting minors from purchasing, renting, or using violent video games, for example, in an arcade, without parental permission. In each case, the courts have struck down such laws, stating that government may not restrict children from viewing violence.

(*Continued*)

Figure 2.3 (*Continued*)

Year	Court Cases/Decisions **Note:** U.S. Supreme Court cases in **BOLD** type	Summary of Case/Outcome
	Granholm, No. 05-CV-73634 (E.D. Mich., Nov. 9, 2005); *Video Software Dealers Ass'n v. Maleng*, 325 F. Supp.2d 1180, 1188 (W.D. Wash. 2004); *IDSA v. St. Louis Co.*, 329 F.3d 954 (8th Cir. 2003); *American Amusement Machine Association, v. Teri Kendrick*, 244 F.3d 954 (7th Cir. 2001); *cert. denied*, 534 U.S. 994 (2001).	
2003	***United States v. American Library Association***, 539 U.S. 194 (2003).	American Library Association sued the United States claiming the Children's Internet Protection Act (CIPA) was a violation of the First Amendment. CIPA requires schools and libraries that receive certain federal aid to block or filter images of child pornography, obscenity, and materials "harmful to minors." The Supreme Court ruled filters on public library terminals are constitutional so long as they can be disabled easily upon request to access lawful materials. The Supreme Court noted that CIPA provisions permitted a library to disable the filter in order to enable access for "bona fide research or other lawful purposes." The plurality noted that any concerns over filtering software's tendency to erroneously "overblock" constitutionally protected speech were dispelled by the ease with which library patrons could have the filtering software disabled.
2003	*Counts v. Cedarville School District*, 295 F.Supp.2d 996 (W.D. Ark. 2003).	Parents challenged school board requirement that children must get parental permission to borrow *Harry Potter* books. Court cited the ***Tinker*** case (see below, 1969) and ruled that there was no evidence that reasonably showed substantial disruption or material interference with school activities if students were allowed unfettered access to the books. Schools may not restrict access to the books based on the ideas expressed, whether religious or secular. The Court wrote that even a minimal loss of First Amendment rights is injurious. Requiring parental permission for certain books can cause a "stigmatization" of children who choose to read the books (seen as "bad books"). *Harry Potter* books were returned to unrestricted shelves in the school library.

Figure 2.3 (*Continued*)

Year	Court Cases/Decisions Note: U.S. Supreme Court cases in **BOLD** type	Summary of Case/Outcome
2001	*Kathleen R. v. City of Livermore,* 87 Cal. App. 4th 684 (Cal. App. 1st Dist. 2001).	Parent sued a public library after her young son accessed pornographic images. The California court ruled that the library had no constitutional obligation to protect children from whatever harm might befall them as a consequence of using the Internet. The public library could keep its open Internet access policy for all ages (no filters), because there is no special duty in a public library to protect children This is a significant difference between public and school libraries with regard to Internet access for children. A school operates "in loco parentis" [in place of the parents] while a public library does not.
2000	*Sund. v. City of Wichita Falls, Texas,* 121 F. Supp. 2d 530 (N.D. Texas, 2000).	Residents of Wichita Falls, Texas, sued the city after the city council passed a resolution that allowed books to be removed from the children's section and placed on a locked shelf in the adult area if 300 adult library card holders signed a petition. The Court ruled that the city improperly delegated governmental authority to private citizens. The resolution provided no standards or review process, and allowed impermissible content-based discrimination. The Court viewed this action as violating the library users' constitutional rights to receive information. *Heather Has Two Mommies* and *Daddy's Roommate* were returned to public library children's open shelves.
1998	*Monteiro v. Tempe Union High Sch. Dist.* 158 F.3d 1022, (9th Cir. Ariz. 1998).	Parent asked school to remove *Huck Finn* from the curriculum because the "n" word harmed her daughter. Court cited *Board of Education v. Pico* (see below, 1982), saying that there is a well-established rule that the right to receive information is an inherent corollary of the rights of free speech and press, and that the students have rights to receive a broad range of information so that they can freely form their own thoughts. Court wrote: "Bad ideas should be countered with good ones, not banned by the courts. One of the roles of teachers is to guide students through the difficult process of becoming educated, to help them learn how to discriminate between good concepts and bad, to benefit from the errors society has made in the past, to improve their minds and characters." *Huck Finn* was not removed from curriculum.
1995	*Campbell v. St. Tammany Parish School Board,* 64 F.3d 184 (5th Cir. 1995).	An individual and a religious organization sued a school board after it removed an academic book on voodoo religion that has specific spells. Court

(*Continued*)

Figure 2.3 (*Continued*)

Year	Court Cases/Decisions Note: U.S. Supreme Court cases in **BOLD** type	Summary of Case/Outcome
		said: "in light of the special role of the school library as a place where students may freely and voluntarily explore diverse topics, the school board's non-curricular decision to remove a book well after it had been placed in the public school libraries evokes the question whether that action might not be an attempt to 'strangle the free mind at its source.'" The parties settled the case before trial by returning *Voodoo and Hoodoo* to the libraries on specially designated reserve shelves. The special shelving solution was part of the pre-trial settlement, not ordered by a court.
1995	*Case v. Unified School Dist. No. 233,* 908 F. Supp. 864 (D. Kan. 1995).	Students and parents sued the school board after it removed a lesbian novel from junior and senior high school libraries. Court found that although the board said it found the book educationally unsuitable (per the *Board of Education v. Pico* case, see below, 1982), in fact it removed the book because school board members disagreed with its ideas. The decisive factor behind the removal was the school board members' personal disapproval of the ideas contained in the book. Further, the school board violated its own materials selection and reconsideration policies. *Annie on My Mind* returned to school library shelves.
1989	*Virgil v. School Board of Columbia County,* 862 F.2d 1517 (11th Cir. 1989).	School board was challenged after removing previously approved textbooks from elective high school class because of objections to vulgarity and sexual explicitness. The Court ruled that the school board could take such action when the removal decision was "reasonably related" to the "legitimate pedagogical concern" of denying students access to "potentially sensitive topics." The school board's decision to remove Chaucer's *The Miller's Tale* and Aristophanes's *Lysistrata* from the curriculum was upheld.
1988	***Hazelwood School Dist.v. Kuhlmeier,*** 484 U.S. 260, (1988).	Students filed suit against the school district after the school principal removed articles on teen pregnancy and divorce from a high school newspaper produced as part of class. Supreme Court ruled that the principal need not tolerate student speech "that is inconsistent with its 'basic educational mission,' even though the government could not censor similar speech outside the school." The rights of students in public schools are not as strong as the rights of adults. Articles

Figure 2.3 (*Continued*)

Year	Court Cases/Decisions Note: U.S. Supreme Court cases in **BOLD** type	Summary of Case/Outcome
		removed from school paper when found inconsistent with educational mission.
1986	***Bethel School Dist. No. 403 v. Fraser***, 478 U.S. 675 (1986).	Student sued school district for violation of his freedom of speech when he was suspended after he used sexual innuendo at a school assembly. The student argued that he did not cause disruption of school activities and referred to ***Tinker v. Des Moines Independent School District*** (see below, 1969). Court ruled that school officials have a responsibility to "inculcate values" and may prohibit student speech before a student assembly that is vulgar, lewd, and plainly offensive.
1982	***Bd. of Education, Island Trees Union Free School District v. Pico***, 457 U.S. 853 (1982).	Students sued the school board after it removed books from school libraries, describing the books as "anti-American, anti-Christian, anti-Semitic, and just plain filthy." In a badly fractured opinion, a plurality of justices on the Supreme Court wrote that school boards may not have the unrestricted authority to remove school library books "simply because they dislike the ideas contained in those books and seek by their removal to prescribe what shall be orthodox in politics, nationalism, religion, or other matters of opinion." Although a majority of justices did not agree to this, the opinion has come to stand in lower courts for the principle that school boards may not remove books from school libraries merely because they disagree with the ideas therein. *Slaughterhouse-Five, The Naked Ape, Down These Mean Streets, Best Short Stories of Negro Writers, Go Ask Alice, Laughing Boy, Black Boy, A Hero Ain't Nothin' But a Sandwich,* and *Soul on Ice* were all returned to school library shelves.
1979	*Salvail v. Nashua Board of Education,* (469 F. Supp. 1269 (D. N.H. 1979).	Student, teacher, and community members sued after the school board removed *MS* magazine from high school library. Court found the board failed "to demonstrate a substantial and legitimate government interest sufficient to warrant the removal of *MS* magazine from the Nashua High School library. Their action violated the plaintiffs' First Amendment rights, and as such it is plainly wrong." *MS* magazine returned to high school library shelves.
1978	*Right to Read Defense Committee v. School Committee of the City of Chelsea,* 454 F. Supp. 703 (D. Mass. 1978).	The Right to Read Defense Committee sued the Chelsea School Committee [school board] after it barred the poetry anthology *Male and Female Under 18* from the high school library because of the

(*Continued*)

Figure 2.3 (*Continued*)

Year	Court Cases/Decisions Note: U.S. Supreme Court cases in **BOLD** type	Summary of Case/Outcome
		inclusion of a sexually explicit poem. Court wrote that although the committee was not obligated to select the anthology, once it did, it created a "constitutionally protected interest." The Court distinguished between the school committee's control over resources in the curriculum [classroom] and those in a school library, saying the school library is "a mighty resource in the marketplace of ideas. There a student can literally explore the unknown, and discover areas of interest and thought not covered by the prescribed curriculum. The student who discovers the magic of the library is on the way to a life-long experience of self-education and enrichment. That student learns that a library is a place to test or expand upon ideas presented to him, in or out of the classroom. The most effective antidote to the poison of mindless orthodoxy is ready access to a broad sweep of ideas and philosophies. There is no danger from such exposure. The danger is mind control." School was ordered to make the whole anthology available to all students at the high school in accordance with standard library procedures.
1976	*Minarcini v Strongsville (Ohio) City School District,* 541 F.2d 577, (6th Cir. 1976).	Students sued the district after the board of education ordered the removal of *Catch-22* and *Cat's Cradle* from the school library. Court wrote that the school board was not obligated to provide a library or choose any particular books, but once "having created such a privilege for the benefit of its students" could not "place conditions on the use of the library which were related solely to the social or political tastes of school board members." Court found the removal of books from a school library is a much more serious burden upon the freedom of classroom discussion than the action found unconstitutional in ***Tinker v. Des Moines Independent Community School District*** (see below, 1969). Court rejected the board's absolute right to remove books from a school library writing, "A library is a storehouse of knowledge. When created for a public school, it is an important privilege for the benefit of students in the schools. That privilege is not subject to being withdrawn by succeeding school boards whose members may desire to 'winnow' the library for books the

Figure 2.3 (*Continued*)

Year	Court Cases/Decisions Note: U.S. Supreme Court cases in **BOLD** type	Summary of Case/Outcome
		contents of which occasioned their displeasure or disapproval." The two books were returned to the school library.
1972	*Todd v. Rochester Community Schools*, 200 N.W.2d 90 (Mich. Ct. App. 1972).	Parent sued to remove *Slaughterhouse-Five*, noting it made reference to religious matters and should not be in the school library or classroom. Court cited Supreme Court opinion *West Virginia State Board of Education v Barnette*, 319 U.S. 624, (1943): "If there is any fixed star in our constitutional constellation, it is that no official, high or petty, can prescribe what shall be orthodox in politics, nationalism, religion or other matters of opinion ... " *Slaughterhouse-Five* returned to school libraries and curriculum.
1969	***Tinker v. Des Moines Independent Community School District***, 393 U.S. 503, (1969).	Three students sued the school district after they were expelled for wearing black armbands to school to protest the Vietnam War. Supreme Court held that students "do not shed their constitutional rights at the schoolhouse gate" and that the First Amendment protects public school students' rights to express political and social views during school hours. Court ruled schools may ban student free speech only if it is reasonably expected to cause substantial disruption or material interference with school activities.

Created by Mary Minow.

CHAPTER 3

Selection of School Library Media Program Resources

The library environment affirms all people regardless of race, gender, religion, political stance, ability and/or economic circumstance. That involves creating an environment in which all learners will see themselves reflected. It also means ordering materials containing viewpoints and perspectives with which one personally does not agree.[1]
—Ginny Moore Kruse, Director Emerita, Cooperative Children's Book Center, School of Education, University of Wisconsin–Madison

Introduction

Selecting school library resources is one of the most critical and controversial responsibilities of a library media specialist. The items selected become part of the print and electronic collection from which students will access information for school and personal purposes. The school library professional must ensure that a policy is in place to guide resource selection. During selection, the school library professional will:

- evaluate the collection to determine where new information is needed and out-of-date material should be removed,
- seek resources to meet the needs of the school community,
- implement the actual selection and acquisition process, and
- de-select or weed materials.

Selection is an ongoing process, often complicated by fiscal limitations, school and community climate, and other constraints. Although many selection policies encompass all instructional resources—textbooks, supplementary classroom resources, and school library materials—this discussion will focus on the selection of resources housed in the school library or selected by the school library media specialist.

The Selection Policy

A board-adopted instructional materials selection policy with reconsideration procedures is the *legal basis* for selection and reconsideration of all instructional materials used within a school, including school library resources. Some states, including Wisconsin and Arkansas, require public school districts to have board-approved materials selection policies and procedures for reconsideration. The American Library Association (ALA) Office for Intellectual Freedom recommends the selection policy as one of the five policies needed to manage a library collection and defend intellectual freedom.[2] The selection policy provides an explanation to the entire school community regarding how and why certain materials are chosen. In addition, a selection policy:

- provides designated staff with guidance for the selection of materials consistent with the educational philosophy, goals, and curricula of the institution,
- ensures the orderly acquisition of resources under a standard set of criteria,
- enables school personnel and the community to remain informed about the selection of instructional and library materials, and
- offers a formal process under which school resources can be reconsidered for meeting district selection criteria.

The most inclusive selection policy is developed with input from a broad representation of members of the school community, including school library professionals, teachers, administrators, students, and parent and board of education representatives. Including the many stakeholders in the policy creation process ensures smooth implementation and support for the document. When completed, the policy will reflect the educational goals and objectives of the district or school and guide the selection of resources to serve its unique student population and curriculum.

 Policy Tip

Wholesale adoption of another district's or school's materials selection policy is not a good idea; however, reviewing the policies of others to gather ideas and provide the basis for discussion is a sound strategy. Many districts and private schools post their selection policies on the Internet, making them readily available.

The ALA "Workbook for Selection Policy Writing" recommends that a selection policy include the following sections:

- the district's **objectives** for obtaining instructional and library media center materials;
- **responsibility for selection** of classroom and library print, audiovisual, and electronic resources;
- specific **criteria for selecting resources** including those that may be considered controversial;
- **procedures for the selection, acquisition, and collection maintenance** process, including the types of materials collected, reviewing sources, consideration of donated and gift items, reevaluation of present resources, and weeding;
- statement of **support for intellectual freedom**; and
- statement of policy with **procedures allowing for the reconsideration of resources** when a formal written complaint is received.[3]

Library Philosophy and Selection Objectives

Selection policies exhibit great diversity. Some begin with an introductory statement or philosophy summarizing the library's role in providing unrestricted access to a wide range of information, the relationship of the library media program to the curriculum, and its place in the education of students. Other materials selection policies start with general, broad objectives that lay out why a district is assembling a collection of materials housed or accessed in a school library media center. This example illustrates a single, very encompassing objective: *to support, enrich, and implement the educational program of the school.* The ALA "Workbook for Selection Policy Writing" provides two more specific objectives:

- "make available to faculty and students a collection of materials that will enrich and support the curriculum and meet the needs of the students and faculty served."
- "provide students with a wide range of educational materials on all levels of difficulty and in a variety of formats, with diversity of appeal, allowing for the presentation of many different points of view."[4]

Responsibility for Selection

Although the board of education or governing authority of the institution is legally responsible for the resources used within a school, it delegates the actual selection of library resources to its professional school library personnel. The school library professional provides leadership in implementing the selection policy, selecting materials based on the criteria, and following the procedures within the policy. Most policies direct the library professional to work collaboratively with other staff members during the selection process. The school library media specialist should confer with content area teachers when selecting materials that complement their curricula. When faculty assist in selection, it is more likely they use the resulting resources and direct students to them. Although others participate in the selection process, strong policies state that the final responsibility for the selection decision rests with the library's professional staff.

Selection Criteria

Selection policies list both general and specific criteria for the selection of print, audiovisual, and electronic resources to ensure that additions to the collection meet selection policy objectives. With respect to a school library media program, the policy encompasses the selection of the physical collection housed within the library facility as well as information services such as fee-based electronic databases and e-books. The library media specialist also selects resources in formats to meet the needs of students with disabilities.

Selection criteria for choosing school library media program resources may include:

- consistent with district and school goals,
- contribute to the curriculum,
- receive favorable reviews or are included in core collection development tools,
- appropriate for the age, interests, emotional development, ability levels, learning styles, and social development of the students for whom the resources are intended, including students with disabilities,
- accurate in terms of content and authority of the author,
- free of bias and stereotyping (e.g., sexism, racism),
- reflect the pluralistic nature of a global society,
- represent the various religious, ethnic, gender, and cultural groups and their contributions to American heritage,
- depict diverse points of view on controversial topics,
- current and relevant,
- possesses aesthetic, literary, or social value,
- logically arranged and organized,
- attractive and appropriate format to effectively support the curriculum,
- provide value to the collection commensurate with cost,
- durable,

- acceptable technical quality for audiovisual and multimedia formats, and

- depth of coverage, search functionality, user-friendliness, technical support, remote accessibility 24/7, and technical criteria for fee-based electronic databases and reference tools.

The previous list is not all inclusive, and other criteria may be added to define future acquisitions to the collection. While the library professional carefully reviews the criteria during the selection process, not every resource will meet all the criteria listed. A resource may still be selected if it fills a need. For example, the library media specialist may choose a poorly written nonfiction book because students need easy to read resources on that topic.

Selecting Materials on Controversial Topics

School library media specialists select materials on a wide range of subjects with a diversity of viewpoints, and the selection policy provides guidance for choosing resources on topics that may be considered controversial. It is impossible to select a resource that does not have the potential to offend someone within the school or larger community. Therefore, library professionals must use the policy's criteria to guide their selection. A conscious effort should be made during the selection process to match the prospective resource with as many criteria as possible. Every resource chosen should be directly defensible because it met one or more of the selection criteria prior to purchase. In effect, a library professional will use the criteria to *guide their selection* and, in the event of a challenge, will also use the policy criteria to *defend the selection.*

One Midwestern public school district directs their library staff in this manner.

Although the board of education recognizes that any item may offend some patrons, selection of resources on controversial topics will not be made on the basis of any anticipated approval or disapproval but rather on the merits of the resources and its value to the collection and patrons.[5]

The administration and board expect its staff to use evaluative selection criteria to provide high-quality resources useful to library users rather than selecting what may be considered by some to be "safe" titles.

Bonnie, a librarian in an independent school in Minnesota, explains her school's philosophy toward controversial topics.

I am a librarian at a Christian, college prep private school and have been here 26 years. When I started, I feared that I would experience censorship and other difficulties with book selection. That has not been the case. Our school's policy is to present students with not only the Covenant viewpoint but also other viewpoints so that they will have the ability to form their own educated opinion. To that end, I have worked hard to present materials on both sides of an issue. We have a selection policy which can be found on our website.[6]

What about the Internet?

Districts treat Internet websites in different ways within selection policies. Some state that websites are not subject to the selection policy, because the educational institution is unable to regulate or control Web content. Other policies describe that the district or school subscribes to a filtering service to comply with the Children's Internet Protection Act (CIPA). Still others note that Internet access is both a right and a privilege and refer to the district's acceptable use policy (AUP) for specific expectations for appropriate and acceptable use of websites by students and staff. One midwestern district acknowledges the students' role in the selection of websites to access: "The student also plays a significant role in the selection of educational materials while searching on the Internet and ... must accept responsibility for accessing materials which are relevant to the educational goal being pursued."[7] However addressed, the policy should acknowledge educationally appropriate Internet resources as legitimate, and school personnel should apply intellectual freedom concepts for gaining access to the sites. Chapter 7 will discuss intellectual freedom and Internet use in schools.

Procedures: The Nuts and Bolts

Having a selection *policy* with objectives and criteria does not guarantee school library personnel will fulfill their acquisition responsibilities in a consistent fashion. Instead, school library staff rely on district *procedures*, a series of sequential steps or guidelines to implement the materials selection policy. Procedures ensure that selection, acquisition, weeding, and replacement are accomplished in a consistent manner. School library media professionals need guidance on the types of resources to be added to the collection; acceptable selection sources to use, such as professional review journals and core collection tools; whether examination or preview is required; and specific directions that outline the acquisitions process. The procedures begin with identifying collection needs, move to initial review of prospective resources, and follow the process all the way to final selection and acquisition.

The procedures section of the policy lays out not only how new resources will be added to the collection but also how old, worn, or inaccurate materials will be withdrawn and replaced. De-selection procedures are needed to avoid one type of covert censorship, whereby a resource is removed dishonestly under the guise of "weeding" because it is offensive to someone. School library media specialists must ensure that the process for evaluating and acknowledging gifts and donations is detailed in the procedures section. Most schools use the same criteria for accepting gifts as they do for newly purchased items.

Support for Intellectual Freedom

The district's commitment to intellectual freedom and protection of students' First Amendment rights is often articulated in its selection policy. Selection policies vary greatly among public and private schools, but the majority include a statement affirming the importance of intellectual freedom in a democratic society and referring to the *Library Bill of Rights* and to the First Amendment of the Constitution of the United States. Frequently, the referenced documents are appended, and their presence sends an unequivocal message to the community: This educational institution stands behind the principles of the U.S. government and society, and its policies protect access to information.

When the *Library Bill of Rights* is referenced in the selection policy, all of its statements and ideas, such as "Libraries should provide materials and information presenting all points of view on current and historical issues" (Article II)[8] become part of what the policy itself asserts. For example, Article II supports the collection development process by requiring the provision of resources on varying perspectives for those served by the library.

Reconsideration of Challenged Materials

No matter how carefully a resource is selected, someone may object to its use with students, question its educational value, and seek its removal from the collection. Therefore, the selection policy must include a means by which questioned resources are reexamined by a formally appointed committee representing the school community. The reconsideration process protects students' First Amendment rights to receive information and, whatever its outcome, upholds democratic principles. Prior to the formal reconsideration process, however, most reconsideration procedures include a step for seeking an informal resolution of the concern. "Informal resolution" does not mean that the principal or media specialist gives in to the demands of the complainant to remove a book or place restrictions on its use. Instead, the library media specialist or the principal listens to the objections of the complainant, explains the school's policy, and articulates the principles of intellectual freedom and access. In other words, they follow the policy. (See Chapter 6 for tips on how to approach this discussion.)

If an informal discussion does not satisfy the complainant, it is standard practice to offer an opportunity to submit a formal written request, detailing concerns with the material and a request for its disposition. Most policies require the complainant to use an official reconsideration form and take no action concerning the resource unless the completed reconsideration form is received. Some policies include a time period for the returning of the reconsideration form after which the matter is considered officially closed. Submission of the official reconsideration form signals the beginning of the formal reconsideration process. The policy should include a statement that the resource in question will not be removed from circulation until the entire reconsideration process is completed.

The policy should lay out the reconsideration process in unambiguous language to ensure the committee understands its responsibilities. The policy also should describe the composition of the reconsideration committee, its basic responsibilities, and the circumstances under which it will work. Some districts also include a list of instructions for the committee and a list of questions to guide discussion. The reconsideration committee is often established as a *standing* committee, ready to act at any time. The committee responsibilities usually require members to:

- read, listen to, or view the challenged work in its entirety
- read reviews and acknowledge awards, if any
- assess the work against established selection criteria
- discuss the work as a group
- seek the opinions of outside specialists and
- prepare a recommendation for the disposition of the work.[9]

Committee recommendations may include retaining the work, restricting its use, removing it from the collection, or moving it to another level.[10]

The reconsideration process commonly offers the complainant recourse to appeal to the superintendent or the board of education if the reconsideration committee's decision is unacceptable. The roles of the superintendent and the governing board should be delineated in the policy. The policy also should name by position the institution's official spokesperson to the media; this action will control and focus the institution's message.

It is conceivable that after experiencing a challenge, those involved will realize the procedures for reconsideration were not sufficiently comprehensive. For example, the level of detail associated with the reconsideration committee's work was inadequate leading to such questions as: Who will chair the meetings? Are the meetings public? May the complainant speak? Are standard questions available to guide the committee's discussion? If deficiencies are apparent, study the weak points and formally submit changes to the school board or other governing authority for approval.

What Should You Do with This Policy?

Once adopted by the board of education or other policy-making body, the materials selection policy should be implemented by school library media specialists in *every* school. As part of policy implementation, the library professionals should introduce the faculty to the policy and invite administrators, students, and parents to participate in the selection process. Reach out to teachers as subject area specialists who have knowledge to share. When faculty have an understanding of the selection process, they will comprehend how decisions are made. This knowledge may eliminate misunderstandings about why some materials are purchased for the library while others are not.

School library media specialists should discuss the selection policy and reconsideration procedures with their principals, who may not understand the fine points of intellectual freedom as it applies to selection or removal of materials in school library media collections. Make an annual appointment with the principal to go through the policy and reconsideration procedures together. By using this proactive approach, the principal will not be caught unaware and violate policy by agreeing to remove a book if a parent complains. The library professional also will have an opportunity to discuss current selection, budget, and collection areas in need of improvement due to age or curricular changes.

Library media specialists should talk to parent groups and library volunteers about the selection process, criteria, and steps they may take if they have concerns about materials. Promoting an open attitude about the selection process may eliminate problems before they occur and pay dividends if a challenge occurs.

 Teaching about Intellectual Freedom

Not every lesson takes place in a classroom. By including students in the selection of library materials, the library media specialist can teach them about how libraries support democracy. She/he can use selection policy criteria such as *reflect the pluralistic nature of a global society* or *free of bias and stereotyping* to enlighten students about the right of all members of a democratic society to view, listen to, and read materials on a variety of topics with diverse perspectives. When students read reviews and discuss possible new materials, they learn firsthand that library resources must reflect many points of view.

Bonnie, an independent school librarian, is proud of including students in the selection process.

"I have developed a club for the school entitled Friends-of-the-Library. It is a student group, which has grown to 45 students. I take them shopping using funds from the library budget and allow them to select books for the library. They are very serious about this responsibility and who better to select what they need in classes than the students in the classes! This has been a great way to sell the library to students (and their parents)."[11]

A policy is only as effective as the people in charge of following it. If the school library media specialist, principal, superintendent, or headmaster/ mistress is afraid of a parent, the media, or a special interest group and gives in to the pressure to remove an item from the collection without following the reconsideration process, *the policy is useless.* The intellectual freedom and First Amendment rights of minors to receive information are weakened substantially, because at least one resource is no longer available to students.

Policies do not have an infinite shelf-life; therefore, develop a schedule for the systematic review of *all* school library policies to ensure currency. An annual review seems too frequent, but initiating a policy review every three years is reasonable. In three years, resources in new formats may be available, requiring some change in selection criteria, or selection tools may change. Beyond these possibilities, when a policy review committee takes a close look at the policy under which *all* library resources are selected, it heightens awareness in the school about the process.

Why Some Books May Fail to Become Part of the Collection

In 1953 Lester Asheim published his well-known essay "Not Censorship But Selection." In it, he examines the difference between selection and censorship by librarians during the selection process. He notes that the selector looks for ways to *include* [emphasis added] a resource; in contrast, the censor comes from a negative perspective, looking for reasons to rationalize his/her decision to *exclude* [emphasis added] the resource from the collection. According to Asheim, the censor looks for "isolated parts rather than the complete whole upon which to base a judgment. Taken out of context and given weight completely out of keeping with their place in the over-all work single words and unrelated passages can be used to damn a book … In other words, four letters have outweighed five hundred pages."[12] Conversely, the librarian, in the role of selector, judges and makes a selection decision based on the *entire content* of the book, looking at the work as a whole. Asheim warns librarians against rejecting a title for the collection based on *anticipated* external pressure and the fear of how it may affect one's job. This act constitutes censorship. Asheim concludes his essay with these powerful words.

> Selection seeks to protect the right of the reader to read; censorship seeks to protect—not the right—but the reader himself from the fancied effect of his reading. The selector has faith in the intelligence of the reader; the censor has faith only in his own.[13]

Asheim's essay remains relevant today. A school library professional may still rationalize not purchasing an item that does not match his/her personal views. As more "edgy" fiction is published and the media reports challenges to these titles, a school library media specialist may find reasons not to add a title to the book order. For every professional who needs to be reminded of

Asheim's timeless admonitions, the essay is accessible to readers on the ALA Office for Intellectual Freedom website.

Self-Censorship

In Chapter 1, the ethical dilemma of self-censorship or pre-censorship was introduced. Pre-censorship differs from censorship in that the material is censored *before* being added to the collection; it is never purchased and made available. Pre-censorship occurs *during* the selection process and may be based on a conscious or unconscious bias against the topic or author by the person selecting materials.[14] The school library professional also may pre-censor based on fear that the resource, if added to the collection, will result in a formal challenge.

School Library Media Specialists: Censors or Selectors?

Unfortunately, no broad national study has determined the extent of self-censorship or pre-censorship by school library media specialists in the United States. There are only snapshots in time. Marjorie Fiske's study of public and school librarians in California reported in 1959 that almost two-thirds of librarians could cite instances where they did not purchase an item because it was considered controversial. In addition, nearly 20 percent said they routinely did not purchase materials if they were *perceived* as controversial.[15] Laura Smith McMillan completed a doctoral dissertation in 1987 researching "Censorship by Librarians in Public Senior High Schools in Virginia." She reported that school library media specialists "were significantly more restrictive with fictional materials than with nonfictional materials."[16]

In 2002 Ken P. Coley studied self-censorship in Texas high school libraries. He reported that 82 percent of the schools in the study showed indications that self-censorship had occurred during the collection development process, and fewer controversial books were selected in small schools than in larger schools.[17]

A survey was conducted by the University of Central Arkansas to determine the extent to which 21 of the most popular gay, bisexual, lesbian, and transgender-themed books published between 1999 and 2005 were owned by public, school, and academic libraries in Arkansas. The results reported "about 21 percent of public libraries, nearly five percent of university libraries, and a shocking less than one percent of school libraries have books containing controversial themes and characters."[18] The researchers believe these statistics reflect a range of reasons—fear of challenges, concern over administrative displeasure, the possibility of job loss, and personal values.[19] While this research was conducted in Arkansas, it likely reflects the fears many library media specialists have about selecting materials on homosexuality.

School library professionals negatively impact collections when they are fearful to select a resource because it may be challenged. They also impact the collection when their selections are based on personal bias or preferences. The bias may be *against* certain topics and *decidedly over-positive* toward others. Kay Bishop in *The Collection Program in Schools,* warns:

> Media specialists should be aware of their own biases and preferences so that personal prejudices do not inadvertently affect selection decisions. A media specialist with a strong belief in higher education may be tempted to purchase more college-oriented materials than items for vocational courses. A media specialist who advocates online searching as a major teaching tool may be overzealous in budgeting for online services. A media specialist whose hobby is cinema may buy numerous materials about movies and equipment for video production. College-preparatory materials, online databases, books on cinema, and video production equipment are all worthy resources; however, the media specialist's personal interests should not unduly influence selection decisions.[20]

The school library media professional must weigh many factors during selection, including his/her fears, biases, and preferences so that the collection will reflect and serve the needs of students and faculty.

A school library media specialist would find it difficult not to allow personal values, beliefs, and biases for and against certain types of materials, as well as fears—whether grounded for not—to impact selection decisions at one time or another. Nearly every library media specialist has wrestled with the temptation of self-censorship when choosing resources for the collection. It is easy to look at the community and *anticipate* a challenge *if* a book on this topic or that hot button issue is selected. However, library professionals cannot see into the future and should not prejudge a book, thinking it may trigger a challenge. As the popular quote by Jo Godwin states, "A truly great library contains something in it to offend everyone."[21] Speaking at a conference on banned books, young adult author Cynthia Grant said, "The best collection is one that always makes you feel slightly uneasy. In other words, if you're doing your job, somebody won't be happy."[22]

"I have from time to time removed books of my own volition from the shelf because I thought I had made a mistake in its purchase."
Anonymous preschool-8th grade independent school librarian[24]

Dr. Rebecca Butler, Associate Professor, Northern Illinois University, speaks for many library professionals when she states, "It always strikes me as interesting that anyone can be a censor and that probably ALL of us are, given particular situations. I believe so strongly in intellectual freedom that I like to think I just COULDN'T ever censor, but I know in my heart that is probably not the case. Any of us could choose to censor something that offends us." [23]

Megan Schliesman, a librarian at the Cooperative Children's Book Center (CCBC) of the School of Education at the University of Wisconsin–Madison, brought the topic of self-censorship out into the open in a commentary, "Self-Censorship: Let's Talk About It."

"As a profession, we don't talk much about self-censorship—why it happens and what we can do about it. And the reality is that one of the biggest challenges librarians may face in choosing books or other materials for a collection are their own fears or biases. We need to encourage one another to talk about barriers that can arise in materials selection openly and honestly, and we need to create environments where these discussions can take place without fear of judgment. In doing so, we might not be able to alleviate everyone's fears, but we can certainly help mitigate them, and decrease the sense of isolation that is certainly a reality for some librarians who feel out on a limb when making material selection decisions.

If fear is at the root of self-censoring behavior, talk about those fears and weigh them against reality. No matter how certain someone is that a book or other item will offend someone, no one knows for certain when—or over what—a challenge may arise. And no library can function effectively if any member of the staff is fearful of making selection decisions. Everyone responsible for materials selection needs to understand their policy: how it supports and empowers them to serve their community, be it students and staff in a school, or the citizens of a community.

Perhaps the most insidious form of self-censorship, and therefore the most difficult to overcome, is that rooted in personal bias. And that's when it's time to be more assertive in affirming a library's responsibility to the diverse members of its community and to the First Amendment rights of everyone it serves. A library collection should reflect the wide-ranging needs and interests found within the community it serves, not those of the librarian(s) responsible for selecting materials. A librarian who is rejecting items on topics or with content that he or she finds personally objectionable is, quite simply, not doing her or his job."[25]

Combating Self-Censorship

The library media professional starts combating self-censorship by laying the groundwork for a climate supportive of intellectual freedom throughout the school. When the school library media specialist proactively builds support *before* a challenge occurs, the fear of challenges diminishes. Take the time to explain the selection process and official selection criteria to teachers, administrators, students, and parents. One single explanation or conversation is not enough. To be effective, a message must be repeated over and over. Advocacy for intellectual freedom within and beyond the school community will be discussed in Chapter 9.

Library media specialists find guidance in *The Code of Ethics for the ALA* about one aspect of self-censorship—bias and personal preferences, stating, "We distinguish between our personal convictions and professional duties and do not allow our personal beliefs to interfere with fair representation of the aims of our institutions or the provision of access to their information resources" (Article VII).[26]

Library media professionals can use the following strategies to successfully combat self-censorship:

- Invite teachers, administrators, students, and parents to be active participants in the selection process.
- Acknowledge that libraries provide choices for their patrons.
- Determine whether a potential resource will make a contribution to the collection.
- Question whether there are students who *need* and *would read* this information.
- Realize that selection often involves choosing to purchase an item containing ideas or viewpoints with which one does not agree.
- Remember that selection does not mean that the library professional personally *endorses* the ideas found in the work.
- Employ numerous reviewing sources and analyze evaluations.
- Compare the reviews for a title against the selection criteria in the materials selection policy and the collection's needs.
- Reread Lester Asheim's essay, "Not Censorship But Selection," concentrating on the ideas: Selectors look for reasons to *include* the resource and make a decision based on the entire content.
- Ask teacher colleagues to read the review(s) and discuss their opinions.
- Seek the views of students both on the topic and the specific resource.
- Confer with other school library professionals about the resource to gain their perspectives.
- Be conscious of personal biases and preferences represented in the library collection by using these strategies and others:
  - Look at a narrow section of the collection retrospectively to analyze whether only one point of view is represented.
  - Look at something you believe to be "truth" and ask if that "truth" is reflected in unconscious bias in the collection.
  - Analyze whether sections of the collection are larger because they reflect the personal interests of the library professional rather than the instruction and recreation needs of patrons.

Administrative Intervention in Selection

In addition to self-censorship, library media specialists face other barriers during the selection process. For example, the supervisor of the library media specialist may implement pre-censorship. Reflecting on an experience with book selection and pre-censorship early in her career, Ginny Moore Kruse, Director Emerita of the Cooperative Children's Book Center of the School of Education at the University of Wisconsin–Madison said,

> In my first school library position I was the "head librarian" in a large junior high school. There was a second full-time librarian on the staff, and we had a full-time library aide, too. These were the so-called "good old days." But not everything was "good." All orders for library materials went to the school district library coordinator who scrutinized each order, line by line. I still have no idea where or why she had the time to do this, but she did, and she literally red-lined any item she decided wasn't necessary.
>
> I always selected books using the guidance of published book reviews in the noted journals of this decade: *School Library Journal, Booklist, The Horn Book,* and the *Bulletin of the Center for Children's Books.* I also used my knowledge of the school's instructional program and paid attention to teachers' requests. The day when I received a copy of my most recent book order and saw that my order for a copy of *The Outsiders,* written by new novelist S. E. Hinton, had been red-lined was the day when I understood first-hand what censorship is, the effect it has, and how it can happen *internally* as well as from outside sources. I protested, showing the professional reviews to back up my request. The students in my school were soon able to check out a library copy of *The Outsiders* after all, but that experience caused the scales to fall from my eyes and permanently changed one dimension of my professional life.[27]

Today, as in Kruse's "good old days," library media specialists still face obstacles when selecting materials for their libraries. One experienced school library professional related:

> After a series of book challenges over a period of several years, the new administration in our school district directed a memo to all media specialists that stated that all material reviews must be approved by school principals before items are purchased. This has resulted in delayed orders. In addition, some items were rejected even though they had favorable reviews in reliable review journals such as *School Library Journal.* The administration did not clarify what they would or would not approve, but it would appear that those items with a slightly "edgier" theme are the items that are rejected. It appears that the administration thinks that they can "appease" a certain segment of the community with this procedure or, as the very least, hope to prevent any challenges from ever occurring. With concern about open enrollment [the practice of allowing students to enroll without charge in any PK-12 public school, including those living outside a district], administrators want to avoid any bad publicity. It is clear that they perceive book challenges as bad publicity.

This new "policy" has also affected the selection of materials by the media specialists. We now are more likely to "second guess" our decisions and to possibly even self-censor our choices. Over a period of time, this type of selection will create a collection that is bland and devoid of any real substance. It will also result in a collection that is lacking balance.[28]

These two examples are not unique, and there are other variations on the theme of supervisors' red-lining book orders. In some school districts, library media specialists are required by the selection policy to post their book consideration files on the library website or have a copy available for parent and community review. In others, library professionals may order only from approved lists. While the input of teachers, students, administrators, and parents is *welcomed* and often mandated by the selection policy, a supervisor or principal pre-censoring a title creates an atmosphere of apprehension for the school library professional. In addition, if the policy states the school library media specialists make the final selection decision, interference in the selection process is contradictory to the policy.

Other Selection Concerns

Proscribed Reading Programs

Because of the increasing popularity of computerized reading management programs such as Accelerated Reader and Scholastic Reading Counts, school library professionals are facing pressure to select and purchase only those books for which computer-delivered quizzes on the books' content are available. This constraint does not take into account the substantial knowledge of the library media specialist regarding what is needed in the collection to support both research and the personal interests of student readers. Selection policy criteria should be applied to purchases supporting the school's reading program just as with any other addition to the library media center collection.

Opposition to Multilingual Resources

Many school library media programs serve students whose first language is not English. In some parts of the country, library professionals are limited by budgetary constraints or discouraged from adding resources in languages other than English by "English only" local sentiment. "Access to Resources and Services in the School Library Media Program: An Interpretation of the *Library Bill of Rights*" states:

> While English is, by history and tradition, the customary language of the United States, the languages in use in any given community may vary. Schools serving communities in which other languages are used make efforts to accommodate the needs of students for whom English is a second language.[29]

In other words, it is the responsibility of the library media specialist to attempt to provide equal and equitable access to resources that match the community's linguistic diversity.

A middle school library media specialist in Pennsylvania eloquently described why resources in languages other than English are needed.

> We have over 40 languages other than English spoken in our school district. Students who speak other languages often benefit from resources in their primary language, even when they are fluent in English. As they are learning English, they especially need access to information and reading materials in both languages. My Spanish copy of *Number the Stars* will be used in conjunction with their classroom copy (in English) to ensure that the students understand the story. My Spanish encyclopedias enable them to complete projects (usually in English) because they understand the science or history involved.... If we are not to "devolve into a society bifurcated into haves and have-nots," then we must provide resources on all levels and languages needed by our patrons.[30]

Opposition to Multicultural Resources

Library media specialists must also provide materials reflecting the ethnic minorities using school library media centers. According to Michele de la Iglesia,

> For the children of a specific ethnic minority, reading positive stories about their own ethnic group can increase self-esteem and make them feel part of a larger society. For children of a "majority" group, reading stories about other cultures can increase their sensitivity to those who are different from themselves, improve their knowledge of the world, and help them realize that although people have many differences, they also share many similarities.[31]

When the school library professional stocks multicultural resources that reflect a community's ethnic minorities, s/he supports the right of students to access to information, protects their intellectual freedom, and prepares them to be responsible citizens in a global society.

Graphic Novels

Graphic novels are book-length comics, include both fiction and nonfiction titles, and cover nearly every genre, including biographies, poetry, history, romance, crime, adventure, fantasy, and science fiction. Their format is appealing to students of all ages, including the segment considered "reluctant readers." The school library professional will find that graphic novels fit under the existing criteria in most materials selection policies, and they are reviewed in professional review sources.[32]

The graphic format does not mean that the content is always mature, violent, or sexually explicit; and library staff must acknowledge that *the combination of words and graphics has a different impact than words alone.* Those opposing graphic novels often focus on the images because they have a powerful impact. In 2006 the National Coalition Against Censorship, the American Library Association, and the Comic Book Legal Defense Fund created "Graphic Novels: Suggestions for Librarians" to assist school and public library youth professionals in selecting, shelving, and defending resources in a graphic format. Available online, the guide asserts that graphic novels "promote visual and verbal literacy, as well as a love of reading."[33]

Whatever the obstacle to selection—self-censorship, administrative intervention, undue pressure to support computerized reading management programs, weak support for bilingual and ethnic resources, or opposition to graphic novels—the library media professional must remember that students have a First Amendment right to receive information. The materials selection policy, adopted by the public or private school's governing board, provides the structure under which materials are added to a collection. Doug Johnson, director of media and technology for I.S. D 77 Mankato Public Schools (Minnesota), gives this sage advice,

> Know your selection policy, select from authoritative reviews, insist on due process if a book is challenged, and make children responsible for their own choices. It's not hard, but it *does* take genuine courage. And it is not only why we need professionals in all our school libraries, but professionals who act professionally.[34]

✍ Key Ideas Summary

This chapter covered a broad range of issues related to developing a materials selection policy and obstacles to selection of materials. To review, here are some of the major ideas:

- A formally adopted materials selection policy is the legal basis for selection and reconsideration of all materials used in a school, including school library media center resources.

- A selection policy describes why and how resources will be added to the school library media program collection.

- A materials selection policy is composed of the following: objectives; responsibility for selection; criteria for selection; direction on selecting materials on controversial topics; procedures for selection, acquisition, and collection maintenance; support for intellectual freedom; and procedures for reconsideration of library resources.

- Implementation of materials selection policies includes explaining the selection process to faculty, administrators, library volunteers, and parent and community groups.

- Students involved in the selection process learn that school library media center collections include materials on a variety of topics from diverse perspectives.

- Selection policies should be reviewed on a regular basis for possible revision.

- Self-censorship, initiated by either the school library media specialist or his/her supervisor, is the act of *not* selecting a resource based on anticipated objection to the title or topic or on personal bias.

- Additional concerns relating to selection may include administrative intervention, pressure to purchase only those books for which reading management program computer-generated tests are available, resistance to providing resources to meet the needs of multilingual students for whom English is a second language, not recognizing the importance of stocking multicultural resources that reflect a community's ethnic minorities, and selecting fiction and nonfiction in a graphic format.

Library Bill of Rights Interpretations

- American Library Association. "Access to Library Resources and Services Regardless of Sex, Gender Identity, Gender Expression, or Sexual Orientation: An Interpretation of the *Library Bill of Rights*"

- American Library Association. "Access to Resources and Services in the School Library Media Program: An Interpretation of the *Library Bill of Rights*"

- American Library Association. "Diversity of Collection Development: An Interpretation of the *Library Bill of Rights*"

- American Library Association. "Evaluating Library Collections: An Interpretation of the *Library Bill of Rights*"

All interpretations may be found at the ALA Office for Intellectual Freedom website: http://www.ala.org/oif.

Recommended Resources

- **American Library Association, Office for Intellectual Freedom, "Workbook for Selection Policy Writing,"** http://www.ala.org/Template.cfm?Section=dealing& Template=/ContentManagement/ContentDisplay.cfm&ContentID=11173

  Aimed specifically at school libraries, the document includes the recommended sections and sample language for a school materials selection policy with reconsideration procedures.

- **American Library Association, Intellectual Freedom Committee Subcommittee on the Impact of Media Concentration in Libraries, "Fostering Media Diversity in Libraries: Strategies and Actions," June 2007,** http://ala8.ala.org/ala/oif/ ifissues/fostering_media_diversity.pdf

  The purpose of the document is to provide all types of libraries with strategies to create and provide access to a diverse collection of resources, including children's and young adult collections and equally diverse library services and programs.

- **Asheim, Lester. "Not Censorship But Selection,** *Wilson Library Bulletin* **28 (Sept. 1953): 63-67.** Also available on the ALA website: http://www.ala.org/ala/oif/basics/notcensorship.htm

  This classic article carefully defines the difference between selection and censorship on the part of the library professional.

- **Bishop, Kay.** *The Collection Program in Schools: Concepts, Practices, and Information Sources.* **Rev. ed. Westport, Connecticut: Libraries Unlimited, 2007.**

  A revised edition of the classic by Phyllis J. Van Orden and Kay Bishop. Of particular interest is the information on policies and procedures, selection criteria, and ethical and intellectual freedom issues related to developing a collection.

- **New York Library Association. "Self-Censorship Checklist,"** http://www.nyla.org/index.php?page_id=444

  The checklist's 18 questions will help library professionals determine if they have ever violated intellectual freedom principles.

- **Reichman, Henry.** *Censorship and Selection: Issues and Answers for Schools.* **3rd ed.** Chicago: American Library Association, 2001.

  Reichman addresses writing a selection policy, censorship of library resources, filtering Internet content, and legal issues and relevant court cases.

Notes

1. Kruse, Ginny Moore, email to author, February 20, 2007.
2. American Library Association, Office for Intellectual Freedom. *Intellectual Freedom Manual,* 7th ed. (Chicago: American Library Association, 2006), 418.
3. American Library Association, "Workbook for Selection Policy Writing," http://www.ala.org/Template.cfm?Section=dealing&Template=/ContentManagement/ContentDisplay.cfm&ContentID=57020.
4. Ibid.
5. Rules for the Selection and Reconsideration of School Media Center Resources, Rosholt School District [Wisconsin], September 12, 2000.
6. Bonnie, email to author, November 13, 2007.
7. Rules for the Selection, Rosholt School District.
8. American Library Association, Article II, *Library Bill of Rights,* http://www.ala.org/ala/oif/statementspols/statementsif/interpretations/Default675.htm.
9. Symons, Ann K., and Charles Harmon, *Protecting the Right to Read* (New York: Neal-Schuman Publishers, 1995), 84–85.
10. Ibid.
11. Bonnie, email to author, November 13, 2007.
12. Asheim, Lester, "Not Censorship But Selection," originally published in the *Wilson Library Bulletin,* 28 (September 1953), 63–67. Currently available at http://www.ala.org/ala/oif/basics/notcensorship.htm.
13. Ibid.
14. Reitz, Joan M., *ODLIS – Online Dictionary for Library and Information Science,* http://lu.com/odlis/search.cfm.
15. Langland, Laurie, "Public Libraries, Intellectual Freedom, and the Internet: To Filter or Not to Filter," *PNLA Quarterly* 62, no. 4 (Summer 1998), http://www.pnla.org/quart/su98/langland.htm#fiske.

16. Coley, Ken P., "Moving Toward a Method to Test for Self-Censorship by School Library Media Specialists," *School Library Media Research* vol. 5 (2002), http://www.ala.org/ala/aasl/aaslpubsandjournals/slmrb/slmrcontents/volume52002/coley.htm.

17. Ibid.

18. Whelan, Debra Lau, "Gay Titles Missing in Most AR Libraries," *School Library Journal* 53, no. 1 (January 2007), 18.

19. Ibid.

20. Bishop, Kay. *The Collection Program in Schools: Concepts, Practices, and Information Sources.* 4th ed. (Westport, Connecticut: Libraries Unlimited, 2007), 170.

21. Godwin, Jo, "Quotation," Liberty-Tree.ca, http://quotes.liberty-tree.ca/quotes_by/jo+godwin.

22. Grant, Cynthia, "Tales from a YA Author: Slightly Uneasy," *School Library Journal* 41, no 10 (October 1995), 50.

23. Butler, Rebecca, email interview with author, January 29, 2007.

24. Anonymous, email to author, November 6, 2007.

25. Schliesman, Megan, "Self-Censorship: Let's Talk About It," *Wisconsin Library Association Intellectual Freedom Round Table Newsletter* XIII, no. 1 (Spring 2007), http://www.wla.lib.wi.us/ifrt/Newsletters/IFRT_Spr07.pdf.

26. American Library Association, Article VII, *Code of Ethics of the American Library Association,* http://www.ala.org/ala.oif/statementspols/codeofethics/codeethics.htm.

27. Kruse, Ginny Moore.

28. Anonymous school library media specialist, email to author, April 17, 2007.

29. American Library Association, "Access to Resources and Services in the School Library Media Program: An Interpretation of the *Library Bill of Rights*," http://www.ala.org/ala/oif/statementspols/statementsif/interpretations/Default675.htm.

30. Markiewicz, Lois, "Libros en espanol? Reader Forum, Letters and Comments," *American Libraries* 38, no. 11 (December 2007), 8.

31. Royce, John, "Walking Two Moons: Crossing Borders with International Literature," *Knowledge Quest* 35, no. 2 (2006), 33.

32. Rudiger, Hollis Margaret, and Megan Schliesman, "Graphic Novels and School Libraries," *Knowledge Quest* 36, no 2 (November/December 2007), 57–58.

33. National Coalition Against Censorship, the American Library Association, and the Comic Book Legal Defense Fund, "Graphic Novels: Suggestions for Librarians," 2006, http://www.ncac.org/graphicnovels.

34. Johnson, Doug, "Don't Defend That Book," *Library Media Connection* 26, no. 1 (August/September 2007), 98.

CHAPTER 4

"The Right to Read"

It is not enough to simply teach children to read; we have to give them something worth reading. Something that will stretch their imaginations— something that will help them make sense of their own lives and encourage them to reach out toward people whose lives are quite different from their own.[1]

—Newbery Medal author, Katherine Paterson

Foundations of the Right to Read

The Freedom to Read, a joint statement of the American Library Association (ALA) and the Association of American Publishers, proclaims, "The freedom to read is essential to our democracy."[2] Legally, school library media specialists protect minors' right to read under the First Amendment and case law. In the First Amendment, freedom of speech refers to more than oral communication and has been interpreted by the courts to include a minor's right to read and receive information and ideas. The four court cases below support the First Amendment rights of minors to read using resources in school library media program collections.

- *Counts v. Cedarville School District* (2003) The school board adopted a policy that required students to have written parental permission to read the *Harry Potter* books because it was concerned that the books promoted disobedience and included witchcraft and the occult. A federal district court reversed the board's decision stating that the board "could not abridge students' First Amendment right to read a book on the basis of an undifferentiated fear of disturbance or because the Board disagreed with the ideas contained in the book."[3]

- *Case v. Unified School District No. 233* (1995) When the school board voted to remove *Annie on My Mind*, a novel about a lesbian relationship, from junior and senior high school libraries, the federal district court in Kansas ruled that they had violated the students' rights under the First Amendment. Through their board testimony, it was clear that their original reason for removal—"educational unsuitability"—masked their true reason: disapproval of the book's content. The school board also was found to have violated its own materials selection and reconsideration policies.[4]

- *Salvail v. Nashua Board of Education* (1979) The school board removed *MS* magazine from a New Hampshire high school library. The U.S. District Court decided that the board "failed to demonstrate a substantial and legitimate government interest sufficient to warrant the removal of *MS* magazine from the Nashua High School library. Their action contravenes [conflicts with] the plaintiff's First Amendment rights, and as such it is plainly wrong."[5]

- *Minarcini v. Strongsville (Ohio) City School District* (1976) The board of education ordered the removal of *Catch-22* and *Cat's Cradle* from the library. The court ruled against the school board, rejecting the board's absolute right to remove books from a school library stating, "A library is a storehouse of knowledge. When created for a public school, it is an important privilege for the benefit of students in the schools. That privilege is not subject to being withdrawn by succeeding school boards whose members may desire to 'winnow' the library for books the contents of which occasioned their displeasure or disapproval."[6]

Within the library profession, there is additional support for the right to read and access information. "Free Access to Libraries for Minors: An Interpretation of the *Library Bill of Rights*" makes a powerful statement related to minors' First Amendment free speech rights. "Children and young adults unquestionably possess First Amendment rights, including the right to receive information through the library in print, nonprint, or digital format. Constitutionally protected speech cannot be suppressed solely to protect children or young adults from ideas or images a legislative body believes to be unsuitable for them."[7]

The ALA and the American Association of School Librarians (AASL) support minors' free access to library resources. Access is one of ALA's "Core Values of Librarianship" and includes providing all patrons with equal and equitable availability to library resources regardless of format.[8] As noted in Chapter 1, the *Library Bill of Rights*, Article V, affirms special protections to minors using libraries stating, "A person's right to use a library should not be denied or abridged because of origin, *age* [emphasis added], background, or views."[9] The school library professionals who wrote *Information Power* articulated that one of a library media specialist's goals is to "become an advocate inside and outside the school for reading and for literacy in print, graphic, and electronic formats."[10] Regardless of format, the right of students and youthful public library patrons to read and receive information is well established.

The Role of School Library Professionals in Student Reading

Knowing the legal and philosophical basis for the right to read is not enough. School library media specialists' personal support of intellectual freedom precepts and their day-to-day practice affect students' access to books and information and have far-reaching implications in their lives. Research gives some insight into school library professionals' attitudes and practices.

In 2004 Sarah McNichol conducted research in the United Kingdom to determine the attitudes of school and youth services public librarians toward intellectual freedom and whether their stated beliefs were carried out in *practice.* McNichol reported in "Attitudes Toward Intellectual Freedom and Censorship Amongst School and Children's Librarians" that while U.K. school library professionals supported intellectual freedom in theory, in their libraries, they practiced censorship in various ways including:

- controlling access to books perceived to have dangerous or controversial ideas,
- labeling materials perceived to be controversial, and
- restricting access to fiction based on age.[11]

One U.K. school library professional openly acknowledged that censorship practices occur. "I think young people should have access to what they want to read because I believe you read to the level that you understand ... so in principle, with lofty ideals, I think there shouldn't be censorship, but in day to day practicalities, we do censor; that's just a fact of being a librarian I think."[12]

Frances Beck McDonald conducted a similar study among school librarians in three midwestern states in 1993 and reported her findings in *A Survey of School Librarians' Attitudes and Moral Reasoning* (Scarecrow Press, 1993). McDonald stated,

> This study revealed that school librarians, *while professing agreement with the principles of intellectual freedom in theory, were not so strongly in agreement with the application of the principles.* School librarians were inclined to be restrictive in all categories of potential censorship: policy, selection, access, and diversity. School librarians showed restrictive attitudes toward selection of resources, responded to perceived influences on their selection decisions, seemed unwilling to enforce policies protecting resources, and were reluctant to provide unrestricted access to items in the collection.[13]

Since McDonald's study was completed over a decade ago, another U.S. study is needed to determine if there is a similar gap today between belief in intellectual freedom principles and actions taken by library media specialists in their programs.

Age and Grade Level Considerations

Information Power directs the school library professional to "Guard against barriers to intellectual freedom, such as age or grade-level restrictions,

Providing Access for Young Patrons

- Ask the student to check out only the number of resources for which s/he can be responsible. The limit is not determined by age, rather by a student's *sense of personal responsibility*.
- Provide large zip-type plastic bags labeled with the child's name to keep the books safe and dry. The books can be placed in children's backpacks and travel to and from school in this manner.
- Provide a fluorescent-colored bookmark with the name of the school library and the date the book is due.
- Supply parents with a library visit calendar, noting the dates of children's regularly scheduled library visits and the dates books are due.

limitations on access to electronic information, requirements for special permissions to use materials and resources, and restricted collections."[14] Unfortunately, in some schools, kindergarten students are not permitted to borrow any books until the latter half of the year for fear they will lose or damage the library materials. Obviously, this practice does not support the extension of intellectual freedom to all patrons regardless of age. Young children love books and should not be denied their First Amendment rights to read based on their year in school.

Elementary students may also be limited in the *number* of titles that they can check out from the school library media center. Similarly, students may not be allowed to freely exchange their books throughout the school week and may be required to wait until their next visit to select another book. Restricting the number of books that can be borrowed at one time or the frequency of school library visits are another barrier to children's right to read.

There is also the potential for restrictions on free selection when young readers choose books beyond their reading abilities, such as a first grader trying to check out one of the *Harry Potter* titles or the *Lord of the Rings*. Should school library media specialists or their teacher refuse to let the child check out the book, apply the "five finger test" (see sidebar), or follow intellectual freedom precepts of allowing the child free choice? There are several factors to consider. Will the child be sharing the book with an adult or sibling who will read the text aloud to the younger child? Is the child looking for the ego boost of carrying a "big book"? Is s/he attracted to the cover, photos, or layout? Sue, a K-8 library media specialist, treats the situation this way, "I have an unofficial rule that students can take *any* book of their choice as long as they also have one or two that I know they can read by themselves."[15]

Many school library facilities are shared by children across a wide range of ages and grades, with varying intellectual, social, and emotional

Selecting the "Right" Book

- The **"five finger test"** is an easy method for determining whether the reading level of a book matches the student's reading ability. Have the student select a page and read. Each time the child struggles or misses a word, s/he raises a finger. When one page is finished, count the number of fingers raised. Five fingers, the book is too difficult; four fingers, the text is challenging but can probably be read with assistance. Two to three fingers raised, the book is just right. One finger indicates the book is too easy.[16]

- In the **"read aloud" method**, ask the child to read the first paragraph or the first page aloud, close the book, and tell a library staff member or another student what happened in the story. If a child can relate accurately what s/he has read, the school library media specialist can feel comfortable confirming this is a "right" book.[17]

development. Children mature at different rates, and age and grade level should not be a determining factor in when a student is ready to read a particular title. To eliminate the potential for restrictions based on age in this type of setting, Sue in a K-8 library counsels,

> We provide a wide variety of materials with a wide range of topics. I strive to have something for everyone. For instance this year, I've made a conscious attempt to purchase graphic novels, because I'm finding they really appeal to students with lower reading levels. We don't restrict students' reading by age; however, we do try to guide them to pick up materials that they can handle.[18]

Elementary libraries may have other limitations based on a student's age or grade level. Laura, mother of an elementary student in New York shared this story of her family's frustration with limitations on their daughter's reading.

> My second grader was tested at the end of last year (1st grade) and found to be reading at a fifth grade reading level. My husband and I are struggling with finding material that is "appropriate" for her age yet challenging to read. Her librarian told her the first week of school she had to remain in the K-2 section of the library and could only check out certain chapter books that the librarian deems appropriate for second graders. Not fair to my child who is interested in Ancient Egypt and mysteries—and some of the material in the section she is allowed to go into—just doesn't interest her or she has already read it. She was told those books are "off limits" to her—the books regarding history and the Little House Series.[19]

> Laura later reported, I have great news in the form of an update to my story. My daughter is completing second grade. Her teacher conducted reading tests last week and told me Katelyn's reading level is "off the charts." Anyway, her teacher went to the librarian and pulled titles of books that are closer to her reading level but appropriate for an 8 year old (like the Nancy Drew mysteries) in content. So—I have a happy ending to what began as a frustrating experience for me and my daughter, and now she loves going to the library each week.[20]

Private schools, like their public school counterparts, have a range of circulation practices. Those with self-checkout are unable to monitor student choices. Some private school librarians feel somewhat constrained because of their religious affiliation. Kevin, a librarian in an independent school in Florida, states,

> My school serves students in grades PS-8th grade. We are an independent, religious-affiliated school. To me this means I need to be careful, mostly in the area of YA fiction. I do put a middle school sticker [on spines] of books I feel are not appropriate for our younger students, but it is not a strict policy. I, myself, make many exceptions for individual students, and if a parent sends a note or comes in, the student may check out the book.[21]

With upper and lower school libraries, Barbara's independent school in Texas actively promotes opportunities for students to engage with literature.

> My school encourages our students to read and expects that the Library Department will program a variety of events, such as Author Visits, Universal Reading Day, Summer Reading Program, Banned Book Week, etc. to lend excitement and value to the habit of reading. No collection is labeled as to reading level, and we have a union catalog which gives all students access to whatever materials they want. Students have full access to both libraries [upper and lower school], which is something we worked hard to provide. We make them feel welcome when they are in either Library."[22]

Hidden Resources and Labeling

Another impediment to free access is created when titles that may be considered particularly controversial or contain content the school library professional deems "mature" are kept in the librarian's office or shelved in another location that requires a student to ask for assistance in obtaining the material. Some schools require student patrons to submit written permission from a parent or guardian before checking out certain books. "Restricted Access to Library Materials: An Interpretation of the *Library Bill of Rights*" warns against creating age-related, economic, linguistic, and other barriers that limit the use of library materials.[23]

Case law from *Counts v. Cedarville School District* in 2003 does not support having a restricted shelf or use of signed permission slips to gain access to the *Harry Potter* books. The court ruled that these restrictions were a violation of the students' First Amendment right to read and receive information.[24] The decision is binding only in that case and only in the Western District of Arkansas; however, it may be considered *persuasive* by other federal courts in future cases. At the very least, having to *ask* to use the material on a restricted shelf or in an area inaccessible to students is a barrier, and one few students may have the courage to cross.

Successful Strategies for Open Access

- Shelve *all books together*, regardless of subject matter, point-of-view, or author's background, according to standard library classification.
- Do not affix labels to prejudice others against books that may be deemed controversial by some. If used, labels should be viewpoint-neutral and designed to direct users toward materials that they may be seeking.
- Use reader guidance to lead students to books matching personal interests, appropriate social and emotional level, and reading level.

There may be situations where not providing open access to resources is reasonable. Some school library media programs shelve materials by format, and not all materials are open and accessible. Audiovisual resources reserved for curricular use by faculty may not be available to students without special permission. Computer games and expensive software have the potential for theft; therefore, these resources may be safeguarded in an area available only to library staff. "Pop-up" books may be shelved to protect them and encourage careful handling. A school library media program collection also may hold archival materials that are rare, delicate, or costly; and users may need authorization from library staff to use them.

Access to information is curtailed even further when a school library media specialist is *required by school policy to create a separate or segregated collection* to house items considered controversial or too advanced in nature for students to use without monitoring. In cases such as these, school officials appear not to trust students to read and analyze information and make up their own minds. However, when youth read and learn about controversial topics, they practice the analytical skills necessary to weigh their choices and make decisions as citizens. According to the ALA's "Labels and Ratings Systems: An Interpretation of the *Library Bill of Rights*," affixing prejudicial labels to items may have the effect of discouraging or restricting users from accessing the materials.[25] Regardless of whether actual labels are placed on the spines of these books, the act of creating a separate collection characterizes the works as *different,* and possibly *dangerous,* in some way.

On the other hand, school library professionals routinely add fiction and nonfiction spine labels to books as "location indicators" to assist patrons. Library supply vendors sell genre adhesive tags, "Accelerated Reader" (AR) stickers, color-coded "dots," and other labels that can be affixed to identify the book's content or reading level at a glance. Adherents to the "no-labeling" philosophy believe that *all* labeling is prejudicial. If a science fiction genre spine label discourages a reader who does not like science fiction from opening and sampling the story, proponents of no labeling conclude the label discouraged the reader and limited his/her access to the book. In a different situation, a student selecting a book with an AR reading level label below the level of his/her classmates, may be embarrassed and teased if others see the label. Even though genre and other labels are applied to help students access materials, consider whether they may have the opposite effect.

The question of what is "appropriate" for children and young adults to read may cause some tension between the intellectual freedom ideal of open access and the practical realities of the child's family values, culture of the community, and the willingness of the school library professional to extend the right to read to all student patrons. According to library educator Gail Dickinson, "I define appropriateness in four ways: reading level, intellectual level, interest level, and emotional level. For each level, you should have evidence on which you base your decision."[26] Sarah Littman, author of *Confessions of a Closet Catholic*, has written, "There are risks involved in allowing young persons relatively free access to a wide range of reading materials.... But we believe there are greater risks in any alternative procedures. Surely we have not, as a people, lost the courage to take the risks that are necessary for the preservation of freedom."[27]

There is disagreement in the profession over *how much* access minors should have to *all* materials in a school library media center collection. Practicing *reader guidance,* in place of rigid restrictions, offers each child a choice based on his/her interests, emotional and social maturity, and reading level. Guiding readers helps each student find "just the right" book and encourages the child to return to the library again and again, creating a lifelong learner.

Reading Level Issues

As schools seek to motivate students to read more and increase reading proficiency, they are purchasing computerized reading management programs such as Accelerated Reader and Scholastic Reading Counts. These programs allow teachers to keep track of the books students have read and their level of understanding using short comprehension quizzes for which points are awarded The more difficult the book, the greater the points offered. In some schools, the points received are used to award incentive prizes for individuals or for classrooms.

While the goals of increasing students' reading skills and encouraging lifelong readers are admirable, *unless carefully administered* the programs can, ironically, become a barrier to students' right to read. Some teachers require that students read *only* those school library media center books on the reading management program's list and more specifically *only* those titles designated at a student's reading level. One of the goals of a school library media program is to support the curriculum. To advance that goal, matching children's reading level to books to be read as part of *classroom* reading instruction or for individual reading skill practice makes some sense. However, there is a difference between instructional reading and reading for pleasure.

Another goal of the school library media program is to provide students with books for personal, recreational reading choices to foster lifelong reading habits. *Restricting* a child's choice of *personal* reading to a limited number of books in the school library media center collection based on his/her reading level, and the availability of computer-generated tests on specific titles, does *not* support students' intellectual freedom or the right to read. When restrictions on selection of personal reading choices occur in the school library media center, the library professional must defend students' rights to freely select what they choose to read. Chapter 9 contains strategies for advocating with teachers about the intellectual freedom of students using the library media center collection.

In a slight variation, the use of computerized reading management programs in high school English and other classes creates another concern on the part of the library professional. Laurie, a high school library media specialist in Wisconsin, expressed her disquiet, noting, "The biggest problem is the limitations placed on students—especially the book reading level. It is frustrating to see kids that want to read a particular book not be able to because it is not at a high enough reading level—even though the content of the book is extremely appropriate. The students get very discouraged, and so do I."[28] It is also difficult for a school library professional to promote new books with good reviews when students feel compelled to confine their book selections to only those included in the reading management program.

In some districts, library media specialists also are being *required* to shelve fiction books by reading level. This practice may confuse students who are learning to find information in school library media centers, and it does not prepare them to use a public and college library. School library professionals also find locating a specific title more difficult. Arranging resources using a nonstandard classification and shelving system places another barrier between the library media center user and the resource.[29]

 Successful Strategies with Computerized Reading Management Programs

- Allow all students to select books for *personal reading* based on individual interest, not reading level or availability of tests in a computerized reading management program.
- Follow selection policy guidelines consistently for all library media program books, including those titles considered part of the reading management program.
- Review the subject matter and events in each title on the reading management program list to ensure it matches the social, emotional, and interest levels of the students using the school library media center, not simply their reading levels.
- Maintain professional practices for organizing the collection such as standard fiction and nonfiction classification and shelving schemes.

Fortunately, in many school districts school library media specialists are an integral part of reading motivation activities, including those associated with computerized reading management programs. Barbara, an elementary library media specialist in Virginia, has been a leader in multiple programs to encourage reading in her school. She states,

> Getting students to read can be challenging these days with the many activities available—television, sports, computers, and electronic games. We need a way to make reading books as appealing, exciting, and rewarding as these other activities. Like other skills, confidence as a reader comes through practice. Our AR [Accelerated Reader] books are only identified with a colored label for each general grade, not specific to the exact level, such as 1.4. The AR books are shelved with all of our other books with fiction shelved by author's last name, and our students are strongly encouraged to read books that are *not* just AR books. Our large collection (over 18,000 books) includes more than 14,000 books that are not AR books. Students are *in no way* limited in the level of AR book they can select.[30]

Barbara involves many parent volunteers who assist students in taking the computerized reading quizzes. They also help with the reward and recognition activities. During these interactions with parents, she notes, "I often give them book suggestions for their children. These suggestions are not confined to AR books, and I feel very strongly that having the AR Program should not restrict children's access to all [library] books. We use it as one of several ways to encourage students to read."[31]

Overcoming Economic Barriers

While public schools are free, tax-supported institutions, there can be economic obstacles to the use of their resources for children and young adults. These may occur in terms of fines for overdue materials, assessments for damaged materials, replacement costs for lost materials, and other possible fees. "Economic Barriers to Information: An Interpretation of the *Library Bill of Rights*" cautions school library media specialists that "All library policies and procedures, particularly those involving fines, fees, or access, should be scrutinized for potential barriers to access."[32] Sadly, in some schools, unpaid library fees may result in punitive actions, such as attendance at special events or recess being denied. The most egregious action is not allowing students to check out books. Charging fines and replacement fees for damaged and lost materials may make sense pragmatically but can pose an ethical dilemma. The library media specialist is responsible for maintaining and *retaining* a collection of print and non-print resources as well as computers and other equipment. However, there are children from low-income families who *cannot* pay fines or replacement costs for lost items. How can the library professional meet his/her fiduciary responsibilities to the school while at the same time serving the needs of the student and teaching responsibility? There is not necessarily a single solution to solve this ongoing area of tension. The library media specialist must handle such matters with sensitivity toward individual students and families.

Debbie, an elementary school library media specialist in an East Coast school library serving K-2 students, states,

> Perhaps I am too lenient at my level, but I understand that students are just building their responsibility skills and sometimes it is no fault of their own when a book is damaged, misplaced, or lost. We will often modify privileges for students who cannot pay for a lost book, by allowing them to check out books for "classroom use." At the end of the year, the slate is wiped clean. We have that policy stated in a written handbook for the K-2 level. I feel a child's perceptions of books, reading, and the library is so much more valuable than the price of a single book.[33]

The child and his/her family will not forget the small kindnesses extended while resolving fines and lost books, and the library media specialist will have protected the student's right to read and access information in the library.

 Successful Strategies for Eliminating Economic Barriers

Seeking a solution with the child and family:

- Discuss with the child the concept of responsibility and your desire to keep the door open to borrowing the library's resources.
- Arrange for a child to pay for a lost item on the "installment" plan.
- Ask a family to donate another paperback or hardcover book in reasonable condition if they are unable to reimburse for a lost item. Note: all materials should meet the criteria outlined in the library's selection policy.
- Offer the option of "working off" the fine or replacement cost for a lost or damaged book, asking the child to help in the library during recess if donating a replacement item is not an option. There are always tasks to be done such as dusting shelves, straightening books, and cleaning library tables.

Ideas for offsetting nonrecoverable costs from lost/damaged library resources:

- Ask the parent organization to establish a small fund to replace library materials that are lost by children who cannot pay replacement costs.
- Use book club bonus titles as collection replacements.
- Seek gently used replacements at rummage or used book sales.

Parents and the Right to Read

The library profession recognizes in ALA's "Libraries: An American Value" statement that it is "the responsibility and the right of all parents and guardians to guide their own children's use of the library and its resources and services."[34] School personnel acknowledge that parents have a right to oversee their child's education. Most parents are genuinely interested in their child's intellectual, social, and emotional development and expect to be part of the educational process guiding the child to maturity. In schools, curricular policies usually give parents the right to request alternative assignments or readings for their children.

Sharon, the parent of a teenage daughter in New York, has strong feelings about intellectual freedom and parents' rights.

> I am a true believer that intellectual freedom should be extended to children of all ages. Not to say that all materials are appropriate for all ages. It is only common sense that parents should be aware of what their young impressionable children are reading. But it is my belief that it is the parents and only the parents that should have the right to monitor their child's reading selections.[35]

Sharon's feelings reflect those of many parents. However, some parents expect the library media specialist to actively assist them in that role. What should a library media specialist do if a parent asks that a child's borrowing choices be limited? For example, parents may request their child not be allowed books on Halloween, ghosts, or witchcraft. Or what if a parent insists that a child not be allowed to check out *any* books, perhaps because the child has a habit of misplacing library books?

These seemingly simple requests can create both practical and ethical problems. It may be impossible for a library professional, paraprofessional staff member, parent volunteer, or student library assistant to remember the restrictions requested by specific parents, let alone monitor what individual students are taking at a given time. Even if the automated circulation system allows such limitations to be entered, self-checkout used in many schools means a child may bypass staff and still obtain a book on the parent's "forbidden topic" list.

More importantly, the *Code of Ethics of the ALA* states, "We uphold the principles of intellectual freedom and resist all efforts to censor library materials."[36] Are requests from parents to restrict access to information or books on specified topics *censorship*? Should school library staff be involved in *preventing* a child or young adult from asserting their First Amendment rights to read or receive information based on a parental request? In *American Amusement Machine Association (AAMA) v. Teri Kendrick*, Judge Richard Posner wrote, "Children have First Amendment rights … People are unlikely to become well-functioning, independent minded adults and responsible citizens if they are raised in an intellectual bubble."[37]

The school library media specialist has a spectrum of options for solving this dilemma. Although rare, some districts have circulation policies stating that parents may request a limitation on their child's reading choices. In this case, the school library professional will follow policy. With no policy in place, s/he can accept the parents' request and insert a note in the circulation system restricting the child's ability to check out materials. The library media specialist may take this action for several reasons. First, s/he may feel parents have a right to guide the reading of their children. Second, it is very difficult politically to resist this type of request.

Some library professionals have found ways to honor parent requests for elementary or middle school students. Jo, a K-6 library media specialist in the Midwest, uses this approach. "I talk to the student about making good choices when I get the note from the parent. If the child brings a book [inappropriate under the parents' guidelines] to check out, I say that he/she will have to make a better choice because mom/dad doesn't think that the child is ready for that particular book yet. If they try again, I tell him/her to put it back and find something else. I don't make a big deal about it."[38] Kathryn, a middle school library media specialist in the Midwest, has another way of lightly reinforcing parent requests. "I am an avid fantasy fan and love to book-talk fantasy and vampire books. However, I always remind students to respect their parents' wishes if they do not approve of certain topics especially when it comes to fantasy literature."[39]

Taking the opposite approach, the library media specialist may refuse a parent's request. As already noted, there are not only ethical but pragmatic reasons for doing so. Gail Dickinson, Associate Professor at Old Dominion University in Virginia, counsels,

> I urge school librarians not to make promises that they cannot keep. The real solution is between the parent and the child. You can try to assist, but you certainly can't promise that a child will not sneak out *Harry Potter* or any book when you are not looking. With self-checkout, this could happen daily. I suggest that the parents be advised to ask their children what library books they are reading, in the same way that they are monitoring television programs or anything else.[40]

By following Gail's advice, a library professional upholds intellectual freedom concepts and makes enforcement of family reading requirements an issue between the parent and child.

Judy, a middle school library media specialist in Wisconsin, agrees.

> The expectation that the media specialist can keep track of each child's parental rules and to take responsibility for them is excessive. I could easily put an "alert"

on the patron's record. I still wouldn't want to set a precedent this way. If a parent has rules for a child to follow when choosing library materials, the parent should hold the child responsible for following those rules. Legally they have a right to check on their child's library records [Wisconsin library records law], so they can follow up on their own.[41]

Lisa, a preK-8th independent school library media specialist in New York, concurs and offers advice in speaking with parents.

If a parent comes to me and says they do not want their child to read *Harry Potter,* I say that they need to tell their child because I cannot keep track of individual families' restrictions. More likely parents will try to restrict a seven year old from taking out picture books because they "should" not be reading "baby books." I have a meeting to talk about freedom to read, the importance of self-selection, and why picture books are an important genre of literature. A few years ago I had a Dad arrive in the library out-of-sorts and demand that his daughter not be

---

 Teaching about Intellectual Freedom

Library media specialists can proactively educate parents about quality children's and young adult literature and encourage them to foster their child's self-selection of independent reading choices. Strategies for reaching out to parents include:

- Initiate a parent reading group that meets regularly to learn about new books that interest children and young adults, trends in children's and adolescent literature, ideas for helping children select books commensurate with their social, emotional, and cognitive development, and skills for discussing books with their children,

- Create a school newsletter column aimed at parents with suggested titles in various genres and tips for sharing the books with children, preteens, and teens.

- Organize a "Back to School" program for parents and students featuring an author, break-out sessions for book sharing discussion, and a book fair.

- Present a "show and tell" new titles book talk for parents at a parent/teacher organization meeting. Describe how materials are selected using the district's material selection policy.

- Develop a parent collection and add books encouraging parents to develop lifelong readers, such as *The Read Aloud Handbook* by Jim Trelease.

Providing opportunities for dialogues about books and reading allows the library media specialist and parents of students to discuss frankly what their children are reading. During those interactions, the library media professional walks a fine line, promoting self-selection choice by children and young adults while at the same time acknowledging the parents' right to guide their children's reading. Despite this balancing act, the positive result may be greater access by students to the materials in the school library collection.

allowed to take out any dog books anymore because they were *never* getting a dog. I was able to jolly him out of it by saying sometimes we have to wait for what we want, that I didn't get my first dog until I was thirty-seven. Then we had the whole self-selection discussion.[42]

In practical terms, a student who really wants to read something will find a way to do so. Kathryn, a middle school library media specialist, shares this story, "I have an 8th grade homeroom student whom I've overheard telling a friend that her father is very restrictive due to religious beliefs. She mentioned that she reads vampire stories at school because dad would never let her read them at home."[43] Jo relates another situation, "I had a girl actually steal a book because her mom wouldn't let her read it. She did bring it back when she was done and couldn't figure out why her mom said she couldn't read it because it 'wasn't really that good.'"[44] Students may hide prohibited books in lockers or desks, move them to a secret spot on library shelves, and devise other ingenious ways to circumvent parental restrictions. While it is acknowledged that parents have the right to direct the reading of their children, the bottom line is that this is an issue between child and parent.

How Budgets Affect the Right to Read

In many districts, school library media program budgets are low or nonexistent. This translates into an inability to purchase new books, update inaccurate resources, or provide electronic reference materials to students. Lack of current information affects students' ability to learn about life in a global society. To have a viable collection, a school library program must purchase one book per student per year to maintain its collection and two per student to grow.[45] The impact of low budgets is seen in the size and age of collections in school libraries. It is estimated nationally that there are 18 books per student in school library media program collections, but schools in economically depressed areas may have fewer than one book per child.[46] Collection age is also of concern. A study of public school library media programs in middle Tennessee revealed that while the average library had 19 books per student, the average age of the books was sixteen years.[47] Another study funded by the New York Library Association found that the average age of books in the state's public school libraries is over 20 years old.[48] Having current, accurate information in the areas of science, health, technology, and others is crucial to students' First Amendment right to receive information and to their education as citizens.

It is no secret that as district financial resources shrink, administrators begin to look at where cuts can be made. AASL estimates that only about 60 percent of school library media programs nationwide have a full-time, state-certified school library media specialist on staff.[49] Because a teacher must be in every classroom with students, school library media specialist and other positions are sometimes reduced or eliminated. This move is made easier because the National Center for Education Statistics (NCES) lists school library media specialists under the broad area of "Support Services-Instruction."[50]

In most instances the elimination of school library professionals starts with elementary schools where children are beginning to read and learning their basic information literacy skills. Continued cuts may lead to situations in which all the elementary library media positions are cut and a single library professional becomes responsible for the library program in all the district's elementary schools. If the cost-cutting continues, professional library staff in middle and high school libraries are affected. In many places credentialed library media specialists are being replaced with paraprofessional staff or parent volunteers.

According to the ALA's "Access to Resources and Services in the School Library Media Program: An Interpretation of the *Library Bill of Rights*," "School library media specialists assume a leadership role in promoting the principles of intellectual freedom within the school by providing resources and services that create and sustain an atmosphere of free inquiry."[51] Chapter 1 delineated the many ways in which school library professionals promote and maintain a climate of intellectual freedom. Without a sufficient number of credentialed library media specialists, students' physical and intellectual access to information is endangered.

> "Credentialed school library media professionals promote, inspire, and guide students toward a love of reading, a quest for knowledge, and a thirst for lifelong learning."
> International Reading Association Board Resolution, May 2000[52]

When there is no longer a school library professional to advocate for the program, hours of access to the facility are frequently shortened. The library may be open only one day per week, or there may be only a few hours when a library staff member is on-site. In some schools, the facilities are locked except when a teacher will accompany students to select books. In others, the libraries are closed with collections boxed and unavailable. In addition, information and technology literacy skills needed to locate and evaluate information may not be taught. Loss of the library media program has a detrimental effect on all students, especially those without the family economic resources to purchase books or obtain Internet access at home. According to Dr. Stephen Krashen, Professor Emeritus at the University of Southern California's Rossier School of Education, there are a substantial number of children in the United States who do not read well. Many of the poor readers are children living in poverty who lack access to books. In addition, schools in low-income areas frequently have inferior collections.[53]

The decreased access to school libraries and their resources is especially disheartening when they may be the *only* library to which a child or young adult has regular access. When school library programs are not viable, teachers may expect students to use public libraries. In many localities a public library with adequate hours, knowledgeable staff, and a current collection is the norm, whereas in others, families must drive many miles to use a library that is open a limited number of hours per week and has a small collection. While unthinkable in the recent past, public libraries and library systems have been facing closure due to lack of local and state financial support. This leaves adult and youth patrons without access to the information they need for their work and personal lives. Even if public libraries are viable in a large urban setting or rural community, minors may not have transportation to visit them.

Harold Howe, former U.S. Commissioner of Education, stated, "What a school thinks about its library is a measure of what it thinks about education."[54] One might add that "what the community thinks about school library media programs is a measure of what it thinks about education." When there is no access to a credentialed school library media specialist, a current collection, and an adequate school library facility, *students' intellectual freedom is affected*, and the future of our democracy may be threatened. As the Greek philosopher Epictetus asserted, "Only the educated are free."[55]

✍ Key Ideas Summary

This chapter covered issues related to students' right to read and receive information and restrictions on that right. To review, here are some of the major ideas:

- The legal basis for minors' right to read and receive information is found in First Amendment free speech rights and case law.

- "Free speech" under the First Amendment refers to more than oral communication and has been interpreted in case law as the right to read and receive information.

- Students are denied their First Amendment rights when access to school library media center materials is restricted on the basis of age, grade level, or reading level.

- Economic barriers, such as late book fines, damaged or lost book charges, or other library fees, lessen access to library materials, especially for students from low-income families.

- Prejudicial labeling and restricted separate collections act as obstacles to students' free access to information.

- Parents and guardians have the right to determine what their children and/or wards may read and should speak with them regarding their reading choices.

- Lack of student access to the services of a credentialed school library media specialist, up-to-date library resources, and an adequate facility severely diminish students' intellectual freedom and their First Amendment right to read.

Library Bill of Rights Interpretations

- American Library Association. "Access for Children and Young Adults to Non-print Materials: An Interpretation of the *Library Bill of Rights*"

- American Library Association. "Access to Resources and Services in the School Library Media Program: An Interpretation of the *Library Bill of Rights*"

- American Library Association. "Free Access to Libraries for Minors: An Interpretation of the *Library Bill of Rights*"

- American Library Association. "Economic Barriers to Information: An Interpretation of the *Library Bill of Rights*"

- American Library Association. "Labels and Rating Systems: An Interpretation of the *Library Bill of Rights*"

- American Library Association. "Restricted Access to Library Materials: An Interpretation of the *Library Bill of Rights*"

All interpretations may be found at the ALA Office for Intellectual Freedom website: http://www.ala.org/oif.

Recommended Resources

- **American Library Association and the Association of American Publishers.** *The Freedom to Read.* http://www.ala.org/ala/oif/statementspols/ftrstatement/freedom readstatement.htm

  This strong philosophical statement on constitutional guarantees of the freedom to read and the continued attempts at suppression or censorship of information was first adopted by ALA's Council in 1953 and has been amended several times, most recently in 2004.

- **"Do Students Have the Right to Read?"** http://www.freedomforum.org/pack ages/first/curricula/educationforfreedom/L05main.htm

  This lesson plan is one of a series of 12 to be used to teach students their First Amendment rights. It includes key concepts as well as several activities to enable students to learn about their right to read. Interdisciplinary ideas, related national standards and benchmarks are included. The site also provides a large number of links and print sources related to the censorship.

- **National Council of Teachers of English. "Students' Right to Read." (1981)** http://www.ncte.org/about/over/positions/category/cens/107616.htm

  While directed toward English teachers, this lengthy essay provides support for the right of students to read a variety of materials with differing points of view.

Notes

1. "Reading Quotes," Richmond School District [Virginia], http://www.rich-mond.k12.va.us/readamillion/readingquotes.htm.

2. American Library Association and the Association of American Publishers, "The Freedom to Read," http://www.ala.org/ala/oif/statementspols/ftrstatement/freedomreadstatement.htm.

3. American Library Association, "Notable First Amendment Court Cases, The Right to Read Freely," http://www.ala.org/ala/oif/firstamendment/courtcases/courtcases.htm.

4. Ibid.

5. Ibid.

6. *Minarcini v. Strongsville (Ohio) City School District*, 541 F.2nd 577 (6th Cir. 1976).

7. American Library Association, "Free Access to Libraries for Minors: An Interpretation of the *Library Bill of Rights*," http://www.ala.org/ala/oif/statementspols/statementsif/interpretations/Default675.htm.

8. American Library Association, "Access, Core Values of Librarianship," http://www.ala.org/ala/oif/statementspols/corevaluesstatement/corevalues.htm#access.

9. American Library Association, Article V, *Library Bill of Rights*, http://www.ala.org/ala/oif/statementspols/statementsif/librarybillrights.htm.

10. AASL and AECT, *Information Power: Building Partnerships for Learning* (Chicago: American Library Association, 1998), 67.

11. McNicol, Sarah, "Attitudes Towards Intellectual Freedom and Censorship Amongst School and Children's Librarians," University of Central England, 2004, http://www.ebase.uce.ac.uk/docs/censorship_report.doc.

12. McNicol, Sarah, "Censorship Practices and Access to Information: Interviews with School and Children's Librarians," University of Central England, 2005, http://www.ebase.uce.ac.uk/projects/censorship_resources.htm [select Followup Interviews].

13. McDonald, Frances Beck, *Censorship and Intellectual Freedom: A Survey of School Librarians' Attitudes and Moral Reasoning* (Metuchen, NJ: Scarecrow Press, Inc., 1993), 134.

14. *Information Power*, 92.

15. Sue, email to author, May 21, 2007.

16. Neumann, Jolen, email to author, March 10, 2007.

17. Coatney, Sharon, email to author, February 24, 2008.

18. Ibid.

19. Laura, email to author, January 8, 2007.

20. Laura, email to author, May 17, 2007.

21. Kevin, email to author, November 6, 2007.

22. Barbara, email to author, November 7, 2007.

23. American Library Association, "Restricted Access to Library Materials: An Interpretation of the *Library Bill of Rights*," http://www.ala.org/ala/oif/statementspols/statementsif/interpretations/Default675.htm.

24. Doyle, Robert P, *Banned Books: 2007 Resource Guide* (Chicago: American Library Association, 2007), 184–185.

25. American Library Association, "Labels and Rating Systems: An Interpretation of the *Library Bill of Rights*," http://www.ala.org/ala/oif/statementspols/statementsif/interpretations/Default675.htm.

26. Dickinson, Gail, "Tough Choices: The Question ... What Should I Do with the *Sports Illustrated* Swimsuit issue?" *Knowledge Quest Web Edition* 35 (September/October 2006), 44, http://www.ala.org/ala/aasl/aaslpubsandjournals/kqweb/kqarchives/volume35/KQW35_1Dickinson.pdf.

27. Littman, Sarah, "Young Readers Deserve a Breadth of Literature," As If! Authors Support Intellectual Freedom, October 18, 2005, http://sarahlittman.com/young_readers_deserve.htm.

28. Laurie, email to author, May 10, 2007.

29. Pappas, Marjorie, "On My Mind: School Libraries Organized by AR or Lexile Scores?" *Knowledge Quest* 33, no. 2 (November/December 2004), 69.

30. Barbara, email to author, May 29, 2007.

31. Ibid.

32. American Library Association, "Economic Barriers to Information Access: An Interpretation of the *Library Bill of Rights*," http://www.ala.org/ala/oif/statementspols/statementsif/interpretations/Default675.htm.

33. Debbie, email to author, May 21, 2007.

34. American Library Association, "Libraries: An American Value," http://www.ala.org/ala/oif/statementspols/americanvalue/librariesamerican.htm.

35. Sharon, email to author, February 8, 2007.

36. American Library Association, *Code of Ethics of the American Library Association,* http://www.ala.org/ala/oif/statementspols/codeofethics/codeethics.htm.

37. Ellison, John, "Intellectual Freedom Quotations," http://www.informatics.buffalo.edu/faculty/ellison/quotes/ifquotesp.html.

38. Jo, email to author, October 4, 2007.

39. Kathryn, email to author, October 5, 2007.

40. Dickinson, Gail, email to author, October 4, 2007.

41. Judy, email to author, October 4, 2007.

42. Lisa, email to author, October 14, 2007

43. Kathryn, email to author, October 5, 2007.

44. Jo, email to author, October 5, 2007.

45. International Reading Association, "Providing Books and Other Print Materials for Classroom and School Libraries: A Position Statement of the International Reading Association," Adopted by the IRA Board of Directors, September 1999, ERIC Document ED436 715, http://eric.ed.gov/ERICWebPortal/custom/portlets/recordDetails/detailmini.jsp?_nfpb=true&_&ERICExtSearch_SearchValue_0=ED436715&ERICExtSearch_SearchType_0=eric_accno&accno=ED436715.

46. Holcomb, Sabrina, "Reader Relief," NEAToday 25, no. 6 (March 2007), 37.

47. Robinson, Dorren, "Libraries," The Community Foundation of Middle Tennessee, http://research.givingmatters.com/papers/2006/9/6/libraries.

48. "School Library Funding, New York State–Old Materials Crisis," March 28, 2008, http://www.ala.org/ala/news/libraryfunding/schoollibraryfunding.cfm.

49. American Association of School Librarians, "The SKILLS Act Talking Points," http://www.ala.org/ala/aasl/aaslissues/SKILLs_Act_TP.cfm.

50. American Association of School Librarians, "Library Media Specialist Instructional Classification FAQ's," http://www.ala.org/ala/aasl/aaslproftools/toolkits/instructionalfaq.cfm#how.

51. American Library Association, "Access to Resources and Services in the School Library Media Program: An Interpretation of the *Library Bill of Rights*," http://www.ala.org/ala/oif/statementspols/statementsif/interpretations/Default675.htm.

52. "School Libraries Work! Research Foundation Paper, Scholastic Library Publishing, 2006, 7.

53. Krashen, Stephen, "The 'Decline' of Reading in America, Poverty and Access to Books, and the Use of Comics in Encouraging Reading," *Teachers College Record*, February 2005, http://www.sdkrashen.com/articles/decline_of_reading/index.html.

54. Ibid.

55. Logan, Deborah, "Quotations about Libraries, Books, and Reading," http://www.deblogan.com/quo2.html.

CHAPTER 5

Privacy in the School Library Media Program

People are not necessarily what they choose to read.[1]
—Stacey L. Bowers, Attorney and Lecturer at Denver Sturm College of Law

Privacy and Confidentialtiy

The word "privacy" does not appear in the U.S. Constitution, although decisions of the Supreme Court have implied its existence for citizens.[2] In a library context, *privacy* is defined as "the right to engage in open inquiry without having the subject of one's interest examined or scrutinized by others."[3] Privacy and *confidentiality* are intertwined. Library records hold personally identifiable information about student patrons. The library media specialist has access to student library records and is often privy, through observation and interaction with students, to additional knowledge about them. "Confidentiality exists when a library [and its staff] ... keeps that information private on their [patrons'] behalf."[4]

The library community has a strong commitment to extending and protecting the privacy of students using school library media centers. This obligation is evident in the policy statements of the American Library Association (ALA) and the American Association of School Librarians (AASL):

- "We protect each library user's right to privacy and confidentiality with respect to information sought or received and resources consulted, borrowed, acquired or transmitted."[5] (*Code of Ethics of the ALA*, Article III)

- "The library community recognizes that children and youth have the same rights to privacy as adults."[6] (AASL "Position Statement on the Confidentiality of Library Records")

Unfortunately, state and federal laws are sometimes at odds with the right of privacy for minors affirmed by the library profession.

Student Expectations of Privacy

Like adult library users, students must feel confident that their privacy will be respected in the school library media center. They should be granted the right to read and borrow free from scrutiny regardless of age. They need to know that library staff will keep confidential the titles of books checked out and interlibrary loan requests made.

Students should also be able to seek information and have the subject of their research remain private. Because school library media centers provide both curricular and recreational resources, it is the one place in a school where a student may freely investigate topics of individual interest. "Privacy: An Interpretation of the *Library Bill of Rights*" reminds library media professionals of their obligation "to an ethic of facilitating, not monitoring access to information."[7]

Disclosing Student Library Records

Apart from ALA policy and ethics statements supporting the privacy of library patrons, there are state and federal laws guarding citizen's privacy. Determining when student library records may be disclosed legally is based on interpretation of state library records laws and federal privacy law relating to students' education records.

State Library Records Laws

Forty-eight states and the District of Columbia have laws that protect the confidentiality of library records. Hawaii and Kentucky do not have specific library records laws, but their attorneys general have written opinions supporting the confidentiality of library records.[8] Current state library records laws may be found at the American Library Association website by searching the term "state privacy laws."

State library records laws protect the privacy of "library users," "a user of library services," and other terms referring to a library patron. The term *minor* is not included in state library record laws except for references in selected states to the release of minors' library records to parents or guardians. Although minors are not mentioned, it can be inferred that minors' library records are protected by state law.

It is *critical* to read an individual state's library record law carefully. In some states, the law may refer only to "public libraries." In those cases, the definition of "public library" is essential, because it may mean that school library media program records are not protected unless shielded in another way, such as district policy. Fortunately, in all but a handful of states, school libraries are mentioned specifically, included through the definition of "public library," or encompassed under "library" records. However, at this time library records laws in Florida, Maine, Connecticut, and Massachusetts do not protect the privacy of school library media program records.[9]

The laws vary in the types of library records protected. Pennsylvania law shields only circulation records.[10] In New York, the library record law has broader coverage and includes "but is not limited to the circulation of library materials, computer database searches, interlibrary loan transactions, reference queries, requests for photocopies of library materials, title reserve requests, or the use of audio-visual materials, films or records ..."[11]

The state laws also vary as to who may access library records. They may include the patron, library staff in pursuit of their duties, law enforcement agents with a proper court order, and parents or guardians. In 15 states— Alaska, Alabama, Colorado, Florida, Georgia, Louisiana, Ohio, New Mexico, South Dakota, Utah, Vermont, Virginia, West Virginia, Wisconsin, and Wyoming—parents or guardians have access to library records of their minor children or wards.[12] However, unless disclosure is *specifically required by law*, minors' library records should remain confidential. Students may not feel comfortable checking out particular resources if they think the titles or choices of topics may be examined by an adult, including their parents. School library media specialists should check their own states' laws to determine protection of school library media center records.

May a school library media specialist provide information on what a student has checked out to a teacher or the principal? There is *no state library records law* that allows principals, teachers, or other school staff access to student library records. Nearly all state library records laws are very specific about to whom records may be released, and teachers and principals are not listed. Releasing any records about students' use of library materials, except for the stated exemptions, is not legal.

In fact, there may be penalties for release of library records by library staff to unauthorized individuals. For example, the Texas Public Information Act (Chapter 552, Texas Government Code) states that those who permit inspection or disclose confidential information [including library records] to unauthorized individuals may be found guilty of a misdemeanor "punishable by: (1) a fine of not more than $1,000; (2) confinement in the county jail for not more than six months; or; (3) both the fine and confinement."[13] Arizona Revised Statutes specify, "Any person who knowingly discloses any record or other information in violation of this section is guilty of a class 3 misdemeanor."[14] Colorado Revised Statutes consider disclosing library records a punishable offense stating, "Any library official, employee, or volunteer who discloses information in violation of this section commits a class 2 petty offense and, upon conviction thereof, shall be punished by a fine of not more than three hundred dollars."[15]

Whether state library records laws shield or fail to protect student library records, the *Code of Ethics of the ALA* directs school library media specialists

**Protecting Student Library Records
and Student Privacy**

- Develop a privacy policy stating who may access library patron records and the circumstances under which records may be released.
- Create and retain as few student library records as possible.
- Train library staff, volunteers, and student assistants about the confidentiality of all library records, instructing them not to examine circulation records of others.
- Teach *all* students to respect the confidentiality of library records—their own and those of others.
- Protect circulation records with passwords and provide different levels of access for students, volunteers, and library staff.
- Configure library automation software to delete student circulation history.
- Fold and staple overdue notices so only the student's name is visible, not the titles of late or unreturned materials.
- Make a conscious effort to purge circulation records on a regular basis as directed by a library records retention policy.
- Refrain from conversations with students on private matters related to their reading or research, especially on sensitive issues in public areas, unless certain the conversation cannot be overheard.
- Protect information gained through student use of school library media program resources and services by not divulging it indiscriminately to faculty, administrators, or others.
- Proactively educate administrators about the confidentiality of student library records under state library records law. Determine how the Family Educational Rights and Privacy Act (FERPA) applies to local school library records.
- Discuss privacy concerns with vendors of any technology and request that they include privacy protections in future software changes.

to safeguard a patron's right to privacy and confidentiality. In a school setting, school library media specialists have the most knowledge of library law and intellectual freedom concepts and bear the greatest responsibility to protect the privacy of their student patrons.

The Family Educational Rights and Privacy Act

The Family Educational Rights and Privacy Act of 1974 (FERPA) is a federal law aimed at maintaining the privacy of students in PK-12 and postsecondary settings. The law applies to all schools that receive funds from programs administered by the U.S. Department of Education. FERPA protects students' "education records" and grants parents the right to view these records maintained by a school until the minor reaches 18, at which time that right transfers to the young adult.[16]

As previously described, most state library records laws explicitly include protecting the confidentiality of school library media program records or the records of any library supported by public funds; however, FERPA does not specifically list school library media program patron records as shielded. Instead, it has a very broad definition of the term "education records" defining them as "those records, files, documents, and other materials which— (i) contain information directly related to a student; and (ii) are maintained by an educational agency or institution or by a person acting for such agency or institution."[17]

Are K-12 school library media program records, such as automated circulation records, Internet use logs, or other library records considered "education records" under FERPA? It all depends on who you ask and his or her interpretation of "education records." Kathleen Wolan, a Program Analyst in the Family Policy Compliance Office of the U.S. Department of Education, states, "In the circumstances you describe [example given: school library media program circulation records], if the records are maintained by a public school or district, and are able to be identified by student, then we'd probably consider them to meet the qualification of FERPA as education records."[18] Although library circulation records and Internet use logs may be considered temporary, according to Wolan, "a school is required to provide the privacy protections of FERPA to education records during whatever period of time the school chooses to maintain them."[19]

Others are less certain of the legal interpretation of FERPA. Deborah Caldwell-Stone, Deputy Director of the ALA Office for Intellectual Freedom and a lawyer specializing in privacy, stated,

> ... we're dealing with two questions: first, whether or not school library media center records are records covered by FERPA; and second, whether the federal law trumps an applicable state library confidentiality law protecting the records' confidentiality. Unfortunately, no court has decided these questions, and, until and unless these issues are litigated in a court of law, the applicability of FERPA to school library records will always be a matter of interpretation and opinion.[20]

Because of the differing opinion, school library media specialists are put in a difficult position regarding the applicability of FERPA to school library media program records. To assist, Deborah Caldwell-Stone counsels,

> I believe that school librarians should strive, in accordance with the *Code of Ethics of the ALA* and the *Library Bill of Rights*, to protect the confidentiality of all library users regardless of age. Like other librarians, they should develop effective policies to protect user privacy, like record retention policies that mandate disposal/ destruction of records once they are no longer needed for the efficient operation of the library. I also believe they should comply with state library confidentiality

laws, especially those state laws that impose specific duties on school librarians. If a parent or student or another party believes FERPA trumps state law, the librarian must then rely upon the legal advice of their school board's attorney when responding to the inquiry.[21]

It should be noted that in 2008 the Vermont legislature enacted a confidentiality of library patron records law that lists the following exception for sharing of library records: "(4) to custodial parents or guardians of a student in accordance with the federal law Family Education Rights and Privacy Act (FERPA) by the library at the school the student attends."[22]

In practical terms, does this mean that a teacher may access a student's library circulation records as an "education record" under FERPA? According to a staff member in the Family Policy Compliance Office, "FERPA permits school officials who have a '*legitimate educational interest*' to review a student's education records. Typically, this means that a school official, who needs to review a student's education records in order to fulfill his or her professional responsibilities, may do so. Schools are required to include the criteria for who is considered a 'school official' and what is considered a 'legitimate educational interest' in the annual notification of rights under FERPA that is provided to parents."[23] A copy of a model notification of parents' rights is available at http://www.ed.gov/policy/gen/guid/fpco/ferpa/lea-officials.html. For the library media specialist, the answer is not black and white but rather subject to interpretation and who the district considers a "school official." The ALA Office for Intellectual Freedom's *Intellectual Freedom Manual* advises school library media specialists concerned about the applicability of FERPA to school library media program records to "identify how their institutions implement this law and its impact on collection and retention of library user records."[24]

The Principal and Student Library Records' Requests

What can a library media specialist do if the principal asks for a list of all books a student has checked out since enrolling in the school? This happened to a middle school library media specialist in a midwestern school district.[25] Given her knowledge of what the student had been reading—books related to drugs, weapons, and war—she surmised that the list might be given to law enforcement officers.[26]

Despite the immediacy of the principal's request, the library media specialist took an hour to review key information. She reread her state's library record law to confirm that school library media program records are protected. As previously noted, state library record laws protect the confidentiality of school library media program records *except* in Florida, Maine, Connecticut, and Massachusetts.[27] Next, she reviewed the state legal requirements under which library records may be disclosed. The law allowed her to reveal the records in the following instances: (1) to the patron, (2) to library staff in pursuit of their duties, (3) to law enforcement officers with a valid, signed court order, and (4) to parents/guardians of youth to the age of 16. The principal was not listed as a person to whom library records could be disclosed.

The library media specialist also reviewed the Family Educational Rights and Privacy Act (FERPA). As previously noted, FERPA has a very broad definition of the term "education records." Although it is unclear at this time whether library circulation records are considered "education records" under FERPA, the law allows the disclosure of the student education records *without written consent* from the parent, guardian, or student over 18 years of age, under very specific circumstances (34 CFR § 99.31). Such disclosure is permitted in order "to comply with a judicial order or lawfully issued subpoena; appropriate officials in cases of health and safety emergencies; and state and local authorities, within a juvenile justice system, pursuant to specific State law."[28] The library professional found herself dealing with two issues: (1) are student library records considered "education records" under FERPA in her district, a question for which she and the principal must depend on district legal counsel for the answer and (2) does the request fit one of FERPA's specific circumstances under which education records may be divulged?

Lastly, she considered the ethics of revealing library records. The *Code of Ethics of the ALA* states that library professionals will protect the confidentiality of library records. Would it be ethical to release a list of books a student has checked out with an expectation of confidentiality?

The library media specialist was also aware that the principal had full knowledge of the circumstances surrounding his request—knowledge she did not have—and may have already consulted legal counsel. A principal has many responsibilities, and *safety* of students and staff is a key concern.

How was the situation resolved? Because of the seriousness of the situation, the library media specialist met quickly with the principal to discuss the legal and ethical aspects of revealing a student's reading history. The principal listened briefly and did not reveal receipt of a court order or refer to legal advice. The principal then repeated the request for the list of books. Given a direct order from her supervisor, the library media specialist reluctantly agreed. Fortunately, before she could comply with the records release, the principal contacted her again and stated, "I no longer need them. We have enough evidence."[29]

In this situation, the library professional took appropriate action by promptly making the principal aware of the laws and ethical issues related to the confidentiality of student library records. However, there was another option she could have exercised before speaking to the principal. She could have contacted the ALA Office for Intellectual Freedom or the American Civil Liberties Union for advice. Before complying she should also have asked the administrator if they could immediately seek district legal counsel's advice on whether the records could be released legally. She also could have asked the principal to provide a written statement indicating that he directed her to release the records. Finally, when the situation was concluded, she could also record the situation for her own file relating her reservations in complying with the request.

Many details about the situation are unknown. The principal might have already gotten advice of legal counsel and weighed the safety of students and staff against the privacy of the library records. Instead of complying with state library records law, he *may have relied* on FERPA's exceptions for safety emergencies or a request within the juvenile justice system. This incident demonstrates the need to *proactively* educate administrators about the confidentiality of school library media center records prior to a crisis. It also illustrates one of the gray areas related to privacy laws and student library records.

The Troubled Student and Privacy

When should a school library media specialist consider violating a student's privacy? Although school library professionals extend the maximum amount of privacy to students, there may be times when library staff must apply common sense rather than ALA policy and ethics statements because of a concern for the student's welfare. S/he may observe a sudden change in personality, dramatic switch in friends, a move toward isolation, or a fixation with information on risky or criminal activity. When this occurs, a first action is to talk to the student casually but confidentially. If, after a period of time, the school library professional is still concerned, s/he may seek advice from the school's guidance counselor, who is also bound by confidentiality. The counselor is an excellent choice for a confidant because s/he may already know the child, have obtained similar reports from other sources, and has training and experience on how to proceed in such a situation.

If the situation appears to be related to a school safety issue, the library media specialist can speak directly to the principal. A principal is responsible for the health and safety of *all* students and staff. If there are indications that the student is actively engaging in potentially dangerous or threatening behavior, the principal will take action to contact the parents and/or the police immediately to protect the well-being of the school community.

A second instance for violating privacy of school library users may occur if the library media specialist observes indications of possible child abuse. All states have child protection laws that require educators to report suspected maltreatment of children. For example, in Pennsylvania, the Child Protective Services Law (23 Pa. C.S., Chapter 63) establishes definitions of child abuse, who is required to report abuse, and the procedures to be followed.[30]

Situations in which a school library professional may violate a student's privacy with just cause are rare. Think carefully before taking actions that will compromise a student's privacy, because students are depending on the discretion of library media program staff. Aside from the circumstances outlined above, a school library professional must keep in mind that there are very strong professional policy statements, such as interpretations of the *Library Bill of Rights* and the *Code of Ethics for the ALA*, that urge library staff to guard the privacy of library users.

Age and Patron Privacy

Does the *age of the patron* make a difference in extending privacy rights? As noted previously, the AASL "Position Statement on the Confidentiality of Library Records" affirms that "The library community recognizes that children and youth have the same rights to privacy as adults."[31] Most ALA policy statements, including the *Library Bill of Rights* interpretations and the *Code of Ethics of the ALA*, do not distinguish between minor and adult patrons. State library records laws and the Family Educational Rights and Privacy Act (FERPA) also do not differentiate between younger and older students unless the student is determined to be an adult (defined in state and federal legislation at varying ages of 16, 17, and 18).

Elementary Students' Privacy

Should age be considered when granting privacy to students in a library? Here are questions to consider. Do young children know that they have privacy rights in libraries, and are they concerned about their privacy? Does it matter if the library media specialist calls out the names of children because they have unreturned library books? Is it a serious breach of privacy for the child if a peer overhears the name of the overdue item? Does it compromise a child's privacy if a teacher assists in locating a student's overdue book? These examples may seem like innocuous situations involving a young child's privacy.

On the other hand, compromising privacy can be a slippery slope. While elementary students may have difficulty remembering to return books or even the titles they checked out, they are worthy of respect as future citizens. How will they learn about privacy in a library unless school library media specialists *begin teaching them now*? One of the expectations of privacy students should have in a school library media center is that *all* will be granted the right to read and borrow free from scrutiny *regardless of age*.

In a practical sense, how can a school library media specialist maintain privacy for a library patron, especially a younger child, while still teaching

Teaching about Intellectual Freedom

School library media specialists can turn ordinary library incidents into "teachable" moments about patron privacy.

- If a student or a teacher is looking for a book or other resource not on the shelf and asks who has checked it out, library staff can explain that information about who has borrowed the item from the library is private, referencing the library program's privacy policy.

- Library professionals can model and teach privacy by making sure their conversations with students about materials and research projects are as confidential as possible.

- Informally educate adults, who become involved in the search for missing library materials checked out by a student, about the library media program's privacy policy and their state's library records laws.

students about their responsibility to return borrowed materials in a timely manner? To the extent possible, the library media specialist needs to work directly with the student to problem solve, which also helps maintain the student's privacy and sense of responsibility. At a certain point, however, parents, guardians, and classroom teachers may need to become involved.

A library media specialist and teachers may use the following consecutive steps to recover elementary students' overdue or missing materials:

1. Send a list of missing books with no user names to a classroom, and ask that everyone search for them.

2. Send a second list with the names of children who still have missing books. Ask the teacher to speak discreetly to the children involved, helping them check their desks or backpacks.

3. Ask the teacher to investigate if the books were lent to friends, thereby moving the search to other students' desks, book bags, or homes.

4. If the missing books are not located, send a friendly, nonthreatening note home about overdue items.

5. Send a second friendly note home (if first not successful) that details the titles(s), due date, replacement cost, and library media specialist contact information.

In reality, there are few secrets among elementary children or with their teachers about what they are checking out. Yet, it is in these situations that school library professionals begin to train young children about their right to privacy in a library.

Middle and High School Student Privacy in the Media Center

The issue of privacy and confidentiality becomes even more important when students reach middle and high school, and their reading and research interests take them into territory that feels very personal to them. The ethic demanding that school library media specialists respect students' right to privacy and not ask *why* information is needed takes on a deeper dimension when the alternative could drive students away from the library media center.

It is the responsibility of the library media specialist to create an atmosphere in which students may seek and use information without fear someone will question their reason or right to information. There may be topics about which teenagers want information but do not feel comfortable asking their parents. Consequently, the school library media center may be the *only* source for accurate information, and a trusted library media specialist may be one individual they can turn to when researching sensitive topics. Any reference question brings a weighty responsibility to abide by the *Code of Ethics of the ALA* and protect students' privacy. It is important to remember that because a student asks for information on abortion, teen pregnancy, drugs and drug use, or some other social issue does not mean that s/he is pregnant, using drugs, or engaged in other risky behavior. Information on equally sensitive topics may be sought for a school assignment or for personal reasons.

In addition to protecting the right of privacy to seek information, it is the library media specialist's responsibility to protect students' privacy during and after the checkout process. This means refraining from comments on what is being borrowed, requested on interlibrary loan, or put on reserve, or discussed in "reader advisory" conversations, and making sure paraprofessional staff, student workers, and parent volunteers do the same. As part of their training in patron privacy, library staff and volunteers also should be told they cannot casually review or discuss library circulation records.

Liz, a library director in an independent girls' day boarding school for grades 6–12 in Massachusetts, states,

> All patrons' library records are kept confidential, and the ALA *Code of Ethics* is part of my collection development policy. I frequently get requests from students to let me know who has book "x" checked out because they also need to use it for a paper, and I always give them the same response: "I will contact the student who has that book checked out and let her know that someone needs to use it." One of the cracks in my system is the fact that I have 14 student pages who also have access to circulation records; though I instruct them in the library's privacy policy, I doubt that they all place as much stock in it as I do.[32]

Middle and high school students have not fully developed their sense of responsibility for returning library materials, and the school library professional should establish preteen and teenager patrons as accountable for missing and overdue items. Personal accountability helps maintain the student's privacy when materials are returned in a reasonable time frame; however, as a last resort, parents may need to become involved. The following strategies can be used in recovering middle and high school students' overdue, damaged, or missing materials while respecting student privacy:

- Give quiet oral reminders.

- Deliver printed notices, folded and stapled for privacy, to the student's homeroom.

- Send an email overdue notice to a student's school account.

- Involve parents in the recovery effort through a mailed notice, telephone call, or other means.

Liz explains her procedures for the return of overdue materials.

Another crack [in the library process] is our billing procedure for unreturned materials. When I send that information to the Business Office, I include the title of the missing book or video, and bills are sent to parents, not students. I have tried just billing a dollar amount but was inundated by calls from parents wanting to know what was missing. Part of me also feels that after three or four unsuccessful overdue notices, I need some help from the parents in retrieving the material. I have also never had to bill for anything other than clearly curricular material. The sensitive stuff is always returned on time—or stolen![33]

Today's preteens and teens appear to have a double standard when it comes to privacy. They want to explore sensitive and intriguing topics without close scrutiny by their parents, teachers, or other adults. In contrast, they also want to use personalized searching and portals (e.g., iGoogle portal). As a result, young people give up some privacy in return for the features, results, and tailored information.

Less savvy middle and high school students show little discretion in what they post about themselves online. A survey conducted for the National School Board Association in 2007 revealed 52 percent of districts report that students providing personal information online is a problem, while only 3% of students agree.[34] Conversely another snapshot of teen privacy from the 2007 Pew Internet & American Life report "Teens, Privacy, and Online Networks" disclosed, "The majority of teens [surveyed and self-selected] actively manage their online profiles to keep the information they believe is most sensitive away from the unwanted gaze of strangers, parents and other adults. While many teens post their first name and photos on their profiles, they rarely post information on public profiles they believe would help strangers actually locate them such as their full name, home phone number or cell phone number."[35] Wherever students are on the privacy knowledge continuum, the library media specialist must teach them how to guard their own privacy in their physical and virtual lives. This instruction may be a part of the information and technology literacy curriculum.

Age may have some place in how school library media specialists extend privacy to student patrons, but First Amendment rights, the *Library Bill of Rights*, the *Code of Ethics of the ALA*, and other policy statements indicate granting privacy is the *right* thing to do. As students grow and mature, providing scrutiny-free access to information and keeping their interests and intellectual pursuits confidential is a matter of keeping faith with them and honoring professional ethical codes.

The Impact of Technology on Privacy

The transition from traditional school libraries with large print collections held within the walls of the facility to school library media centers with print, nonprint, electronic subscription database, and Internet resources exemplifies the way in which technology has changed the library media program. While resources have become more accessible, technology has also made personal data held in the library media program's record-keeping systems more vulnerable to exposure.

In 1977 the U.S. Privacy Study Commission wrote, "The real danger [to privacy] is the gradual erosion of individual liberties through automation, integration, and interconnection of many small, separate record-keeping systems, each of which alone may seem innocuous, even benevolent, and wholly justifiable."[36] Prior to the pervasive use of technology, school records were paper-based and held in offices scattered throughout the facility. As data collection and management became electronic and systems integrated, access to information became easier and schoolwide. Armed with passwords and sufficient levels of access "rights," an authorized individual (teacher, principal, technician) can check a student's attendance, disciplinary reports, grades, email account, library records, lunch room account, and bus route. An individual's use of subscription databases and Internet use can be followed. While the examples that follow relate to use of technologies used in a library media center, the responsibility for student privacy is also held by many other staff. This is an encouraging sign because it means the school library professional will find allies among those who are also charged with maintaining record confidentiality.

Library Automation Systems and Privacy

When automation systems were first installed, school library media specialists thought only of the convenience and release from the drudgery of filing checkout cards and typing overdue lists. Originally it was believed that when an item was checked in, the link between the patron and the book or other library resource borrowed was broken; in many cases, this was erroneous. Depending on software configuration, library staff can not only determine the current borrower but also learn who checked it out previously—from the most recent person to a staff-designated number of earlier borrowers. These records will remain in the system indefinitely unless purged. Some library media specialists want this type of information; it allows them to trace recent borrowers if damage is discovered after the item is returned. Conversely, it can also be used to determine who is reading selected types of books.

In the early days of automated circulation systems, no one imagined how the program features would evolve and present an even greater threat to the privacy of school library users. Today's programs allow easy access to data once available only through laborious use of a separate utility program or hand collation. Patron checkout histories, beginning with the first item borrowed by the student through the present day, are now readily available at the click of a mouse. According to Pat, a middle school library media specialist in Washington, by selecting "checkout history" he is able to view *every title checked out by a student*, its barcode number, and the date of checkout.[37]

While Pat can disable this feature to protect the circulation history of the student, he has been reluctant to do so.

> I have had occasion to use this information in conjunction with classroom teachers looking for the truth about what certain students claim they have read versus what they have actually checked out. I do not share the entirety of the list, only sharing the YES or NO on titles in question.[38] He sees yet another positive side of the checkout history feature. I have had students ask me what they checked out in the past. One in particular comes to mind. She is a migrant student and reads voraciously. When she found out she had checked out 52 books in one year, she crowed about it to her friends and bragged about how well she was doing. To me, that is worth it.[39]

Pat trains student assistants about library privacy and provides each with a brochure that includes guidelines for being a volunteer. The brochure emphasizes such key points as:

- "Student aides are not to use the circulation program to look at other students' information, either personal or academic.
- Library aides will not give out information about other students' library circulations to anyone."[40] Note: Library automation systems can limit access to patron information for student aides and parent volunteers.

According to Gwen, a middle school media specialist in Virginia, students are able to access their own circulation records from any Internet accessible computer. This means they can learn what items are checked out, when they are due, and put others on reserve. Are there any privacy concerns associated with this new freedom for students? In some schools, patron library numbers are the same as student lunch numbers. While this may make it easier for students to remember, it also means that there is a greater chance for the number to be learned by others. To Gwen's knowledge, students have not shared their patron library numbers nor played tricks on each other by checking out "interesting" items to one another.[41]

Biometric technology is also being used by library automation programs to identify library patrons for the purpose of checking out materials. Biometics refers to "technologies that measure and analyze human body characteristics, such as fingerprints, eye retinas and irises, voice patterns, facial patterns, and hand measurements, for authentication purposes."[42] In the case of library automation, the biometric technology involved is the Universal Finger Identification System (UFID). The system takes measurements of an individual's finger, uses software to identify specific data as "match points," converts and stores the information as a numeric value in a database, and uses the "match points" biometric data to compare when a live, human finger touches the finger reader/scanner at a circulation desk.[43] For those with concerns about patron privacy issues, according to Bob Engen, president of Educational Biometric Technology, actual fingerprints are not stored, only the measurements of the fingerprint; therefore, an individual's fingerprint cannot be generated from the data stored.[44]

Why should the advances in automation systems concern school library professionals? The *Code of Ethics of the ALA* states in Article III. "We protect each library user's right to privacy and confidentiality with respect to information sought or received and resources consulted, borrowed, or transmitted."[45] School library media specialists must take steps to ensure that the *readily available information* about student patrons' use of library resources is protected from teacher and administrator inquiries, parent and student volunteers, and students who may be at a circulation computer involved in self-checkout of their library materials. If school library professionals are serious about students' privacy, they also must consider how *the automation system and each upgrade* will affect the confidentiality of library records and take pro-active measures to protect them.

RFID in School Library Media Programs

Radio Frequency Identification (RFID) technology, which automates library circulation, inventory management, and antitheft security for resources with a single tag, is being implemented in public and academic libraries across the United States; however, it is still rarely used in school library media centers. RFID is "a method of identifying unique items using radio waves."[46] An RFID system consists of three parts: the tag (transponder), the reader (receiver), and the application (circulation, inventory, and security systems) that uses the data read by the reader from the tag. The tag, which may be active or passive, has a chip and an antenna and contains information identifying the resource. The reader is composed of a radio frequency module, a control unit, and an antenna to communicate with the tag. RFID readers can "read" or communicate with tags at varying distances.[47]

RFID technology has the advantage of allowing libraries to combine a number of functions using a *single*, paper-thin adhesive label that can be applied to a library book or other resource. Multiple items can be checked out and in simultaneously, because unlike barcodes, RFID tags do not require direct contact or line-of-sight scanning.[48] There are two positive results: checkout/in is faster, and the repetitive motions associated with checkout/in are reduced, thus lessening the potential for workplace injuries by library staff. The technology also is capable of sorting library resources for return to the proper area of a library. Library materials are protected from theft without addition of another security tag placed in the resource; and there is more efficient management of the inventory process, no longer requiring the physical handling of each item. RFID is an attractive technology because the combined features can lead to greater efficiency of library management tasks, freeing the library professional to work directly with patrons.

Privacy concerns surrounding the use of RFID focused on libraries placing "trackable" chips [within RFID tags] on circulating library resources that, following checkout, might be read by unauthorized individuals using RFID readers allowing the collection of information on library users' reading habits and other activities without their consent or knowledge. There was also concern that vendors had not addressed the privacy issues sufficiently.[49]

Because of concerns over the possible misuse of RFID to collect information about patrons' use of library materials, in 2005 the ALA Council approved the "Resolution on Radio Frequency Identification (RFID) Technology and Privacy Principles." In 2006 in an effort to assist libraries during implementation of the technology and to protect patron privacy, the ALA Intellectual Freedom Committee approved the "RFID in Libraries: Privacy and Confidentiality Guidelines," which detail policy considerations and the best practices for libraries utilizing RFID. Both documents are available on the ALA website. In December 2007 the National Information Standards Organization (NISO) RFID Working Group, comprised of librarians, software and hardware producers, and representatives from the publishing industry, released a lengthy report, "RFID in U.S. Libraries," that included privacy concerns related to the technology and presented a list of 10 recommendations with several to protect library patron privacy. [http://www.niso.org/publica tions/rp/RP-6-2008.pdf] As the technology changes, privacy advocates will continue to monitor changes in light of preserving patron privacy.

RFID and Privacy in School Library Media Centers

Use the following strategies when implementing RFID technology:

1. Educate the school and local community about the use of RFID technology in the library media program.
2. Address privacy issues and concerns with vendors during the procurement and implementation process.
3. Include RFID technology use in the library program's privacy policy.
4. Limit the data included on the RFID tags.
5. Delete personally identifiable information collected by the RFID system.
6. Use encryption to protect library patron and resource data.
7. Continue library media program staff training on privacy issues.[50]

Because of its cost, major school library automation vendors have been discussing RFID but have not put its development on the fast track. According to the *School Library Journal* and San Jose State University 2006 Automation Survey, over half of the school library media professionals who responded expressed no interest in RFID.[51]

When the cost of RFID technology drops, more schools may move from traditional barcodes and electromagnetic theft detection systems to RFID. At that time, as with any new technology, school library professionals must be cognizant of the possible implications for patron privacy and take proactive measures.

Surveillance Cameras and School Library Media Centers

In many schools surveillance cameras record activity in entrances, hallways, classrooms, the cafeteria, the library, computer labs, parking lots, the perimeter of the facility, and on school buses. Activities taking place can be monitored at a central location. The general consensus is that the locations selected for security cameras are limited to public spaces where school staff and students *have no reasonable expectation of privacy.*

With the tragedy at Columbine High School in 1999 as well as more recent incidents of school violence, school administrators in urban, suburban, and rural schools have been turning to a variety of surveillance devices including cameras in an effort to improve security for students and staff in public schools. Alice Rose, principal of Perrymont Middle School (Virginia), said, "Anything that we can do that will create an atmosphere where the students feel safer is a very worthy thing to do. Everybody feels better when you know that there are proactive steps being put in place to ensure that students are in a safe environment."[52]

While the surveillance cameras provide administrators, faculty, students, and parents with a sense of relief, when placed in a library they may impinge on school library media center patrons' expectations of privacy. Whether there is intrusion on patrons' privacy depends on camera placement and the clarity of the recorded image. Cameras directed at entrances/exits, general seating areas, or computers may record students and staff entering, leaving, and working, not the specific materials that are being used. To protect the privacy of students, the school library professional should request that a camera not be aimed at the circulation area(s) and sections of book stacks. Surveillance of some portions of the stacks may keep students from seeking out information on sensitive topics.

A school district must have a policy stating the purpose for surveillance of students and staff. Implementing guidelines should include where surveillance devices will be located, how they will be used, who may view the recordings and for what purposes, record keeping on the viewing of recordings, and how long recordings will be retained. Students, staff, and school visitors also should be apprised of the fact that surveillance technology is being used. The role and responsibility of the school library media specialist with regard to the use of *any* technology in the media center is to assess its impact on patron privacy and advocate for the privacy of students and staff as they use the facility and its resources.

Computerized Reading Programs and Student Privacy

Computerized reading management programs, such as Accelerated Reader, allow teachers and library media specialists to keep track of the books students have read and whether they successfully passed the book tests. According to Judith, a library media specialist serving grades 4–8 in Florida, "Databases like AR, Read 180, and other similar programs, maintain lists of what book tests a child has passed or failed for years. If someone wanted to see who read a book and took the test on it, even to the day and time that the test was taken, that information is retained until the database administrator removes it. Most people don't know this record exists unless the database administrator shares the info with them. This is often not a librarian, but the books can be from the library/media center. So this is something of a 'shadow' library record for a student."[53]

There is another privacy concern related to the reading programs. In some school library media centers, a colored spine label denoting a book's reading level is affixed to each book that is part of a reading management program. While labeling spines of books with their reading levels may be seen as useful to students, there is a negative aspect involved in announcing the book's reading level publicly. When a child selects a "labeled" book, others may see the child's reading level from the book chosen. This is *personal* information that should be kept confidential among the child, his/her family, and teacher. When children learn the reading levels of their peers, there is a tendency to use this information to tease, harass, and bully.

Labeling the collection in this manner affects students' privacy when selecting library resources and thereby threatens their intellectual freedom.

Whether we are aware of it, many technologies commonly employed in school library media programs have the potential to impact the privacy of students and faculty using the facility. From the automation system to RFID tags to surveillance devices to computerized reading management programs, it is the responsibility of the school library media specialist to fiercely guard the privacy for all library patrons.

Privacy and Confidentiality Policies

One of the critical actions a school library media specialist can take to protect the privacy of student library users is to work with the school administration to create a policy on the confidentiality of school library media program patron records and a policy on patron privacy. Two policies are needed because each policy has a different purpose. A confidentiality of library media program records policy is written *for staff* and aimed at directing the actions of the library professional and support staff, student assistants, and adult library program volunteers. Its goal is to maintain confidentiality for all types of patron records. A privacy policy, on the other hand, is written *for library users* and describes how library staff will protect and ensure their privacy in the school library media center. Both policies should be approved by the board of education.

AASL has developed a "Position Statement on Confidentiality of Library Media Program Records," which includes significant ideas to guide library professionals as they develop confidentiality and privacy policies including:

- "The members of the American Library Association, recognizing the right to privacy of library users, believe that records held in libraries which connect specific individuals with specific resources, programs or services, are confidential and not to be used for purposes other than routine record keeping.

- School library media specialists are advised to seek the advice of [legal] counsel if in doubt about whether their record keeping systems violate the specific laws in their states."[54]

The ALA also has two policy statements that are useful as supporting documents—"Confidentiality of Library Records" and "Confidentiality of Personally Identifiable Information about Library Users." These policies state the responsibilities of library staff in maintaining the confidentiality of patron personally identifiable information and records related to usage of library resources both within and outside a school library media center. Both policies are available on the ALA Office for Intellectual Freedom website.

A confidentiality of school library media program records policy should include the following:

- rationale for maintaining library program records;
- the importance of library staff protecting the confidentiality of library media program patron records;
- relevant state or federal library records laws relating to the release of library records containing personally identifiable information about patrons;
- rules and procedures to ensure confidentiality of patrons records, secure the data, and ensure their integrity; and
- training about privacy issues for all library staff.

In addition to the policy language, documents from professional associations should be referenced and attached to provide reinforcement for the local policy.

A privacy policy for the school library media program relies on many of the same intellectual freedom concepts, laws, and policy statements as the confidentiality policy. Basic considerations to address in a privacy policy include:

- a definition of privacy and why it is critical to student library patrons;
- notice of intention by library staff to protect the privacy of patrons and the confidentiality of their library records;
- a reference to the state's library record law, to whom and under what circumstances library records may be legally released, and whether parents and/or guardians may access their child's/ward's library records;
- a statement on whether student library records are considered "education records" and as such accessible to "school officials" (defined by FERPA) and parents;
- a description of the type of personally identifiable information collected about patrons and how library staff use the information, secure the data, and if it is purged when no longer needed;
- information on when and how students may access their own library circulation records;
- a statement advising students of their right to privacy when using a school library media center;
- recourse for a student patron if he/she feels personal privacy has been violated in the library; and
- a plan for training students and staff about protecting personal privacy.

Supporting documents for a privacy policy may include ALA's "Privacy: An Interpretation of the *Library Bill of Rights*" and the ALA and AASL policy statements described previously.

Formal approval of both policies by the board of education or other governing body ensures that the policies will be official. Furthermore, it protects patrons and directs library staff in their work. In addition, because state library records laws differ in each state and not all state library records laws protect school library media center patron records from disclosure, it is crucial that district policy address how school library media center patron records will be protected in situations where state law is silent.

Resources are available to help develop both policies. Sample privacy and confidentiality policies may be found in *Privacy in the 21st Century: Issues for Public, School, and Academic Libraries* published by Libraries Unlimited in 2005. While ALA does have a sample privacy policy online as part of its online "Privacy Toolkit," its language is more general and suited to public libraries.

Records Retention

The purpose of library records is to manage library resources efficiently. Library records may include but are not limited to circulation records; interlibrary loan records; public access computer/Internet signup lists or automated logins; temporary files, cookies, and use records created during Internet searching; virtual or email reference interviews and queries; and server logs. Once statistical data such as how many books were circulated during a school year has been obtained, the raw information that connects a user to an item or service should be erased, shredded, or expunged. Library and technology staff should develop a schedule and specific guidelines to destroy nonessential personally identifying data or files of library records that are no longer needed.

There are two important concepts to bear in mind regarding library records.

- The shortest possible retention of records helps ensure patron privacy.
- Library records should be destroyed when they are no longer needed.

A school library media center staff member cannot produce records if they are no longer available, nor can they be vulnerable to unauthorized disclosure. According to Judith, a library media specialist serving grades 4–8 in Florida, "We made the conscious decision not to retain any [computerized circulation] records beyond that of immediate use. It has not been inconvenient except in the rare occasion when I need to know who has damaged a book that was checked in before we realized it had been damaged. At that point the record is lost. We do retain records of lost/missing/damaged/overdue items; those items become part of a different discussion regarding access."[55]

A library records retention policy is another key document supporting the privacy of school library program users. According to Deborah Caldwell-Stone, Deputy Director of the American Library Association's Office for Intellectual Freedom, "Record retention policies assure that records due to be erased or shredded actually are erased and shredded, and they also provide evidence of the library's everyday practices, should anyone question why a record has not been retained."[56]

When creating this policy, the school library media specialist must consider his/her state's record retention schedule for school districts. The schedule lists the records that districts must retain and the length of retention. While school library media program records may not be specifically mentioned, the state document will give an overview of the types of records that must be preserved and may provide useful insights for developing a library records retention policy. If the type of library record is not specifically noted and there is no broad language that may include the record, school library media staff may dispose of the information.

A library records retention policy should include:

- a statement outlining the concept of destroying unnecessary records on a regular basis,
- an explanation of how record disposal follows local school policy as well as state and federal laws, and
- guidelines for the destruction of each type of record.

The library records retention policy should be approved by the board of education or governing body. A sample library media program records retention policy with guidelines for record retention may also be found in *Privacy in the 21st Century: Issues for Public, School, and Academic Libraries.*

Privacy Advocacy Training

The library media specialist is involved in privacy advocacy training for three groups: (1) library staff and volunteers, (2) teachers and administrators, and (3) student patrons. Once the privacy, confidentiality of library records, and records retention policies have been developed and adopted by their institution's governing body, all library media program staff and volunteers should receive training to allow them to implement the policies correctly. The library professional should include information about state library records law, the Family Educational Rights and Privacy Act (FERPA), and ALA library policy statements such as "Privacy: An Interpretation of the *Library Bill of Rights*" and the *Code of Ethics of the ALA.*

Privacy and the *Bill of Rights*

4th Amendment: "The right of the people to be secure in their persons, houses, papers and effects, against unreasonable searches and seizures, shall not be violated, and no warrants shall issue but upon probable cause, supported by oath or affirmation, and particularly describing the place to be searched, and the persons or things to be seized."

5th Amendment: "No person shall be held to answer for a capital or otherwise infamous crime, unless on a presentment or indictment of a grand jury, except in cases arising in the land or naval forces, or in the militia, when in actual service in time of war or public danger; nor shall any person be subject for the same offense to be twice put in jeopardy of life or limb; **nor shall be compelled in any criminal case to be a witness against himself,** nor be deprived of life, liberty, or property, without due process of law; nor shall private property be taken for public use, without just compensation."[57]

School library media specialists protect student patrons' privacy best when they teach students how to guard their privacy both online and in day-to-day life. As part of this training, school library professionals should encourage students to realize that citizens have privacy rights under the Fourth and Fifth Amendments to the *United States Constitution* [*Bill of Rights*] as well as under state and federal laws. Another instructional tool the library professional can use is the library media program's privacy policy. An effective policy will enlighten library users regarding the data collected about them, how it is used, and how their privacy will be protected. Library professionals must also educate school administrators and teachers about student privacy rights under state and federal laws. Advocacy for all facets of intellectual freedom is described in Chapter 9.

Final Thoughts on Privacy

Privacy in school library media programs is an evolving principle based on state and federal law and policy statements from the ALA. It is not an easy principle to defend because the majority of patrons in library media centers are minors. State library records laws do not universally protect the patron records of students in public schools, nor is federal privacy legislation such as the Family Educational Rights and Privacy Act clear in the status of school library records. However, the library profession has guides such as the *Library Bill of Rights* and its interpretations and the *Code of Ethics of the ALA* that strongly support granting the maximum privacy possible to library patrons regardless of age. Every school library media specialist must strive to attain these professional statements and ethics.

✎ Key Ideas Summary

This chapter covered a broad range of issues related to privacy and confidentiality in school libraries. To review, here are the major ideas:

- Students have two expectations of privacy and confidentiality when using a school library media center. The first expectation is that *all* students will be granted the right to read and borrow free from scrutiny regardless of age. The second is the right of students to seek information and have the subject of their research remain private.

- State library records laws, or opinions from attorneys general, protect the confidentiality of school library media center records except in Florida, Maine, Connecticut, and Massachusetts.

- There are differing opinions regarding the applicability of the Family Educational Rights and Privacy Act (FERPA) to school library media center records; and until this issue is decided in court, the matter will be subject to interpretation and opinion.

- The school library media specialist in an elementary library can make the principles of privacy and confidentiality work in a practical way.

- When extending privacy to middle and high school student patrons, consider their First Amendment rights, the *Library Bill of Rights* and its interpretations, the *Code of Ethics of the ALA*, and other policy statements that indicate granting privacy is the *right* thing to do.

- Library professionals should be aware of the impact technology has on library records and take proactive steps to ensure confidentiality.

- There may be grave situations where a library professional will violate a student library user's privacy because of a concern for the student's or others' welfare.

- Protect patron privacy and the confidentiality of library records by working with school administrators to create three policies: a confidentiality of library media program records policy, a library privacy policy, and a library records retention policy. Seek adoption by the institution's governing body.

- Retaining minimal library records for the shortest period of time helps ensure patron privacy.

- Three groups—library staff and volunteers, teachers and administrators, and student library program patrons—should receive privacy advocacy training.

Note: Much of this chapter's content originally appeared in the "Privacy Matters" columns published by *School Library Media Activities Monthly*.

Library Bill of Rights Interpretations and Policy Statements

- American Library Association. "Privacy: An Interpretation of the *Library Bill of Rights*"
- American Library Association. *Code of Ethics of the American Library Association*
- American Library Association. "Policy on Confidentiality of Library Records"
- American Library Association. "Policy Concerning Confidentiality of Personally Identifiable Information and Library Users"
- American Library Association. "Questions and Answers on Privacy and Confidentiality"

All interpretations, policy statements, and the *Code of Ethics* can be found at the ALA Office for Intellectual Freedom website: http://www.ala.org/oif.

Recommended Resources

- **Adams, Helen R. "Privacy Matters" columns,** *School Library Media Activities Monthly,* **September 2006–.**
  One-page columns related to privacy in school library media centers are featured in each issue.

- **Adams, Helen R., Robert Bocher, Carol Gordon, Elizabeth Barry-Kessler.** *Privacy in the 21st Century: Issues for Public, School, and Academic Libraries.* **Westport, Connecticut: Libraries Unlimited, 2005.**
  Chapter 5, "Privacy Issues in School Library Media Centers," discusses in depth the issues related to privacy for students using the media center. The volume includes a model privacy policy, records retention policy, and privacy audit chart developed specifically for use in school media programs.

- **American Library Association, "Privacy Toolkit,"** http://www.ala.org/ala/oif/iftoolkits/toolkitsprivacy/privacy.htm
  These extensive privacy resources include a model privacy policy, instructions for undertaking a privacy audit, references to federal and state privacy laws, and strategies for protecting patron privacy during law enforcement requests for records.

- **Association for Library Service to Children (ALSC),** http://www.ala.org/ala/alsc/alsc.cfm
  ALSC is concerned with the intellectual freedom of children and young adults and provides resources aimed at helping them understand their rights including library privacy and confidentiality of minors' library records. Check the ALSC website for the most recent materials.

- **Family Educational Rights and Privacy Act (FERPA)**
  An easily understood summary of the provisions of the legislation may be found at http://www.ed.gov/policy/gen/guid/fpco/ferpa/index.html

- **National Forum on Education Statistics, "Forum Guide to Protecting the Privacy of Student Information: State and Local Education Agencies," NCES 2004-330. Washington, D.C.: March 2004.**
  The primary purpose of this document is to help local education agencies and schools develop adequate policies and procedures to protect the confidentiality of information about students and their families.

- **Woodward, Jeannette.** *What Every Librarian Should Know about Electronic Privacy.* **Westport, Connecticut: Libraries Unlimited, 2007.**

  Covering the broad spectrum, the book explores topics such as protecting the privacy of children and young adults, use of RFID technology, a step-by-step plan for protecting electronic privacy, privacy education, and advocacy for privacy.

Notes

1. Bowers, Stacey L., "Privacy and Library Records," *The Journal of Academic Librarianship* 32, no. 4 (July 2006), 377.

2. Minow, Mary, and Tomas A. Lipinski, *The Library's Legal Answer Book.* (Chicago: American Library Association, 2003), 166.

3. Office for Intellectual Freedom, American Library Association. *Intellectual Freedom Manual.* 7th ed. (Chicago: American Library Association, 2005), 402.

4. Ibid.

5. American Library Association, Article III., *Code of Ethics of the American Library Association,* American Library Association, http://www.ala.org/ala/oif/statement spols/codeofethics/codeethics.htm.

6. American Association of School Librarians. "Position Statement on the Confidentiality of Library Records," http://www.ala.org/ala/aasl/aaslproftools/position statements/aaslpositionstatementconfidentiality.htm.

7. American Library Association, "Privacy: An Interpretation of the *Library Bill of Rights,*" http://www.ala.org/ala/oif/statementspols/statementsif/interpretations/Default675.htm.

8. American Library Association, "State Privacy Laws Regarding Library Records," http://www.ala.org/Template.cfm?Section=stateifcinaction&Template=/ContentManagement/ContentDisplay.cfm&ContentID=14773.

9. Ibid.

10. Ibid.

11. Ibid.

12. Ibid.

13. Texas Public Information Act (Chapter 552, Texas Government Code), § 552.352. Distribution or Misuse of Confidential Information.

14. Neuhaus, Paul, "State Laws on the Confidentiality of Library Records," Arizona Revised Statutes, Section 41-1354, http://library-privacy.wikispaces.com.

15. Ibid. Colorado Revised Statutes, Section 24-90-119.

16. "General, Family Educational Rights and Privacy Act (FERPA)," http://www.ed.gov/policy/gen/guid/fpco/ferpa/index.html.

17. Cornell Law School, *U.S. Code Collection, Family Educational Rights and Privacy Act, Title 20, Chapter 31, Subchapter III, Part 4, X 1232g.* "Family Educational and Privacy Rights," http://www.law.cornell.edu/uscode/html/uscode20/usc_sec_20_00001232—g000-.html.

18. Adams, Helen R., "Privacy Matters: Family Educational Rights and Privacy Act (FERPA) and Library Media Records," *School Library Media Activities Monthly* 23 no. 3 (November 2006), 35.

19. Ibid.

20. Ibid.

21. Ibid.

22. S.220, AN ACT RELATING TO THE CONFIDENTIALITY OF LIBRARY PATRON RECORDS, CHAPTER 4. LIBRARY PATRON RECORDS, § 172. LIBRARY RECORD CONFIDENTIALITY; EXEMPTIONS, (5), http://www.leg.state.vt.us/docs/legdoc.cfm?URL=/docs/2008/bills/passed/S-220.HTM

23. Campbell, Ellen, Family Policy Compliance Office, U.S. Department of Education, "Two Questions Regarding FERPA," email to author, July 5, 2006.

24. *Intellectual Freedom Manual*, 328.

25. Anonymous, email to author, July 7, 2007.

26. Ibid.

27. American Library Association, "State Privacy Laws."

28. "General, Family Educational Rights and Privacy Act (FERPA)."

29. Anonymous, email to author, July 7, 2007.

30. Pennsylvania Department of Public Welfare, "Child Abuse Neglect," http://www.dpw.state.pa.us/Child/ChildAbuseNeglect.

31. American Association of School Librarians. Position Statement on the Confidentiality of Library Records.

32. Liz, email to author, Nov. 12, 2007.

33. Ibid.

34. National School Board Association, "Creating & Connecting: Research and Guidelines on Online Social—and Educational—Networking," July 2007, http://www.nsba.org/site/docs/41400/41340.pdf.

35. Pew Internet & American Life Project, "Teens, Privacy, and Online Social Networks," April 18, 2007, http://www.pewinternet.org/PPF/r/211/report_display.asp.

36. "Privacy Quotes, Liberty-Tree.ca, http://quotes.liberty-tree.ca/quotes/privacy.

37. Pat, email to author, October 2, 2007.

38. Ibid.

39. Ibid.

40. "Guidelines for [name removed] Middle School Library Aides," 2007.

41. Gwen, email to author, October 4, 2007.

42. Biometrics definition, SearchSecurity.com, http://searchsecurity.techtarget.com/sDefinition/0,,sid14_gci211666,00.html.

43. Ibid.

44. Wieneke, Nancy, "Finger ID System to Facilitate School Food Service," *Clintonville Tribune-Gazette*, January 18, 2007. http://skyward.com/DeptDocs/Marketing/Public%20Website/News_Articles/Clintonville%20Tribune%20-%20Finger%20ID.pdf.

45. *Intellectual Freedom Manual*, 245.

46. Adams, Helen R., Robert Bocher, Carol Gordon, Elizabeth Barry-Kessler, *Privacy in the 21st Century: Issues for Public, School, and Academic Libraries* (Westport, Connecticut: Libraries Unlimited, 2005), 128.

47. Ayre, Lori Bowen, "Position Paper: RFID and Libraries," August 19, 2004, http://galecia.com/included/docs/position_rfid_permission.pdf.

48. SearchNetworking.com Definitions http://searchnetworking.techtarget.com/sDefinition/0,,sid7_gci805987,00.html.

49. Ayre, Lori Bowen, 9.

50. Givens, Beth, "RFID Implementation in Libraries: Some Recommendations for 'Best Practices,'" 2004, Privacy Rights Clearinghouse, http://www.privacyrights.

org/ar/RFID-ALA.htm and the American Library Association, Intellectual Freedom Committee, "RFID in Libraries: Privacy and Confidentiality Guidelines," June 27, 2006, http://www.ala.org/Template.cfm?Section=otherpolicies&Template=/Content-Management/ContentDisplay.cfm&ContentID=130851.

51. Fuller, Daniel, "School Library Journal & San Jose State University 2006 Automation Survey," *School Library Journal,* October 1, 2006, http://www.schoollibrary journal.com/article/CA6376081.htm.

52. Meola, Olympia, "School Security: Camera Systems Part of $2.7 Million Safety Plan," *Richmond Times-Dispatch* (VA), July 1, 2007, EBSCO Newspaper Source (accessed Nov. 12, 2007).

53. Judith, email to author, August 24, 2007.

54. American Association of School Librarians. "Position Statement on Confidentiality of Library Records," http://www.ala.org/ala/aasl/aaslproftools/position statements/aaslpositionstatementconfidentiality.htm.

55. Judith, email to author, August 26, 2007.

56. Adams, Helen R., et. al, 112-113.

57. *U.S.Constitution. Bill of Rights.* http://www.law.cornell.edu/constitution/constitution.billofrights.html.

CHAPTER 6

Challenges to School Library Media Program Resources

Censors don't want children exposed to ideas different from their own. If every individual with an agenda had his/her way, the shelves in the school library would be close to empty.[1]

—Judy Blume

Defining Censorship

When an individual or a group raises concerns about a particular library resource—its topic, the ideas expressed, or the language used in dialogue or description—a variety of actions may be initiated, including one termed *censorship*. According to the American Library Association, "Censorship is the suppression of ideas and information that certain persons—individuals, groups or government officials—find objectionable or dangerous."[2] In 1986 the ALA Intellectual Freedom Committee developed definitions to clarify the terminology surrounding concerns about resources in libraries:

- **"Expression of concern:** An inquiry that has judgmental overtones.
- **Oral complaint:** An oral challenge to the presence and/or appropriateness of the material in question.
- **Written complaint:** A formal, written complaint filed with the institution (library, school, etc.), challenging the presence and/or appropriateness of specific material. [Note: This is also known as a *challenge*.]
- **Public attack:** A public disseminated statement challenging the value of the material, presented to the media and/or others outside the institutional organization in order to gain public support for further action.
- **Censorship:** A change in the access status of material, based on the content of the work and made by a governing authority or its representatives. Such changes include exclusion, restriction, removal, or age/grade level changes."[3]

Chapters 1 and 3 stressed that just about anyone, including library professionals, may find it difficult to support intellectual freedom for minors in all instances, and just about anyone may become a censor.

Why Censorship Occurs

Annually the ALA Office for Intellectual Freedom (OIF) reports the "Top 10" most challenged books as reported to its office. According to its challenges database, between 2000 and 2005 there were over 3,000 challenges recorded.[4] The reasons cited most often for challenges are:

- Offensive language
- Sexually explicit
- Unsuited to the age group
- Violence
- Occult and Satanism
- Homosexuality
- Political or religious viewpoints.[5]

Although the number of reported challenges is substantial, OIF staff estimate that for *each* challenge reported, as many as *four or five are undisclosed.* Challenges go unreported because of lack of knowledge about the ALA challenge support services, fear of reprisal, a feeling of isolation, and insufficient experience to respond proactively during a challenge.

Joan Bertin, former executive director of the National Coalition Against Censorship, explained an additional rationale for censorship.

> Most people say they believe in the First Amendment, but when you get down to specifics it's clear that many people don't really understand it. They want the First Amendment to protect the material *they* like, but not necessarily what *you* like. Some people object to sex or violence, others are offended by what they consider to be disrespectful of religion, or parental authority, or the government ... But given the wide range of opinion, if everyone had the right to veto what he or she didn't like, nothing much would be left.[6]

In recent years the number of challenges reported to the ALA has fluctuated but is lower than in the 1980s. Judith Krug, director of the ALA Office for Intellectual Freedom, cited two possible reasons for the decline, "Librarians are better prepared to organize community support on behalf of a book, and would-be censors are focusing more on online content."[7] A third reason for the decline may be that school library professionals have been overwhelmed fighting cuts to staff, budgets, and programs, or a library media specialist may no longer be present in the school.

Censorship from "Outside" the School

At one time, challenges were mostly local in origin. However, as described in Chapter 1, the Internet now allows organizations with an "agenda" a means to inform visitors to their websites about "bad books" in schools and libraries. After posting lists of "suspect" books, the groups urge parents to check local school libraries for these books and make their feelings known to school administrators and school board members.

Having a Web-based online public access catalog (OPAC) makes information about school library media program resources accessible to students and staff. While a definite advantage to library users, the accessibility also creates a risk for potential challenges. *Anyone* with an Internet connection can find out what is held in the library media program collection. A potential challenger can search a school OPAC for copies of the books deemed "questionable" without physically entering the library media center.

Parents are by far the largest group attempting to censor resources in school library media programs. According to the ALA's Office for Intellectual Freedom, there were 1,800 parent-initiated challenges between 2000 and 2005.[8] Frances Beck McDonald, an intellectual freedom advocate and library educator, explained why some parents attempt to censor:

> While some of the onslaught against the First Amendment stems from deeply held religious beliefs, other attempts to restrict access stem from concerned parents trying to protect their children from unpleasant depictions of human behavior. These parents seek a verbal and visual world in which nothing will be scary, nothing will be silly, nothing will be unpleasant, and nothing will be real. They rally to remove resources they view as threatening to the cocoon in which they wish to raise their children.[9]

Parents may also fear their children will copy actions they read about. As a result, books with behaviors some parents consider inappropriate, such as swearing or questioning parental authority, or risky, such as drug use or sexual activity, can be targeted as modeling unacceptable behavior.

Library professionals may consider written requests to remove a book or other resource from a library as impinging on the rights of many to satisfy one or a few. However, it is essential to also think about reconsideration of the challenged item as part of the local democratic process. Complainants are entitled to request a review of collection materials, and their concerns should be treated with courtesy and respect.

Censorship "Inside" the School Community

ALA's Office for Intellectual Freedom's Challenge Database discloses that teachers and administrators were responsible for nearly 500 challenges between 2000 and 2005.[10] Most policies allow district employees as well as other residents to question the appropriateness of resources in school library media programs.

Although the numbers of internal school challenges are significantly fewer than those initiated by parents, school library media specialists find it more difficult to respond to censorship attempts especially if the person initiating the complaint is the principal. As the educational leader of the school, the principal exercises great power over staff, budgets, and programs. The principal may have little understanding of the First Amendment and how the courts have ruled on minors' rights to receive ideas and information in a school library media center. Principals may not be thoroughly familiar with the criteria under which library media program resources are selected or the formal process for responding to concerns about those resources. As a result, principals frequently act to remove materials they consider inappropriate or about which they have received complaints.

In 1991 Dr. Dianne McAfee Hopkins, Professor Emerita, School of Library and Information Studies, University of Wisconsin–Madison, published a study that analyzed the outcomes to challenges in secondary school library media programs in terms of retention, restriction, or removal of resources and reported these sobering results regarding challenges initiated by principals:

- Most were oral (as opposed to written) challenges.
- The school's formal reconsideration process was not followed in a majority of cases.
- 75 percent of challenges ended in removal or restriction of the resource.[11]

Hopkins found that when principals initiated a challenge, the school library media specialist was less likely to inform others of the challenge or to seek support and advice from those in a position to help. Eugene Hainer, a former school library media specialist and current Director of the Colorado State Library, concurs, "It's often a matter of job security. Years ago, there was a book series called *The Stupids*. My principal at the time told me to get it off the shelves. No discussion. Just do it."[12] Hainer opposed the removal, but was forced to comply. "If you have a choice between your paycheck and doing what's right," he said, "it can be a tough choice."[13]

Hopkins' study also sought to determine the key factors that influenced the retention of library media program materials in public secondary schools. Those found to be statistically significant include:

- "the existence and use of a board approved materials selection policy,
- internal and external support provided to the librarian during the challenge,
- overall support for the retention of challenged material, and
- the form of complaint, with written complaints being more likely to result in retention than oral complaints."[14]

Hopkins' findings emphasize the importance of library media specialists working toward full and consistent implementation of the materials selection policy from selection of resources to their reconsideration; actively seeking support when a challenge occurs; and requiring written requests for reconsideration. Those who do, experience greater retention of challenged materials.[15] While her research was completed in 1991, the strategies for retention remain valid today. Unfortunately, many school library media specialists facing challenges do not seek support during a challenge. W. Bernard Lukenbill's study "Censorship: What Do School Library Specialists Really Know?" conducted in 2002 found that 45 percent of Texas school library media specialist respondents would not turn to outside help such as the Texas Library Association, the ALA, the ACLU, or a personal lawyer for assistance with a challenge, although 55 percent of those who returned surveys said they would seek assistance.[16]

There are three other groups who may be responsible for censorship attempts in schools—teachers (already noted earlier), students, and school library media specialists. For example, in a rural district in Wisconsin, a high school freshman filed a formal request for reconsideration on Stephen King's *Different Seasons* because she did not want her younger siblings to be exposed to the violence and prison rape scene in the novella *Shawshank Redemption*. The challenge ended with the district's reconsideration committee recommending retention of the book.

As described in Chapter 3, school library media specialists struggle with self-censorship in selection of materials, fearing the collecting of "edgy" fiction, graphic novels, and fiction and nonfiction on controversial topics may result in challenges. When resources are in the collection, a phone call from a parent or discussion with a principal about a "troubling title" may result in "covert" censorship. Secretly removing a resource from the collection is certainly against district policy, because it deprives students of their First Amendment rights to access information; and it is a violation of the *Code of Ethics*.

Library Media Specialists Tell Their Stories

What occurs during an oral complaint or challenge is best told by those who have had that experience. The stories of public, private, and international school library professionals—Cassandra, Lisa, Barbara, Kathy, and Ruth—illustrate how challenges occur and are resolved.

Cassandra's Story

Cassandra Barnett is a media specialist in a public high school in Fayette-ville, Arkansas. Fayetteville schools experienced multiple challenges during 2005 and 2006.

In spring of 2005, the district librarians received a terse email from the McNair Middle School librarian: "A parent called this morning and is coming today to get the policy and forms to challenge *It's Perfectly Normal* by Robie Harris." A Christian group on the radio had said it promoted homosexuality. The parent also requested a list of all "questionable" books in the collection. Although the librarians did not comply, the parent obtained a list from another source, and this led to other challenges.

Following district policy, a reconsideration committee was formed to look at three sex education titles for teens and preteens: *It's So Amazing* and *It's Perfectly Normal* by Robie H. Harris, and *The Teenage Guy's Survival Guide* by Jeremy Daldry. Their recommendations included:

- *It's So Amazing*–remain on the shelf for all students.

- *It's Perfectly Normal*–reassign to the elementary and middle school level parent libraries, and retain it in the general collection for junior high.

- *The Teenage Guy's Survival Guide*–should not be in any elementary collection (it wasn't), and recommend it be placed in the middle schools' parent libraries.

The recommendations from the reconsideration committee changed the fundamental nature of the Fayetteville School District parent libraries as prescribed by the Arkansas Parent Involvement Act 630 passed in 2003. The materials available through the parent library are intended to focus on parenting, and their circulation is not restricted to parents. While the reconsideration committee's recommendations did not technically violate policy, they created a "restricted" shelf, an idea which a federal district court in Arkansas had ruled violated student First Amendment rights in the Counts v. Cedarville School District, 295 F.Supp.2d 996 (W.D. Ark. 2003). Note from author: Different aspects of this case are described in Chapters 2 and 4.

After meeting with the parent, the superintendent moved the **three titles** to the parent libraries, and the school board accepted his recommendations. The superintendent did not follow district policy when he met with the parent, responded to her email and phone calls, arbitrarily changed the recommendation of the reconsideration committee to the board, and placed all titles in the parent libraries. The superintendent apparently believed that, if he responded to the parent's concerns, she would be satisfied. Unfortunately, it seemed to fuel her enthusiasm for objection. The superintendent eventually realized that the best approach was to follow the district policy, something the school librarians had urged.

During that summer, the parent complainant released an announcement to the newspapers that she had identified 70 books with "vile and gratuitous sexual premises," and she urged that a parental review board be appointed to "audit" and label (like the MPAA film rating) every book in every library in our district. She also formed the group Parents Protecting the Minds of Children and created a website showing illustrations and text from the "offensive" books.

Rating Library Materials

The Motion Picture Association of America (MPAA) voluntary rating system on content in films and television programming is frequently suggested as a way to also rate other types of media including library books. The MPAA system evaluates the depictions of violence, sex scenes, drug use, language (expletives, sexual references, and other types of more "adult" terminology), and adult themes for films shown in theaters, on television, as well as on home entertainment media.[17] Common Sense Media (CSM) also has a rating system. CSM is a nonpartisan, nonprofit organization that reviews films and television programming, video games, music CDs, books, magazines, and websites to assist parents in selecting media appropriate for children and young adults. According to the CSM's "Common Sense Beliefs," the organization believes in "media sanity, not censorship."[18] On the other side of the issue, ALA's "Labels and Rating Systems: An Interpretation of the *Library Bill of Rights*" states unequivocally that adoption or enforcement of any rating systems by a library to determine the appropriateness of resources, including websites, for youth violates the *Library Bill of Rights*.[19]

The ensuing community uproar resulted in a board decision to call a town meeting in the fall of 2005 to provide a forum for everyone's concerns. Simultaneously a special board meeting was arranged to reconsider the board's decision on the three originally challenged books. As a result of presentations by both high school librarians and the district's attorney and the overwhelming support of the community, the board rescinded its decision, voting 4-3 to accept the original recommendations of the reconsideration committee. In addition, the board charged the superintendent with the task of forming a committee to revise the selection and reconsideration policy.

In the meantime, the original parent complainant filed additional challenges: *Push* by Sapphire and *Deal With It* by Esther Drill. The reconsideration committees recommended that these books be retained in their respective libraries with open access by students. The superintendent and the board accepted their recommendations. The parent has taken no further action on her published list of objectionable titles.

While the local newspapers adopted a neutral view in **reporting,** the columnists were somewhat divided as either for or against what the parent was trying to do. Television reporting stuck to the basic information without much editorializing. Unfortunately, the school district was not assertive in presenting a point of view that supported intellectual freedom or corrected misinformation.

During this period, a very conservative local talk radio station devoted itself to preaching about the liberal/wicked ways of the public schools and its librarians. Although many attacks were personal, and there were even nasty phone calls, I tried to remain focused on my job and told myself that these people didn't really know me, so how could they accurately reflect who I am. **To remain professional and stick to the facts about collection development and my role as a school librarian was the hardest thing I have ever had to do.**

There are no formal book challenges being considered in the Fayetteville Public Schools at this time. The materials selection policy with reconsideration procedures has been revised, and administrators and librarians have had training on the new policy.[20]

The Fayetteville School District's *reconsideration procedures* were given particular scrutiny during the policy revision process. The procedures now outline that:

- Reconsideration requests may be submitted from the first day of school to the last student contact day in March [leaving time for the request to be considered before the end of the school year].
- No more than two requests for reconsideration may be accepted from a concerned person at a time.
- A maximum of four books may be under reconsideration at any time.
- Material that has been through the reconsideration process may not be reconsidered again for five years.[21]

The *selection procedures* were also revised to include providing a list in each school's media center and on each library media program's website of those materials that have either been selected or are under consideration for acquisition. A "Parent Preview" opportunity is required for new resources the day before they are shelved in the fall and again in the spring. Items that are acquired in between are made available to students without preview.[22]

 Lessons Learned

Cassandra Barnett provides the following advice for school library media specialists based on her experiences.

- "Be visible promoting the library media program *before* a challenge occurs.
- Keep your selection policy with reconsideration procedures up-to-date.
- Educate members of your school community about the selection policy and reconsideration process to ensure everyone understands.
- Follow the policy, and be sure that everyone involved is following it.
- Seek local allies—faculty, students, and community members—who support intellectual freedom.
- Bring in your own big guns! There are state and national organizations ready to help you.
- Retain your professionalism, speak only to the issues, and show respect for the complainant.
- Do your homework: know your policy and the law, develop talking points, and identify misinformation and inform the public.
- Realize that you are not alone! There will be community members, parents, faculty members, and students who believe in what you do. Rely on them to help defend students' First Amendment right to receive information."[23]

Challenges in Private Schools

Private schools also experience attempts at censorship. Lisa, an independent school library media specialist in New York, explains that she has had titles challenged by teachers, graduate students, and parents at least once a semester.

> The top titles are the *Goosebumps* [series], *Captain Underpants* books, *Drawing Manga* books, any books by Robie Harris, and individual titles like *There's a Girl in My Hammerlock*. I usually have a one-to-one conversation with the individual. I listen to their concerns and thank them for supporting the freedom to read. The person generally understands why that title is in the collection and available. I also give them the written collection development policy. We do have a reconsideration form that, when completed, goes to the reconsideration committee consisting of the Dean, the Library Director, a parent representative, and me. In the past ten years no challenge has gone that far.[24]

As in public schools, attempts to remove resources from private school libraries can occur at any time and having a selection policy and a review process in place is not a guarantee against challenges or censorship. Barbara, an independent upper school (grades 9–12) librarian in Texas, described one of her experiences:

> We had an interesting situation develop last year. The Headmistress informed the middle school librarian that a specific book would be removed due to a request by a board member. The middle school librarian at that time was young, as was our second lower school librarian who had also just been hired. They were offended that the process for reconsideration had not been followed. As department chair, I waited a couple of days for a little clarity on all sides, and then I requested a meeting of the Library Department and the Headmistress. It was one of the best meetings. At some point the Headmistress's files had been cleared of the Collection Development documents, including the Request for Reconsideration. We presented her with the recently revised document and had a lively and forthright discussion about the importance of the process as a protection for intellectual freedom. We all left the meeting feeling much better. The young librarians had witnessed a powerful example for their professional lives in how to have a productive discussion, and the Headmistress promised the process would be used if another challenge should arise.[25]

While many private schools have materials selection policies with reconsideration processes, like their public school counterparts, the outcome depends on the leadership and understanding of intellectual freedom exhibited by the school's director or headmaster/mistress. Students in private school *may not* legally have the protection of the First Amendment unless granted by state law, local ordinances, or institutional rules. Therefore, it is critical that private school library professionals educate their administrators about the importance of making information from a wide range of viewpoints accessible to all students to enable them to develop into critical-thinking citizens in a democratic society.

Censorship in International Schools

Like their public and private school counterparts in the United States, school library media specialists in international schools also deal with intellectual freedom issues such as materials challenges, tension in resource selection, and filtering. However, there are also additional factors that have an impact on intellectual freedom. Ann Symons, intellectual freedom advocate and currently a middle and high school library media specialist at the Anglo-American School of Moscow, states, "Local values, politics, religion, and culture all have a role to play in defining an international school community. In their recruiting specifications, some private schools require that the librarian espouse their school community's religious values, and that the collection reflect those values as well."[26]

Another significant difference is that students in private international schools outside the United States are not shielded by the First Amendment, the source of legal protection for students' right to read and receive information in America. In international schools, guardianship of students' intellectual freedom comes from several sources: a board-approved materials selection and reconsideration policy, reliance on the American Library Association documents such as the *Library Bill of Rights* and the *Code of Ethics for the American Library Association,* and the knowledge and ethical stance of the library media specialists.

 What Is an International School?

"International schools are independent schools that operate autonomously in countries around the world, often serving the children of personnel employed in diplomacy, foreign service, multinational corporations, and the military. While the instruction is usually in English, each school and its library situation are unique."[27]

Religion and cultural traditions may have an impact on the collections of school libraries in international schools. A story from the Middle East illustrates this point:

While working in Saudi Arabia a few years ago I had to be careful as materials were ordered. All orders went through the department of ministry and every book was inspected. Then any books with the cover having exposed female arms or legs were colored with a black marker. Also any pictures of any other religion, other than Muslim, were also blackened (i.e. crosses on the tops of buildings). Then the big one was that pages would be torn out of books, picture books were especially targeted. For example, in *George Gets a Medal* the middle 4 pages were torn out because they depicted pigs. Also in non-fiction books if they referred to certain time periods and history that was not in agreement with the ministry, these pages were also ripped out.[28]

Over the years, regional territorial conflicts and the fictional depiction of the country's citizens have had an impact on intellectual freedom in a Christian school in Asia where Kathy is a teacher and preservice school library media specialist:

Being an American working overseas in a private international school, I technically do not have the traditional recourse to intellectual freedom concepts and First Amendment rights. My current school in Asia has autonomy for the most part. However, I am aware of two incidences when the country's government did step in and request changes to resources, a sequence of events that would not have transpired at a stateside school.

In the first instance more than twenty years ago, our school was directed to cross off "Sea of Japan" on every map, atlas, and textbook and to rewrite "East Sea." The directive stemmed from a regional territorial dispute.

A more recent challenge presented itself in the spring of 2007 over a novel studied in the 7th grade. A parent expressed concern to the middle school principal about how citizens and soldiers in the army of the host country were portrayed in the novel. The principal then met with a committee involving 7th grade teachers and the school library media specialist to discuss how the book was being used in class. The library media specialist was included because the book was also present in the libraries on the campus.

The concern was not confined to only the school community. The book was also being discussed in the local media and in the English newspapers in the country. There were emotional articles about how citizens [of the Asian country] were portrayed in the book. The country's Ministry of Education became involved and met with our headmaster. The decision was made to voluntarily withdraw the book from the curriculum as an expression of goodwill. One librarian voiced her concern that no effort was made to retain the book, but the administration's viewpoint was that we are guests in the country and should respect its government's wishes. Interestingly the book remained in the libraries, and there was no discussion of removing it. The only issue was that the book was required reading.[29]

Ruth, a school library media specialist working in an American international school in Taiwan, had a similar experience related to the effect of regional politics and current laws on her school's library:

Taiwan, a young democracy of just fifty-eight years, has made significant progress toward greater intellectual freedom. At one time under martial law, all information about mainland China was prohibited or literally cut from a book or encyclopedia set for political reasons. Although this activity happened as little as fifteen years ago, it does not happen now. On the other hand, there are some seemingly archaic laws that still exist from this period. The library department still pays an annual fee to a government office whose job it is to "inspect" all our imported films to ensure that we have no subversive material or messages in the media. The inspection seems cursory, but the law still exists. I have never had anything refused or rejected as illegal during customs inspections.[30]

However, Ruth also sees some differences in comparison to intellectual freedom in public schools in the United States:

I find challenges to intellectual freedom to be less of an issue in some ways than I did while working in the United States. For instance, I have not encountered a single challenge although our library carries many, if not most, of the titles that have been challenged in United States' schools. The teachers also have more discretion to use materials, particularly videos of varying ratings, in their classrooms. For example, "Schindler's List" (rated R) is a movie that I recall could not be considered for classroom use in my stateside school but is shown here quite appropriately in the context of a world history class.[31]

As Kathy noted, patrons in international schools do not have protection under the First Amendment of the U.S. Constitution. School library professionals also need to take into account the laws of the host country as well as local cultural and religious customs. Therefore, an international school's policies, including the materials selection and reconsideration policy, must provide guidance and support against censorship. The library professional will also rely on the *Library Bill of Rights*, its interpretations, and the *Code of Ethics of the ALA*.

Challenges to School Library Media Program Resources

Most school library professionals dread the "C" word—*challenges*. School library media specialists can prepare for a challenge, but the actual moment when a parent or principal says, "I would like to talk to you about this book," can be heart-stopping the first time it occurs. Suddenly, there is the realization that one has done all the preparation possible to defend against attempted removal or restriction of school library media program resources. From this moment on, it is a matter of following the reconsideration process.

Preparing for a Challenge

Library media specialists all hope not to have a challenge, but "hope" is not a strong preparation strategy. Therefore, a library media specialist begins preparing for a challenge on the first day s/he is employed. Proactive steps a school library media specialist can take to prepare for a potential challenge include:

- Create a materials selection policy that includes a *formal process* for reconsideration of school library media program resources, and ask that it be officially approved by the institution's governing body. Note: In some schools this occurs at the school level and in others at the district level.

- Post the officially approved materials selection policy on the school's and the library media program's Web pages to inform the broader community of how resources in the library media center are chosen and to deflect possible concerns.

- Become thoroughly familiar with the reconsideration process.

- Work with administrators to clarify any steps or responsibilities in the reconsideration process that are not clear.

- Arrange with administrators for opportunities to educate teachers, students, and parents about the process of selection and reconsideration materials in the media program collection.

- Advocate for maintaining a standing reconsideration committee, ready to act at any time.

Having a current materials selection policy with reconsideration procedures is critical for two reasons. First, the reconsideration process provides a formal means by which a resource about which a concern has been raised may be officially reviewed. Second, selection criteria can be used to provide a rationale for why the resource was initially selected. In Chapter 3, the components of a material selection policy are described, including a process for the reconsideration of materials already in the collection.

Megan Schliesman, librarian at the Cooperative Children's Book Center (CCBC), School of Education, University of Wisconsin–Madison, recommends developing a flowchart or list of steps outlined in the policy for responding to a complaint or challenge and noting who is responsible for each.[32] When a concern is voiced, having a visual reminder of the reconsideration process available ensures that a critical step is not missed in the turmoil that often accompanies a challenge.

Maintaining a standing reconsideration committee is a sign of the seriousness with which the school board and administrators view challenges to library media program resources. It is also a signal that school staff will not be caught unaware and are ready for a challenge at any time. Having the committee meet annually to review its charge, the reconsideration procedures, the role of each committee member, the timeline under which reconsiderations are managed, and to elect a chairperson and secretary is well

Teaching about Intellectual Freedom

The library media professional can cultivate an awareness about challenges, the intellectual freedom principles involved, and the process by which they are handled. Educational strategies include:

- Request time during staff development opportunities to examine and discuss the resource reconsideration process. Explain minors' First Amendment rights in a school library media center.

- Teach students about (1) the First Amendment right of citizens [e.g., teachers, students, parents, community members] "to petition the government for a redress of grievances" [e.g., register a written complaint about school library materials]; (2) the reconsideration process to review the item; (3) the First Amendment rights of minors to receive information and ideas in a school library; and (4) intellectual freedom principles opposing censorship. This is a lesson in the democratic process.

- Describe the selection and reconsideration processes to parents and community members in a variety of public forums such as parent-teacher organization meetings, student orientations, school newsletter articles, and on the library media program's Web pages.

- Post the materials selection policy with the review process and citizen request for reconsideration form on the library media program and district Web pages.

- Assist administrators in seeking students, parents, and community members willing to serve on a district/school reconsideration committee.

- Provide training for reconsideration committee members: outlining minors' First Amendment rights, district selection criteria and the acquisitions process, and the role and responsibilities of committee members, and introducing intellectual freedom statements such as the *Library Bill of Rights*, which may be referenced in the materials selection policy.

worth the time. If a challenge occurs, the committee can proceed confidently with its tasks.

Larra Clark, former manager of media relations for the ALA, advises, "Don't wait for the worst-case scenario. Get prepared now. Build positive relationships with parents, community members, school staff, and the media. Get a reputation for being open, honest, and accessible."[33]

Challenging Times

The ALA has strong policy and ethics statements to guide a library media specialist faced with a censorship attempt. "Challenged Materials: An Interpretation of the *Library Bill of Rights*" states that any challenged material that meets a library's material selection policy shall not be removed "under any legal or extra-legal pressure."[34] *Extra-legal pressure* has two meanings. The first is "threat of legal action or pressure by community members or organized groups that results in the banning of library materials." The second definition includes "requests from law enforcement without a proper court order and actions taken by personnel in positions of authority (e.g., elected officials, school officials) to remove or restrict access to library materials or services without following library policies and procedures."[35]

Recently, a new tactic has been used by censors; it includes filing charges under criminal obscenity laws and alleging that a book is obscene under the law or that a school employee has violated a state's "harmful to minors" law by providing "obscene materials" to a minor.[36] In one instance in 2007 in Howell, Michigan, the Livingston Organization for Values in Education (LOVE) petitioned the board of education to remove Toni Morrison's *The Bluest Eye*, Richard Wright's *Black Boy*, Kurt Vonnegut's *Slaughterhouse Five*, and Erin Gruwell's *The Freedom Writers Diary* from the eleventh grade language arts curriculum. When the board voted to retain the titles on the list, LOVE filed a complaint with a local prosecutor, the Michigan Attorney General, and an attorney with the U.S. Department of Justice, claiming that the books are obscene and violate laws against child pornography and child sexual abuse. The Michigan Attorney General and the U.S. attorney found there was no merit to the charges.[37] While the charges may not be successful, the action can cause unwanted media attention, legal costs for the district and staff member, and the possibility of loss of employment for the teacher or librarian involved.

Despite the strategies used, it is essential to recognize that those who bring an oral complaint or formal written challenge using the district's reconsideration of resources form have that right. The First Amendment guarantees that citizens have the right to "petition the Government for a redress of grievances."[38] In this case, the government is represented by public schools and the "grievance" is a concern about resource(s) in the school library media center collection. Those who question library materials may be employees, students, parents, or other citizens, and their opinions deserve respect. While library and school staff may not agree with the request to remove or restrict the resource, a district's reconsideration process sets in motion another evaluation of the resource. Although all complaints, oral or written, are acknowledged by school staff, only a *formal written complaint* should lead to the full reconsideration process.

 U.S. Constitution, First Amendment

"Congress shall make no law respecting an establishment of religion, or prohibiting the free exercise thereof; or abridging the freedom of speech, or of the press; or the right of the people peaceably to assemble, **and to petition the Government for a redress of grievances.**"[39]

Larra Clark, former manager of media relations for the ALA, advises, "Assume that most adults want to protect minors from information and topics they believe may be hurtful or harmful—whether that is racist language, swear words, or sexual information. This isn't a bad instinct; it just can't be generalized beyond one parent's child or children. *Harry Potter* is an example. Many people can easily understand why another parent might love it or hate it—and why, despite that love or hate, the book should be available in the library as a choice. Acknowledge that it is good for parents to be concerned about THEIR children."[40]

When faced with a formal written challenge about a library media collection resource, a school library professional should take these steps promptly:

- Review the school's selection policy and reconsideration procedures.
- Take time to think through the process—do not respond immediately.
- Examine the formal *written* complaint or notes about an oral complaint.
- Prepare a one-page memo for the principal to present facts about the resource in question and discuss the situation with him/her.
- Contact the ALA Office for Intellectual Freedom (OIF) for assistance through its challenge support service.
- Check ALA policy statements such as the *Library Bill of Rights* and the *Code of Ethics of the American Library Association*. [Copies are available in Appendix A.]
- Gather information such as reviews and a list of awards.
- Investigate if the title has been challenged elsewhere.
- Reread or view the questioned item.
- In the case of a formal written challenge:
  - Maintain the item in the collection during the reconsideration process.
  - Obtain copies of the work for the use of reconsideration committee members.
  - Prepare packets of information for the reconsideration committee that may include reviews and awards, an analysis on how the questioned item meets selection policy criteria, why the material is needed in the collection, and other items as specified by district policy.
  - Seek support from local and state-level First Amendment advocates including professional library associations.
  - Seek support and guidance from your colleagues in the school library profession.

Gail Dickinson, former school library media specialist and current library educator, recommends that after receiving a written complaint, the school library professional prepare a memo for the principal or other immediate supervisor. The one-page document could include a brief summary of the plot or challenged resource's content, the selection criteria met by the

Strategies for Positive Communication with Concerned Individuals or Complainants

The first contact between the school library media specialist and a complainant may be in person, over the telephone, or via email. If an expression of concern or oral complaint is made in person, there are strategies that can be used to ensure successful communication with the concerned individual(s).

- Establish eye contact, and smile.
- Be a courteous "active" listener: acknowledge that you understand the concerns; listen more than you speak; and clarify what you do not understand.
- Make no commitment to appease the complainant.
- Describe the library's role in providing access and information to all users and the parent's or guardian's role in monitoring the reading and library use of their child(ren) or ward(s).
- If the complainant is not satisfied, describe the process for reconsideration of a library resource, and offer to provide the reconsideration form.[41]

In some cases, through informal discussion the complainant's objections may be resolved during the initial contact. Having someone listen to his/her concerns is often all the individual seeks.

---

resource, quotes from reviews, a summary of the reconsideration process, and why it is critical that the reconsideration process be followed. In challenges to school library media program resources, courts look at whether the administration and board have followed formal district policy, rather than ignoring the review process. The memo may also refer the principal to important First Amendment court cases such as *Board of Education v. Pico* and others found on the ALA Office for Intellectual Freedom website.[42] Reinforce the information sent to the principal with a follow-up meeting to gauge the principal's support. As part of the conversation, review the roles the principal, school library media specialist, the reconsideration committee, and others will take *if* a formal, written complaint is filed.

The complainant may be impatient and seek to circumvent the district's policy by contacting a higher authority, such as the district administrator or a school board member. If the challenge becomes the basis for a lawsuit, the extent to which district process was followed will be a consideration in the court's decision. Emphasize to administrators that, if the district board-approved policy is not followed, the district may be in legal jeopardy. As Gail Dickinson notes, the approved reconsideration process is to be followed "so that the district does not end up as a footnote in a school law text."[43] The step-by-step process also provides structure in an emotionally charged and potentially chaotic situation.

The Reconsideration Committee at Work

The purpose of a reconsideration committee is to review the formally challenged material and make a recommendation for its disposition. After a formal complaint has been received, the reconsideration committee is appointed unless a standing committee already exists. Policy will determine who appoints the committee and its composition. The committee usually includes administrative or supervisory representation, one or more classroom teachers at different levels, school library media specialists, and parents. Some policies also include a member of the board of education or a high school student if the challenged resource is a part of the high school library media center collection. All members of the reconsideration committee should read, view, or listen to the work in question and form an objective judgment. Under some district's reconsideration guidelines, the committee is instructed to keep in mind the broad principles of students' right to read and learn rather than focusing solely on the defense of the individual material. The committee's deliberations are conducted in a public meeting usually termed a "hearing." As noted in Chapter 3, administrators should provide concrete instructions to the reconsideration committee to ensure that members understand their responsibilities for following both the letter and spirit of the review process. Some districts also supply a list of general questions to guide the reconsideration discussion and recommendations.

Achieving a smoothly coordinated reconsideration hearing requires planning. Strategies for conducting a successful hearing include:

- Announce the hearing, and conduct it as a public meeting with committee members and observers in attendance.

- Review the written list of instructions for the reconsideration committee prior to the hearing. If supplied, a list of questions to guide discussion should also be examined.

- Appoint a member of the committee to take official minutes for the group.

- Record [audio] the proceedings to ensure clarity and accuracy should questions arise later.

- Register observers and committee members as they enter the room.

- Seat the official reconsideration committee separately from the complainant and observers. This is symbolic: The committee is present to conduct business; the complainant is present to address the committee and listen. S/he should not be seated as if a committee member.

- Allow the complainant and others opposing the resource as well as defenders of the work to speak following preestablished ground rules, including a time limit per speaker.

- Discuss the merits and deficiencies of the work [among the committee members] and determine the committee's recommendation for the disposition of the resource in question. Options may include retaining the work, restricting its use, removing it from the collection, or moving it to another level.

- Conduct votes publicly by show of hands.

- Record the committee's recommendation in writing, including minority and majority views, and forward it to the appropriate administrator or body (i.e., superintendent and/or school board) as determined by policy.

- Retain all formal documents, notes, audio recordings, and decisions related to the formal challenge.[44]

The reconsideration committee performs a valuable service by objectively analyzing material to which there has been a formal challenge and providing an impartial recommendation. The committee's work is part of the democratic process that allows citizens to question books and other resources in the library media program collection.

Every committee has its own dynamic, and the strength of feeling for and knowledge of intellectual freedom principles in general may affect the outcome. The position of the person who challenged the book or other resource may also have an impact on the decision. For example, the complainant may be an influential parent or community member or even, as already noted, the principal. This should not matter, but it can, especially if the reconsideration committee does not have a firm understanding of its role and of the First Amendment rights of minors.

Removing a resource from a library media program collection has serious implications for the First Amendment rights of minors, but it is equally important that a democratic discussion take place as part of the resource review. In the end, following the reconsideration process is a triumph for intellectual freedom.

Lea's Story

School library professionals often find themselves weighing minors' right to information against other factors and finding that intellectual freedom is not a simple black-and-white-concept. Lea, director of Learning Resources, in a suburban Texas district, shared her thoughts related to challenges.

"Everyone should have the right to access information especially that which interests them. I have always advocated for not removing library books or not denying access to that which a student needs to complete a research project or has a desire to know. In my career as a building librarian I had at least four books officially challenged. All but one remained on the shelf. I still cringe about the one removed, but that's history."

"When dealing with intellectual freedom and minors, however, the issues become cloudy. So, maybe there are some boundaries to that wide open door. Directing a kindergartener to resources of a sexual, graphical, or mature nature just wouldn't be ethically responsible. The notion of 'age appropriateness' has to be considered. Many selection policies state this criterion which grays the issue of intellectual freedom considerably."

"Last year in our suburban school district, a book challenge brought this issue up in such a way that it was hard to keep the lines between intellectual freedom and parents' rights from blurring. The challenged book was deemed too intense for the middle school students by the reconsideration committee unless parents granted written permission to read the book. The book was NOT removed—that would have been an all out war with librarians. The book was placed under restrictions for checkout. This created a very difficult position for librarians who felt the book was age appropriate and should be openly accessible to middle school students. The mental anguish of our administrators to find a solution to the complainant's position, balancing parents' rights, and the intellectual freedom issues created more mental anguish for the middle school librarians. Fighting against removal would have been easy. Fighting against a parent's involvement in the reading selection of their child is rather difficult. Fighting against an administration which didn't remove the book is also difficult."

"I would like to be considered a champion of intellectual freedom and children's rights to have the information needed. But, as any responsible person knows, that does not mean access to anything and everything. With library collections selected according to established guidelines and professional practices by professional librarians, I think we can offer our students what they need. Dealing with challenges is just part of the job."[45]

Seeking Support

According to Dianne McAfee Hopkins' research, one of the key factors in retention of library media program materials is obtaining internal and external support. It is interesting to note, however, that while many forms of assistance appear to be readily available to school library media specialists, Hopkins found that 50 percent did not seek support locally and 88.4 percent did not ask for help outside the district.[46] It is critical that the school library professional solicit local, statewide, and national backing when resources are challenged. At the local level, the library media professional and close allies can ask students, faculty members, parents, and community members who support the First Amendment rights of minors to write letters to the editor, attend the reconsideration hearing, and speak at a school board meeting.

One of the unknown factors in the beginning of a challenge is how the principal will react if s/he thinks the library media specialist is talking to someone about the situation. Megan Schliesman, a librarian at the Cooperative Children's Book Center of the School of Education at the University of Wisconsin–Madison, fields calls for help with challenges from both school and public librarians. She understands there is usually only one library professional in each school media center, and that individual may feel isolated. "Many school library media specialists fear that telling someone what is happening [a challenge] may make the situation worse, but it is important to overcome that fear and reach out."[47] One of Megan's strategies is to gently ask the caller to consider whom she/he can trust professionally to keep discussion about the challenge confidential. She suggests it may be other school library media specialists in the district or a public librarian, all fellow professionals who are knowledgeable about minors' First Amendment rights, the principles of intellectual freedom, and the ethics of the situation.[48] Once the challenge is known in the community, the school library media specialist may feel more comfortable in openly soliciting support.

If the library professional does not feel confident speaking openly to others within the local school or community, the state library or department of education may employ a school library consultant whose responsibilities include offering counsel and resources to school library media specialists facing challenges. Many state library organizations also have intellectual freedom committees that offer support when a challenge occurs. For example, the Wisconsin Educational Media and Technology Association's (WEMTA) Intellectual Freedom Action Network supplies trained members who have experienced challenges themselves and are willing "to provide confidential collegial support and a sounding board to other professionals facing a resource challenge, filtering issues, and/or other technology related intellectual freedom issues."[49]

At the national level, the ALA Office for Intellectual Freedom (OIF) offers a challenge support service to help librarians when written complaints, public attacks, or preemptive censorship occurs. ALA staff will assist with actual or potential challenges to books, magazines, other library resources, and Internet access. All challenges reported to ALA are kept confidential, and support is provided regardless of whether an individual is an ALA member. Challenges may be reported online or by telephone.

Beyond ALA and the library community, there are other pro–First Amendment organizations, such as the American Civil Liberties Union, that will also offer assistance during attempts to censor school library resources. See Appendix B for a list of these groups with their contact information.

During a challenge, the school library media specialist also needs confidential emotional support. Cassandra Barnett alluded to the personal attacks she experienced and the negative phone calls she received. She stated that remaining professional throughout the lengthy multiple resource challenges *"was the hardest thing I have ever had to do."*[50]

In the midst of confrontations that polarize the community and may make local or even national headlines, school library professionals find ways to maintain a sense of normalcy and emotional balance. Another library media specialist who also faced multiple challenges noted:

> I did have a very good support system in place—family, close friends, and several co-workers who supported me throughout the ordeal. We formed a group of interested people and called ourselves "Save Our Books," otherwise known as SOB. These people were intelligent, open-minded individuals; and we met several times throughout the ordeal. I remember many, many phone conversations with friends where we discussed the "next move." These people attended all public meetings, and we were usually able to 'unload' to each other after each frustrating event. I think that it would have been much more difficult for me had I not had such a tremendous support group that was made up of such reasonable people. We talked and emailed constantly. I am also fortunate to be married to a person who listened and empathized.[51]

Sometimes support develops over time through a proactive stance on the part of the library media specialist. Sue, PS-8 library media specialist, experienced two successive challenges from parents of first-time preschool and kindergarten children. Realizing that the parents were hypersensitive to everything related to their children's school activities, including their choice of library materials, she turned these incidents into positive learning opportunities for other parents. She attended orientations for parents of preschool and kindergarten children and spoke about the library program, its wide range of resources to serve the needs of very young children through eighth graders, and offered parents an opportunity to visit the library and help their children select their reading choices. Sue also spoke about the responsibility of parents in guiding the reading of their children. There were two results. First, there was much goodwill and support generated for the library media program. Second, there have been no other challenges to elementary library program resources in the school.[52] Sue opened a line of communication with parents and started building bridges between parents of early elementary students and the school library media program. Without explicitly stating it, she conveyed the image of a professional and approachable library media specialist.

It cannot be repeated too frequently; the time to develop allies for the library media program is *before* a challenge occurs. Ideally, support for the library media program and its collection begins on the library media specialist's first day on the job. Information about developing an advocacy program for supporting intellectual freedom is found in Chapter 9.

Principals and Intellectual Freedom

According to Fran Roscello, former consultant in the School Library Media Program at the New York State Education Department, the school library media specialist is *the expert* in the school when it comes to all library media program matters including intellectual freedom. S/he supplies the principal with information an administrator may not have but that is necessary to avoid making errors. Most principals do not receive training on intellectual freedom concepts in their coursework; therefore, it is imperative for the library media specialist to help the principal understand the legal and ethical issues involved.

Roscello stresses that the school library professional must establish him/herself as an expert from the first day on the job. The principal gains respect for the library professional when the individual does not bother him/her with minor details but rather contributes positively to the overall goals of the school. When a challenge occurs, the library media specialist must emphasize to the principal that the board-adopted policy is a legal document representing due process which must be followed.[53]

Not all principals follow district policy when confronted with an individual complaining about a resource in the school library media collection. Gwen is a middle school library media specialist in Virginia, and her principal decided to ignore district policy. Gwen received a note from her principal asking her to cancel a subscription to a gaming magazine and remove copies from the collection. The basis of his directive was an oral complaint from a parent. Gwen requested a meeting with the principal to discuss the situation, and over the weekend, prepared by studying the materials selection policy criteria, discussing the situation with other library media specialists, and determining how to persuade the principal to comply with the district's reconsideration process.

During the subsequent meeting she emphasized why the magazine had been selected and its popularity with students.

I explained that we can't just pull something every time someone has an issue with it.[54] She also expressed her selection philosophy stating, "I don't agree with all the viewpoints represented in my library, but it is my charge to provide a wide variety of materials that appeal to many different children and represent many different viewpoints in our culture."[55]

Following the meeting, Gwen mused,

All those other things I do that I don't have to do, that make the school look good, are not only an investment toward every child's education, *they are coins in the principal's bank*. I think I may have cashed them all in today. It was a very difficult meeting. The principal still does not think the magazine should be in the collection, but he is willing to allow the process to play itself out. I ended the meeting by telling the principal about a $500.00 grant we will be receiving from Wal-Mart for our history and geography collection. I was glad to tell him when he asked, that I did fill out the grant paperwork, write a letter, and make numerous phone calls in order that we could receive that money. Maybe I have a few more coins back in the bank.[56]

It took courage for Gwen to confront the principal's initial unwillingness to follow policy and to defend her students' right to read, and there are multiple positive results. The principal was reminded of the district's library resources reconsideration policy and why it is important not to mollify one parent. He agreed to follow policy by calling the parent who originally complained and explaining the district's policy not to remove items without a formal written challenge. If the parent completes the form, the reconsideration process will go forward. Reflecting on the situation several days later, Gwen stated, "It isn't always easy to live out the things that we believe, but it is important to try."[57]

Working with the Media

From her experience in journalism, public relations, and her work as the former manager of media relations for the ALA, Larra Clark has advice on working with the media for school library media specialists and administrators. She recommends, *"Take every media request seriously, prepare your key messages and examples, and repeat them."*[58] She cautions the school or district's spokesperson: *"Nothing is 'off the record.'"*[59] She adds that with blogs and interactive media so accessible, almost anyone can send a message to hundreds of readers. "Be careful with all your communications. By this, I don't mean to be afraid. Too often people approach the media with trepidation instead of excitement. *Every interview is an opportunity to communicate and raise awareness about your library* ... It's important to remember that the reporter is not your audience. The readers and listeners—parents, teachers, or school board members—are your audience."[60]

The ALA Office for Intellectual Freedom provides librarians with tips for managing the message.

- Be knowledgeable about the media source conducting the interview or to which you are submitting a letter or article; appeal to its audience.
- Prepare a simple, concise message with no more than three key points.
- Develop a list of the questions—simple and tough—that may be asked, and practice your responses.
- Respond to inaccurate statements immediately with positive facts, stories, and quotes demonstrating library access and service.
- Look and sound professional, friendly, and upbeat.
- Acknowledge errors and correct them immediately if you misspeak.
- Proactively call to update your interviewer before a story is published or for a follow-up article.[61]

District policy should identify who will represent the school or district when speaking to the media during the reconsideration process. It may name the individual by title or state that a spokesperson will be appointed by the superintendent. Designating a single spokesperson during a challenge will eliminate divisive and conflicting viewpoints from being shared.

Final Work

When the reconsideration process has been completed, file an online report of the challenge and its result with the ALA Office for Intellectual Freedom. Reports are kept confidential and will be used by the ALA in gauging the status of intellectual freedom in U.S. schools and for determining the top 10 banned books of the year.

In addition, ask the reconsideration committee to help analyze the materials selection policy and the review process for weaknesses and inconsistencies. Examine the selection policy criteria to determine if revisions could increase access to resources. If flaws are found in the policy, it is essential to determine whether this is the best time to make changes, or whether time needs to pass before a revision process is undertaken. Timing is everything, and if the school has a very conservative governing board, beginning an intellectual freedom advocacy program may be the best, first step toward policy revision, which can then come later.

What if the Challenge Succeeds?

For a number of reasons, some challenges end with a *change in the status* of the resource. The process may have been cut short by an administrator unilaterally removing the item from the collection or restricting its use. The reconsideration committee may determine the work does not meet district selection criteria and that the selector made an honest error in judgment. The ideas in the work may not fit the social and emotional levels of the students using the collection. As a result, the committee may recommend the work be removed from the collection, moved to a collection at a different level, or place restrictions on the item's use.

Conversely, the reconsideration committee may recommend retention of the challenged resource, but its decision is reversed by the superintendent and/or board of education. They may order the item removed from the school library media center collection. The board, administrators, and district legal counsel must be very sure that a decision to change a reconsideration committee's recommendations or remove an item from the collection is not made on the basis of disapproval of the resource's content or ideas expressed. In the *Bd. of Education, Island Trees Union Free School District v. Pico,* 457 U.S. 853 (1982), Justice Brennan wrote in the plurality opinion:

Local school boards may not remove books from school library shelves simply because they dislike the ideas contained in those books and seek by their removal to prescribe what shall be orthodox in politics, nationalism, religion, or others matters of opinion.[62]

There are two possible actions those defending the work may take when a challenge is successful. They may accept the decision but also increase their advocacy efforts for access to information for minors. Or they may choose to initiate legal efforts to overturn the board or administrative decision. Because law suits are complicated, expensive, and frequently very lengthy, they are generally undertaken with the assistance of an organization whose purpose is to defend First Amendment rights, such as the American Civil Liberties Union.

Do School Library Media Specialists Lose Jobs over Challenges?

Whether a challenge succeeds or fails, there may be some lingering rancor in the community and within the school. As a result of strong support for students' access to information and the concepts of intellectual freedom, a school library media specialist may choose to leave a position or be "encouraged" to do so by administrative and community actions. Although the individual was not fired, the controversy has made his/her presence in the area and on the job untenable.

In other circumstances, the consequences may be more blatant. According to Barbara, an independent upper school librarian in Texas,

> I have had calls from [independent school] librarians who had been asked to quickly remove a book (usually small private schools—both Catholic and independent) and, without procedures in place, they have no way to defend the right to keep the material on the shelf.... I have seen private school librarians threatened with job loss if they didn't remove certain books, and I have seen a librarian fired for selecting a title that had been listed on an area list of best books she had participated in developing.[63]

In some ways, private school librarians have less recourse than public school library professionals. There are no unions or state and federal agencies to support those unfairly dismissed in private schools. According to Debbie, a former administrator in an independent school,

> Public school librarians are government employees whose free expression is better protected under the First Amendment. Librarians employed in private schools are private sector employees, often with "at will" contracts. Their First Amendment rights are subject, to a much greater extent, to an employer's discretion.

Sometimes the courts have protected speech in the private sector (for example when a private company has a contract with the government), but the case law is inconsistent, even vague. So a private or parochial school librarian may be less willing to risk a court test which, even when successful, could make future employment in other private schools problematic.[64]

The situation can be similar in international schools. A library media specialist working in a school library in Vietnam commented, "Educators in international schools have little if any legal recourse when the school doesn't fulfill its contractual obligations or arbitrarily decides that an employee hasn't fulfilled hers or his, or in any grievance or dispute for that matter."[65] Ultimately, the international library media specialist, like his/her counterparts in public and private schools in the United States, must follow the school's policies, including the materials selection and reconsideration policy, and personally determine the degree to which he/she will uphold intellectual freedom principles.

Confronted with uncertain consequences, the school library professional faces a difficult ethical and personal decision. In some cases, s/he may be forced to concede because of financial or other circumstances. A school library professional may be the sole support of a family and risking the potential loss of a job will create a financial hardship. There may be family considerations. The individual may have children and not want his/her family subjected to the media attention, adversarial atmosphere, or personal

 Leroy C. Merritt Humanitarian Fund

Library professionals *in any type of library* who suffer job loss or discrimination in hiring based on their defense of intellectual freedom may apply for limited financial assistance from the Leroy C. Merritt Humanitarian Fund. Established in 1970 in memory of Dr. Merritt, the fund provides support to librarians who, in the trustee's opinion, are:

> "Denied employment rights because of defense of intellectual freedom; that is, threatened with loss of employment or discharged because of their stand for the cause of intellectual freedom, including promotion of freedom of the press, freedom of speech, and the freedom of librarians to select items for their collections from all the world's written and recorded information."[66]

School library media specialists are eligible to apply for Merritt Fund support, and at least one has received assistance. Though not an official part of the ALA, information about the Merritt Fund is available on the Office for Intellectual Freedom website.

attacks. After weighing the situation, taking a stand may come down to knowing that one did all that was personally possible at the time.

Remaining Up to the Challenge

School library professionals and their allies have fought many battles to preserve the intellectual freedom of minors using school library media centers, and more remain. As censors find new tactics to attempt to remove materials from school library media program collections, the school library media specialist must protect and defend access to the collection through the reconsideration process. Being a school library media specialist requires solid knowledge about the First Amendment as applied to school libraries; familiarity and internalization of intellectual freedom principles; and the personal courage to step forward and speak. Each individual must weigh how far s/he is willing and able to protect minors' First Amendment rights. In the end, following policy and doing one's best is all that can be expected.

✎ Key Ideas Summary

This chapter covered a broad range of issues related to challenges to school library media program resources and the role of the school library professional in defending against censorship. To review, here are some of the major ideas:

- Both internal and external attempts to remove or restrict school library media program resources occur for reasons ranging from offensive language to the occult and homosexual themes.

- Ensuring that the school or district has a board-approved materials selection policy with a reconsideration process is a critical step in being prepared for potential challenges.

- Hopkins' research on the outcomes to challenges in secondary school media centers found that complete and consistent implementation of the materials selection policy, seeking support during a challenge, and requiring written reconsideration requests led to greater retention of challenged materials.

- Educating administrators, teachers, parents, students, and the community about the principles of intellectual freedom and minors' First Amendment rights to receive information is an effective way to develop allies *before* a challenge occurs.

- When a written or oral complaint occurs, prepare a one-page memo for the principal summarizing the resource's content, how the resource meets selection criteria, pertinent information from reviews, an outline of the reconsideration process, and why it is crucial to follow policy.

- The responsibility of the reconsideration committee is to read, view, or listen to the work in question and form an objective judgment. In some districts, the committee is instructed to keep in mind the broad principles of intellectual freedom rather than focusing solely on the defense of the individual resource.

- For formal challenges, conduct a public hearing and allow observers on both sides of the issue to speak following preestablished ground rules.

- Designate a single institution spokesperson to speak to the media, prepare carefully for any media contact, and understand that nothing is "off the record."

- Retain all documents and notes related to the reconsideration committee's deliberations and the final decision of the superintendent or governing board.

- A challenge may succeed despite the best efforts of the school library professional and First Amendment supporters.

- Challenges may create an aftermath of negative feelings on both sides, and school library professionals may find their present position uncomfortable, untenable, or worse.

Library Bill of Rights Interpretations

- American Library Association. "Challenged Materials: An Interpretation of the *Library Bill of Rights*"

- American Library Association. "Free Access to Libraries for Minors: An Interpretation of the *Library Bill of Rights*"

All ALA *Library Bill of Rights* Interpretations are available on the ALA Office for Intellectual Freedom website: http://www.ala.org/oif.

Recommended Resources

- **American Civil Liberties Union Foundation of Texas, "Free People Read Freely: Annual Reports on Banned and Challenged Books in Texas Public Schools,"** http://www.aclutx.org/projects/bannedbooks.php

  Annually the ACLU Foundation of Texas submits "open records requests" to every school district and charter school in Texas, seeking information about books that have been banned or challenged by a parent, teacher, administrator, or student in schools in the last year. The resulting report lists the title, author, reason for the challenge, result and current status of a formally challenged book (banned, its use restricted, or accessible to students), and whether the book was in the library collection or on a curricular reading list. Informal challenges are also reported.

- **American Library Association, "Coping with Challenges: Strategies and Tips for Dealing with Challenges to Library Materials,"** http://www.ala.org/ala/oif/challengesupport/challengesupport.emf

The Office for Intellectual Freedom has compiled a comprehensive set of links to assist school library professionals in the areas of communicating effectively with a complainant and the media, applying the principles of intellectual freedom, using the materials selection policy to protect students' access to information, preparing for a challenge, and understanding the reconsideration process.

- **As If! Authors Support Intellectual Freedom,** http://asifnews.blogspot.com
  This blog incorporates comments on censorship attempts and provides links to the websites of many young adult authors who support intellectual freedom.

- **Doyle, Robert P.** *The Banned Books 2007 Resource Book.* **Chicago: American Library Association, 2007.**
  Published every three years, this reference includes a descriptive compilation of books which have either been censored or against which attempts have been made to censor, a summary of notable First Amendment court cases, an extensive compilation of quotes on the First Amendment, recommendations for dealing with challenges, and suggested activities to promote intellectual freedom.

- **Hopkins, Dianne McAfee.** *Factors Influencing the Outcome of Challenges to Materials in Secondary School Libraries: Report of a National Study.* **Prepared under Grant #R039A9004-89, U.S. Department of Education, Office of Educational Research and Improvement, Library Programs. Madison: University of Wisconsin–Madison, School of Library and Information Studies, 1991**.
  "Toward a Conceptual Path of Support for School Library Media Specialists with Material Challenges," *School Library Media Quarterly* **1, 1998,** http://www.ala.org/ala/aasl/aaslpubsandjournals/slmrb/slmrcontents/volume11998slmqo/mcafee.htm
  The first resource reports the findings on Hopkins' research on the factors that influence the outcome of challenges to resources in school library media centers. The second describes research that addresses the question of why some school library media professionals reach out for support during a challenge while others do not.

- **Lukenbill, W. Bernard. "Censorship: What Do School Library Specialists Really Know? A Consideration of Students' Rights, the Law, and Implications for a New Education Paradigm,"** *School Library Media Research* **10, November 2007,** http://www.ala.org/ala/aasl/aaslpubsandjournals/slmrb/slmrcontents/volume10/lukenbill_censorship.cfm
  An extensive study conducted in 2002 in Texas, the researcher reported on the level of judicial knowledge school library media specialists acknowledge relating to federal court decisions impacting minors' First Amendment rights and censorship of school library media center resources. The study also focused on how school library professionals perceive their obligations to follow the law and protect students' First Amendment rights to receive information.

- **Reichman, Henry.** *Censorship and Selection: Issues and Answers for Schools,* **3rd ed. Chicago: American Library Association, 2001.**
  A classic title, Reichmann discusses the "who, what and why" of censorship of school library and curricular resources; provides guidance in developing a materials selection policy; describes the preparation for a challenge and the reconsideration process; and defines the legal basis for defending against challenges.

- **What If? Questions and Answers on Intellectual Freedom,** http://www.education. wisc.edu/ccbc/freedom/whatif/archives.asp

    Maintained by the Cooperative Children's Book Center (CCBC) at the University of Wisconsin–Madison, "What If?" is a question-and-answer forum for teachers, school and public librarians, and others in the library and education fields. Visitors may submit a question confidentially, and CCBC staff will answer it in a thoughtful manner emphasizing how "the principles of intellectual freedom are carried out in practice." The answer archive can be sorted by relevancy to classroom, school and public library, self-censorship, and "other" issues.

Notes

1. Blume, Judy, "In Their Own Words: Authors Talk About Censorship," http://www.randomhouse.com/teens/firstamendment/authors.html

2. American Library Association, "Intellectual Freedom and Censorship Q & A," http://www.ala.org/ala/oif/basics/intellectual.htm.

3. American Library Association, "Definitions to Clarify Terminology Associated with Challenges," http://www.ala.org/ala/oif/challengesupport/challengesupport. htm#definitions.

4. American Library Association, "OIF Censorship Database 2000–2005, Challenges by Type," http://www.ala.org/ala/oif/bannedbooksweek/bbwlinks/challengesbyinstitutions20002005.pdf.

5. Ibid.

6. Blume, Judy, ed., *Places I Never Meant to Be: Original Stories by Censored Writers* (New York: Simon & Schuster Books for Young Readers, 1999), 15–16.

7. Associated Press, "Number of Books Facing Challenge Drops to All-time Low," September 29, 2006, First Amendment Center, http://www.firstamendmentcenter.org/news.aspx?id=17460.

8. American Library Association, Office for Intellectual Freedom, "OIF Censorship Database 2002–2005, Initiator of Challenge," http://www.ala.org/ala/oif/bannedbooksweek/bbwlinks/challengesbyinitiator20002005.pdf.

9. McDonald, Frances Beck, *Censorship and Intellectual Freedom: A Survey of School Librarians' Attitudes and Moral Reasoning* (Metuchen, New Jersey: Scarecrow Press, 1993), 2.

10. "OIF Censorship Database 2002–2005, Initiator of Challenge," http://www.ala.org/ala/oif/bannedbooksweek/bbwlinks/challengesbyinitiator20002005.pdf.

11. Hopkins, Dianne McAfee, "School Library Media Centers and Intellectual Freedom," http://www.ala.org/ala/oif/iftoolkits/ifmanual/fifthedition/schoollibrary. htm.

12. Halls, Kelly Milner, "What Our Teens Read: Who Should Decide?" *Denver Post*, September 26, 2004, http://www.kellymilnerhalls.com/content/blogcategory/101/51.

13. Ibid.

14. Hopkins, Dianne McAfee, "Factors Influencing the Outcome of Challenges to Materials in Secondary School Libraries: Report of A National Study," University of Wisconsin–Madison, School of Library and Information Studies, 1991, http://www.eric.ed.gov/ERICDocs/data/ericdocs2sql/content_storage_01/0000019b/80/23/3e/42.pdf.

15. Hopkins, "School Library Media Centers and Intellectual Freedom."

16. Lukenbill, W. Bernard, and James F. Lukenbill, "Censorship: What Do School Library Specialists Really Know? A Consideration of Students' Rights, the Law, and Implications for a New Education Paradigm," *School Library Media Research*, 10 (November 2007), www.ala.org/ala/aasl/aaslpubsandjournals/slmrb/slmrcontents/volume10/lukenbill_censorship.cfm.

17. "What do the ratings mean?" Motion Picture Association of America, http://www.mpaa.org/FlmRat_Ratings.asp.

18. "Ten Common Sense Beliefs," Common Sense Media, http://www.common-sensemedia.org/about_us.

19. American Library Association, "Labels and Rating Systems: An Interpretation of the *Library Bill of Rights*," http://www.ala.org/ala/oif/statementspols/statementsif/interpretations/Default675.htm.

20. Barnett, Cassandra, email interview with author, March 8, 2007.

21. Fayetteville, "Arkansas School District, Administration Regulations for Policy #6.15," http://www.fayar.net/admin/hr/Policies07.htm.

22. Ibid.

23. Barnett, email interview.

24. Lisa, email to author, October 14, 2007.

25. Barbara, email to author, November 7, 2007.

26. Symons, Ann, "Intellectual Freedom: A Lonely Task Without the First Amendment," *KQ on the Web* (November/December 2007), http://www.ala.org/ala/aasl/aaslpubsandjournals/kqweb/kqarchives/volume36/362/362symons.cfm.

27. Adams, Helen R., "Have MLS, Will Travel," *American Libraries* (November 2005), 54, http://www.ala.org/ala/alonline/selectedarticles/adams.pdf.

28. Ibid.

29. Kathy, email to author, November 8, 2007.

30. Ruth (pseudonym), email to author, November 29, 2007.

31. Ibid.

32. Schliesman, Megan, "April IF Message from the CCBC," Wisconsin Educational Media and Technology Association list, April 6, 2007.

33. Clark, Larra, email interview with author, April 13, 2007.

34. American Library Association, "Challenged Materials: An Interpretation of the *Library Bill of Rights*," http://www.ala.org/ala/oif/statementspols/statementsif/interpretations/Default675.htm.

35. American Library Association, Office for Intellectual Freedom. *Intellectual Freedom Manual*, 7th ed. (Chicago: American Library Association, 2006), 496.

36. "ALA Intellectual Freedom Committee Report to Council," Midwinter Meeting 2008, Philadelphia, PA (January 16, 2008), 2.

37. Hartinger, Brent, "Howell, Michigan Books Not Obscene," As If, March 8, 2007, http://asifnews.blogspot.com/2007/03/howell-michigan-books-not-obscene.html.

38. U.S. Constitution, First Amendment, http://www.firstamendmentcenter.org/about.aspx?item=about_firstamd.

39. Ibid.

40. Clark, email interview.

41. American Library Association, "Coping with Challenges: One on One," http://www.ala.org/Template.cfm?Section=dealing&Template=/ContentManagement/ContentDisplay.cfm&ContentID=11111.

42. Dickinson, Gail, "The Challenges of Challenges: What to Do? Part II," *School Library Media Activities Monthly* XXIII, no. 6 (February 2007), 22–23.

43. Ibid.

44. *Intellectual Freedom Manual*, 7th ed., 424–426.

45. Lea, email to author, March 1, 2007.

46. Hopkins, Dianne McAfee, "Toward a Conceptual Path of Support for School Library Media Specialists with Material Challenges," *School Library Media Research* 1, 1998, http://www.ala.org/ala/aasl/aaslpubsandjournals/slmrb/slmrcontents/volume11998slmqo/mcafee.cfm.

47. Schliesman, Megan, telephone interview with author, August 15, 2007.

48. Ibid.

49. Wisconsin Educational Media and Technology Association, "Intellectual Freedom Network," Intellectual Freedom Plan, http://wemtaonline.org/se3bin/clientgenie.cgi.

50. Barrett, email interview.

51. Anonymous, email to author, August 15, 2007.

52. Sue, telephone interview with author, August 15, 2007.

53. Roscello, Fran, interview by author, Washington, D.C., June 23, 2007.

54. Gwen, email to author, November 28, 2007.

55. Ibid.

56. Ibid.

57. Ibid.

58. Clark, email interview.

59. Ibid.

60. Ibid.

61. American Library Association, "Coping with Challenges: Dealing with the Media," http://www.ala.org/Template.cfm?Section=dealing&Template=/Content-Management/ContentDisplay.cfm&ContentID=11111.

62. Doyle, Robert P., *Banned Books: 2007 Resource Guide.* (Chicago: American Library Association, 2007), 185.

63. Barbara, email to author, November 7, 2007.

64. Debbie, email to author, January 9, 2008.

65. Adams, 55.

66. Leroy C. Merritt Humanitarian Fund, http://www.ala.org/ala/ourassociation/othergroups/merrittfund/merritthumanitarian.htm.

CHAPTER 7

Intellectual Freedom and the Internet in Schools

Filter a website, and you protect a student for a day. Educate students about online safety in a real world environment, and you protect your child for a lifetime.[1]

—Christopher Harris

Federal Laws That Impact Internet Access

In December 2000 Congress passed the Consolidated Appropriations Act (PL 106-554), which included the Children's Internet Protection Act (CIPA) and the Neighborhood Children's Internet Protection Act (NCIPA). CIPA requires that elementary and secondary schools that accept discounted services under the federal Schools and Libraries Program of the Universal Service Fund [a.k.a. E-rate Program] or direct federal funding through the Elementary and Secondary Education Act (ESEA) certify that they have installed "technology protection measures" or filters on *all computers used to access the Internet* by minors and adults to protect against *visual depictions* of child pornography, obscenity, or material "harmful to minors" as defined under federal law. (For purposes of this chapter, the terms "filtering," "blocking," and "technology protection measures" are used interchangeably.) CIPA further requires that schools certify the existence and implementation of an Internet safety policy and that this policy must include monitoring the online activities of minors. Under CIPA and NCIPA, minors are considered to be those less than 17 years of age.[2]

NCIPA applies only to schools and libraries receiving E-rate discounted services and specifies that schools must create and implement an Internet safety policy that addresses the following:

i. "access by minors to *inappropriate matter* on the Internet and World Wide Web;
ii. the safety and security of minors when using electronic mail, chat rooms, and other forms of direct electronic communications;

iii. unauthorized access, including so-called 'hacking,' and other unlawful activities by minors online;

iv. unauthorized disclosure, use, and dissemination of personal information regarding minors; and

v. measures designed to restrict minors' access to materials harmful to minors."[3]

While CIPA defines the term "harmful to minors," NCIPA does not provide a definition for "*matter inappropriate for minors.*" Instead, it allows the local school board or governing body to determine what is and is not inappropriate for minors to access under its Internet safety policy, often referred to as an acceptable use policy or AUP. In fact, NCIPA specifically prohibits any department or agency of the federal government from defining what is "inappropriate for minors."[4] After developing the Internet safety policy, schools are required to give public notice and hold a public hearing on the proposed policy.

In addition to CIPA and NCIPA, many states have filtering laws that apply to schools. Most call for school boards to adopt Internet use policies to prevent minors from accessing sexually explicit, obscene, or harmful materials. Some also require the installation of filtering software on school computers and may tie eligibility for specified types of state funding to compliance. Others, such as Virginia, require instruction in Internet safety.[5] The statutes vary widely, so library media specialists must know their individual state's filtering laws. One source for this information is the National Conference of State Legislatures website [http://www.ncsl.org/programs/lis/cip/filterlaws.htm].

Controlling Internet Access in Schools

Since schools were required to comply with CIPA requirements by July 1, 2002, filtering of Internet access for minors has become pervasive. In November 2006 the National Center for Education Statistics (NCES) published "Internet Access in U.S Public Schools and Classrooms: 1994–2005." In its 2005 survey, NCES found that 99.6 percent of public schools with Internet access used the following methods to restrain students from either inadvertently or willingly visiting Internet sites that do not support the school's educational missions:

- filtering or blocking software,
- teachers or other staff monitoring of students,
- written contract signed by parents,
- written contract signed by students,
- monitoring software,

- honor codes, and

- access only to the school's intranet.[6] Note: An intranet is defined by NCES as "a controlled [closed] computer network similar to the Internet but accessible only to those who have permission to use it."[7]

In 2005 *School Library Journal* collected spending information from the 2004–2005 school year in 529 school library media programs across the country. The resulting data found that 98 percent of the schools reporting had acceptable use policies. The number of school library media programs using filtering software rose to 98 percent in 2005, from 69 percent in 2002.[8]

How Filtering Affects Access to Information

There are two serious issues related to controlling Internet access in schools. The first is the capriciousness of filters themselves. While filtering software has become more sophisticated in recent years, in the second edition of *Internet Filters: A Public Policy Report*, published by the Brennan Center for Justice in 2006, the authors concluded that "Filters continue to block large amounts of valuable information."[9] After reviewing studies covering 2001–2006 to determine filters' effectiveness, they reported that filters both over- and under-blocked legal content.

Most "technology protection measures" include a combination of both mechanical (computer software) and human evaluation of sites. For the most part, filtering company staff are involved only minimally in the filtering products offered to schools. Because thousands of new Web pages are created daily, staff are able to review only a small percentage to determine what encompasses the three federally prohibited types of visual depictions—obscenity, child pornography, or images harmful to minors. Schools purchasing the filtering product do not know companies' political, religious, sexual, or other ideologies or biases; and filtering product staff decisions may be subjective. As a result, there is much over-blocking of legal visual images and *text*. During the suit filed by the American Library Association (ALA), the American Civil Liberties Union (ACLU), and others challenging the constitutionality of CIPA in *public libraries*, evidence provided in court demonstrated "filters wrongly block tens of thousands of valuable Web pages."[10]

Chris Hanson, senior national staff counsel for the ACLU, stated,

The law [CIPA] presents serious First Amendment problems with respect to filtering at public schools for the same reasons that it does for public libraries. Blocking software restricts students and others from accessing constitutionally protected material. There is no software product that purports to make decisions based on any legal category. These companies admit that they create their own categories of material that is [*sic*] not based on legally recognized categories.[11]

Filters create frustration for teachers and students trying to research topics frequently blocked by filters as described in real experiences by school library media specialists later in this chapter. Students with no home access to the Internet also are at a disadvantage compared with students using unfiltered home access.

Filtering Decisions at the Local Level

The second serious issue related to controlling Internet access is how administrators and technology departments are using filters to limit student access to Internet information and sites far beyond what is *required* under CIPA. Although CIPA requires that schools prevent minors from accessing *visual depictions* of child pornography, obscenity, or material "harmful to minors," under NCIPA schools may also locally determine what is "inappropriate for minors" to view under their Internet safety policy (AUP). As a result, more *constitutionally protected* information may be inaccessible to students and staff, depending on how wide or narrow a school defines the phrase "inappropriate for minors." As previously noted, NCIPA prohibits the federal government from defining "inappropriate for minors." In two informal surveys in 2006, Mary Ann Bell, a library educator at Sam Houston State University, collected anecdotal evidence that some schools have banned the use of search engines in classrooms, while others are either forbidding Internet use or severely limiting it. In other cases, blogs, social networking sites, and video games were blocked because they were not considered to be "for instructional purposes." At one school, automobile sites are blocked to discourage recreational use of the Internet, although books related to hobbies are included in the school collection.[12]

Similar situations are reported across the country. While book challenges continue to occur, obtaining access to websites with *legal* information is the most recent school censorship battle. According to Sandra, a high school library media specialist in the Midwest,

We have a technician and a filtering system determining access. If access [to a site] is needed, a teacher or I must send an email. The technician will determine its merit, and then block or deny the request. Any site with the word "blog" is now filtered, even nytimes.com.[13] Throughout the spring semester, Sandra had a running discussion with administrators and the IT director. At one point, A student requested access to the official site of Playstation's game "God of War" for an informative speech. I emailed this request to the IT staff. Access was denied.[14] When Sandra met with the IT director about this issue the response was, "The student has a bad track record." Sandra replied, "I don't deny any students access to resources because of a bad circulation record. We have the technology to allow a student access to one site for a day." This student could have had access to the information he needed.[15]

When May Filters Be Disabled?

As noted in Chapter 2, disabling filters for students to access *legal informa-tion* is dependent on the type of federal funding the school or district is receiving. Currently, recipients of the Elementary and Secondary Act (ESEA) federal funding under 20 USC 6777 (c) may allow authorized school staff to disable the filter for both adults and minors "to enable access for bona fide research or other lawful purposes."[16] However, under 47 USC 254 (H), recipients of the E-rate program may only unlock filters *for adults* engaged in bona fide research.[17] Nevertheless, if a district over-blocks beyond the requirements of CIPA, district staff may unblock for minor students engaged in legitimate research an over-blocked site that does not include visual depictions of child pornography, obscenity, or material legally defined as "harmful to minors." If in doubt, school personnel should check if state filter-ing legislation and district policies may be more restrictive, and seek advice from legal counsel.

Anita, a library media specialist for grades 6–12 in Wisconsin, lamented her experiences with district filters and how they negatively affect faculty instruction and student learning.

Last week I started teaching my website authenticity unit to find that once again, all my examples of misinformation and biased websites had been blocked by the school filter. I had to justify why I was requesting a website on smokers' rights be opened to 8th graders. I was using it for students to debate whether this would be a good source for a Health class paper.

After listening to students and staff complain to me since the beginning of school about the new filter, I finally went to my principal. I asked him to please define the purpose of the filter. I understand that we must filter and protect our students from harmful websites to comply with CIPA. But when it was decided to block "shopping" websites, we disregarded high school students doing reports on companies for Business Education, students collecting a collage of the latest fash-ions for their Fashion and Design class, and the Automobile Repair class students who come to the library to look up auto parts for the cars they are fixing up at home.

I'm in the library—I see EVERYONE'S students. My room is their resource area. I can't anticipate everything students will need to look up before they come in and test the websites to see that they are open. My virtual library is shrinking. Sources that used to be available are now blocked. As soon as one inappropriate item shows up at a website, the entire content of the website is lost to us.[18]

Terry, an elementary school library media specialist in the Northwest, vented her frustration with not being able to access worthwhile Internet sites.

> At the present, if I want to access (or have my students access) a website that has, for whatever reason, been "filtered out," I must rely on the intervention of an individual at the district level and then wait for WEEKS for a response. Instructional time is a precious commodity. It is counter-productive for me to structure lessons that are stimulating, appropriate, and engaging for my students only to be stymied by the lack of authority to "unblock" a site that I have researched and KNOW is safe and important to my students' learning.[19]

Why is access to the Internet and its wide-ranging educational sites being either limited or prohibited? Rationale for either setting filters at a very high level to allow little access or totally preventing the Internet from being used is based on *fear for the safety of children and young adults*. There have been widespread media accounts of online predators. Some fear is justified; however, a recent study by the Crimes Against Children Research Center, "Online 'Predators' and Their Victims: Myths, Realities and Implications for Prevention," points out inaccuracies in those accounts. The study, based on interviews with 600 local, state, and federal law enforcement officers and over 3,000 telephone interviews with youthful Internet users found:

- "The publicity about online 'predators' who prey on naïve children using trickery and violence is largely inaccurate."

- "Internet sex crimes involving adults and juveniles often fit a model of statutory rape—adult offenders who meet, develop relationships with, and openly seduce under-age teenagers—than a model of forcible sexual assault or pedophilic child molesting."[20]

- "Most online sex offenders are adults who target teens and seduce victims into sexual relationships. They take time to develop the trust and confidence of victims, so that the youth see these relationships as romances or sexual adventures. The youth most vulnerable to online sex offenders have histories of sexual or physical abuse, family problems, and tendencies to take risks both on- and offline."[21]

The researchers concluded: More research is needed about the online sexual behavior involving youths, knowledge about victims and potential victims, and the impacts of different types of prevention messages and strategies. Researchers recommend using "developmentally appropriate prevention strategies that target youths directly and acknowledge normal adolescent interests in romance and sex."[22]

Officer Joshua Wilson has been investigating Internet crimes for the New London, Wisconsin, police department for three years, as well as providing presentations to parents and students on Internet dangers. He says, "Filters at school are one small way to protect our children from the dangers presented with the Internet. Unfortunately, many [students] know ways to defeat the filters and access what they want to anyway. We need to be teaching students about the dangers involved with the Internet."[23]

In addition to the fear of online sexual predators, there is also the fear that filters will not block an image that is inappropriate in an educational setting. This happened in an elementary school computer lab in the Midwest. For a class project, the students were researching "pets"; and despite the filters in place, several children inadvertently retrieved visual images of "two legged pets." This is not an isolated incident. In a 2006 report from the Crimes Against Children Research Center, researchers found that among the 1,500 minors surveyed, 42 percent reported being exposed to online pornography within the previous 12 months. From that group, 66 percent said the exposure was unintentional and was the result of misspelled Web addresses, pop-up ads, or email spam. For 9 percent, this accidental exposure to pornography occurred at school.[24] These examples support the findings of filter *under-blocking* reported by *The Internet Filters: A Public Policy Report* cited earlier in this chapter. As a result of incidents such as this, administrators are extremely concerned about the safety of children and young adults using the Internet in their schools. Those in charge also fear that parents may either complain or file legal action against districts for failing to keep their children safe.

There is a third reason why schools limit Internet access beyond what is legally required—misuse of the resource by students. In 2006 an Alaskan school district restricted its students to websites with domain names ending in .gov or .edu, websites that have been approved following a teacher's request, or subscription-based databases. The action was taken because the district found itself fighting a losing battle with students who were using a site dedicated to helping students defeat the district filtering software.[25] According to District Public Information Officer Traci Crotteau, "Students are visiting everything from pornographic and sadistic Web sites, to bomb making and gun Web sites. And some students are spending excessive amounts of time on these sites."[26] A district report found that over a 10-day period, students at the district's five high schools spent less than 40 percent of their time in productive, educationally appropriate sites and more than 60 percent in places such as game, music, and video sites.[27]

The district believed its responsibility was to protect students using the Internet. Director of Management Information Services Marie Burton commented, "The ban was not something done lightly. It was something that was needed to protect our kids…. If the problem is not reined in, the Internet could become a liability for the district rather than an asset."[28]

Joel's Story: An Administrator's Perspective

The Alaskan district is not alone is trying to balance students' access to the Internet, requirements under CIPA, and concerns of parents that their children be safe online. Administrators, technology staff, and library media specialists across the country struggle daily with how to provide safe access to Internet resources for students who are minors. Joel, director of Information Services in a large midwestern district, shared his perspective on the use of filters and student access to the Internet.

As a technology administrator, I struggle with how intellectual freedom applies to the Internet. Without any other factors involved, intellectual freedom would contrast easily against filtering. However, the Internet is quite different from school library collections in that essentially there are no selection criteria; and some of the material is illegal to minors. Our school librarians decide what to include "in" our collections, but we decide what to keep "out" of our student's Web browsers. In some ways, this is not so different to me.

While intellectual freedom might apply without restriction to a public library, schools bear an additional responsibility of working with minors. It is because of our underage population that restricting access to pornographic [or other inappropriate] material makes sense. While it also might contrast against intellectual freedom, I think it is the right decision. There is a false sense of security with the use of the filters on our network. It is amazing how quickly the kids work their way around the system. Within my first two weeks on the job, I had written up two students for accessing pornographic material on school computers.

Two issues come to mind in relation to access to the Internet. For a while, our filtering system was set so high that we could not even access our school's web page! This has been corrected but for a period of about a month, no sites were available to the students. The other issue with the Internet is that some parents do not allow their students to use the Internet due to questionable information they may access.

As educators and library media specialists we may not agree with the decisions of parents in regard to what they will allow their children to read or access via the Internet. For me, the best way to deal with such parents is to provide them the opportunity to articulate their position and to offer their reasons for their decision. I never try to sway them. I respect their decisions and, as much as possible, I try to honor their requests.

I agree with the ALA that the best protection for young people is in teaching them to evaluate information, think critically about the information they receive, and how to make decisions about the materials they view.[29]

The decisions made by school district staff related to filtering are not made easily, and district administrators and IT staff are aware that no "technology protection measures" offer 100 percent security from cyber-garbage. Filters also must be set in a way that is neither too strict nor too lenient, nor discriminatory for segments of the school population, such as those who may be lesbian, gay, bisexual, or transgender. Whether the decisions to filter more heavily are done out of fear of online predators, parent complaints, the threat of legal action, or the response to student actions, the entire issue of filtering is another gray area for library media specialists within the realm of guarding intellectual freedom.

Terri's Story: Filtering from One Perspective

Terri, a high school library media specialist in the Southeast, shares her experiences with students and staff in a filtered environment. She is employed where, in addition to CIPA, state law also requires filtering in public schools.

I haven't felt that the intellectual freedom of our students has been compromised unduly through the use of filters. The year after the school shooting in my previous district (3 students killed, 5 injured) I had a student who was doing a project on comparing the weapons carried by foot soldiers in World War II to those carried during Vietnam, and every weapon site was blocked. It was a knee jerk [reaction] to the situation, and I was able to get that taken care of with a few phone calls. Other than that, we have been able to find most legitimate information. Once in a while a site is blocked, let's say on the occult, but there are five more that are not blocked. So we've been able to get around it. I did have a student who was doing research on the effects of pornography who talked to me about unblocking some sites to aid in his "research." I explained to him that we could do research on sky diving without actually [jumping out of a plane] doing it and the same could be said about this topic. We laughed, and moved on.

All users—students and faculty—sign an Acceptable Use Policy [AUP] form which is kept on file at each school. For grades K-5, parents complete and sign AUP's for their children. Beginning with sixth grade, students and their parent/guardian sign the paper, and it is valid until they graduate from high school.

I would say that our filters are set at medium [restrictiveness]. They are placed at different levels depending on the subject, and so some are higher than others. For example, pornography category would be set at high, and games would be set at light. I haven't found sites about abortion or being gay that are blocked. However, some sites closely related to these topics might be blocked under the "personals" category.

We are a very small school so teachers can request that filters are disabled for a particular site by calling or emailing me. I contact the district technician, and he "opens" the requested site. Depending on his availability, it could be a matter of minutes or up to a day or so if he is tied up in another school. We rarely do this since the sites that are needed by teachers are very, very infrequently blocked. Filters on staff computers are set at a lower level than students, so there hasn't been an issue with opening sites.

If a student accesses a site that is unacceptable, I keep it pretty low key especially if it is accidental. I just say something like, "Well, it's a good thing we are all so mature here." I really think that we have taught kids what is unacceptable to access at school and what is okay so they don't try it [to bypass school filters] as much as they used to. Also, the majority of our students have Internet access at home. I did an informal survey at my school, which has over 50 percent free/reduced lunch, and about 85 percent of the kids do have access at home. The other 15 percent can go to friends' houses, so they can satisfy their natural curiosity outside the school.

At our school, social networking sites such as Facebook and My Space are blocked, but blogs and wikis are not. The issue with social networking is that the schools have not seen any educational importance in those sites. As these sites evolve, if teachers and administrators begin to see these as educational opportunities, we will probably get them allowed.[30]

It would appear that the filtering system in Terri's district has been set at a less restrictive level and also that she has been willing to take action to ensure students' access to information. Terri's experience with filtering has been relatively positive, but in other districts this is not always the case. In some, administrators, IT staff, teachers, library media specialists, students, and parents are at odds over the use of the Internet even though many acknowledge it as having extraordinary educational resources. The comments of Joel, an administrator responsible for both technology and library media program services; and Sandra, Anita, and Terry, library media specialists trying to gain access to sites; and Terri who "works around" the filters, demonstrate the ways educators are trying to balance state and federal laws and the realities of the Internet with intellectual freedom and ethics statements. Where schools have been successful in protecting minors' First Amendment rights, collaboration, cooperation, and staff awareness have been key.

Betty's Story: No Filters

Although nearly 100 percent of all public school districts in the country filter Internet access, there are those very few that have chosen other means. Betty is the district library media coordinator and elementary library media specialist in a medium-size Midwest suburban school district. Her district chose not to filter and has forgone federal discounts for Internet access under the Schools and Libraries Program of the Universal Service Fund (E-rate). Betty states,

In our district, we have a very strong belief in privacy, intellectual freedom, and personal responsibility. We want to prepare our students for the real world and that includes teaching them appropriate Internet usage. That means that they need to learn to be careful, think about their actions, consider why they are using the Internet, and the ramifications of that use. Our policies state that teachers are to pre-select instructional websites for students, and we are trying to provide numerous pre-selected resources on our district and building Web pages. Internet, indeed all computer use, in our schools is for instructional purposes. We do not expect our students to have time to "surf" because they are to be actively engaged in instruction during the school day. Teachers have a responsibility to direct, guide, and instruct students in the use of all instructional tools.

Originally [when the proposal not to filter first became public], we had a strong supporter in a Catholic elementary school principal. Sister G. spoke boldly about intellectual freedom and about children learning in a real environment. Interviewed for a regional newspaper, she stated: "If they have no freedom, they have no way to make the right decisions." That public support goes a long way in a small community!

While we do not purchase a filtering product, we block a number of sites with our firewall. [Note: A firewall is software with a dual purpose. It protects the resources of a school network from intruders, and it controls access for school users to resources outside the school's network.[31]] Anyone may recommend a site for blocking. The site is then reviewed by library and technology staff, and a determination will be made to block or not. Usually, it is not too hard to make that decision.

Every staff member is held responsible for monitoring student computer use on a daily basis. The Student Code of Respect and Responsibility is the guide for all student behavior, including computer and Internet use. Students and staff members are held accountable to the district's Telecommunications Use Policy [AUP]. For poor student computer behavior, serious steps are taken, including denial of computer use, detention, and up to and including suspension. Online harassment or cyberbullying issues also are handled according to our Student Code of Respect and Responsibility. Administrative personnel—principal, human resource director, buildings and grounds directors, or others—are responsible for disciplinary actions of staff who may misuse the Internet.

The district relies on education and teaching responsible use of the Internet. All teachers are expected to include Internet safety instruction at the point of use. Mini lessons are taught whenever Internet use is included as part of a lesson. In the elementary grades, students learn about passwords, confidentiality, and privacy. In the middle school, mini courses are team taught by library media staff and classroom teachers. There are benchmarks on Internet safety included in our Information Literacy and Technology Curriculum.

Policy indicates that students are always to use district-designated resources first, and when exhausted, they may move to pre-selected Internet sites. We try very hard to give the students very relevant and direct resources for their instructional needs. We purchase online databases and have access to subscription-based online resources provided by the State.

Beginning in middle school there is a distinct change in the approach to the use of school computers and students' personal responsibility. They are given a series of introductory lessons on computer use and issued "computer permits." Strict guidelines and penalties are delineated for inappropriate use that includes bullying, accessing inappropriate sites, and wasteful use of resources. For example, an inappropriate site might be a commercial site on a hobby if the class is supposed to be researching on political campaign sites. There is a real push to teach safe and appropriate Internet use before high school, where students have so much more freedom in all their schoolwork.

This issue about not filtering Internet content has come up at school board meetings whenever we present the Technology Plans or discuss policies dealing with computers. Usually the technology director and I answer questions and fully disclose our philosophy and directives, including anecdotal stories to make points about access, learning, and success. We have two high school student representatives to the school board, and they are always very supportive and helpful with this discussion. They give real examples and explain students' attitudes. No parents have made an issue of this [no district Internet filtering]. The board and the community trust our staff. We have not had many problems with students' misuse of the Internet.[32]

No school can control content on the Internet; however, *any* school may choose the path described by Betty. It takes leadership, proactive fore-thought and planning, and courage by administrators, technology staff, library media specialists, faculty, and the board of education. It requires sub-stantial investment in staff development. It necessitates trust by the commu-nity. Finally, not filtering demands faith in the idea that educating students to make ethical decisions and letting them make mistakes during Internet use will prepare and protect them outside the school in an unfiltered world far better than a commercial filtering product.

Private School Thoughts on Filtering

In private schools, the decision of whether or not to filter is a local one based on the school's philosophy of education, safety concerns for the stu-dent body, and whether or not it accepts federal or state funding. For exam-ple, State Code in Virginia requires the following under § 22.1-70.2. "Acceptable Internet use policies for public and private schools." The law further states, "In addition to the foregoing requirements regarding public school Internet use policies, the principal or other chief administrator of any private school that satisfies the compulsory school attendance law pursu-ant to § 22.1-254 and accepts federal funds for Internet access shall select a technology for its computers having Internet access to filter or block Inter-net access through such computers to child pornography as set out in § 18.2-374.1:1 and obscenity as defined in § 18.2-372."[33]

Cathy, an independent school librarian for grades 6 through 12 in north-ern California, firmly declares,

No filtering! The school is adamant about this—the Board of Trustees, the admin-istration, the tech department, the librarian (me). This was the policy before I arrived, and I can say with confidence that it isn't likely to change. Filtering isn't in keeping with our school philosophy. The kids are taught effective search skills, and we discuss what to do when an unexpected website comes up. Plus a lot has to do with how lessons are designed and what the kids are looking for on the Internet. We have a good variety of databases, and I put together pathfinders for a variety of curriculum units which helps guide the students to appropriate websites.

Our upper school students often find themselves searching for topics that could bring up some pretty questionable material. The senior Anatomy and Phys-iology classes do a final project on "any anatomy topic of interest." This has gen-erally been the opportunity for them to do scientific-oriented presentations on risque topics: breast/penis augmentation, birth control (I judged a presentation where everyone put condoms on bananas), s&m—just about anything they can imagine as long as they deal with it from a medical/scientific approach. We also have kids of all grades who research First Amendment topics including pornogra-phy, assisted suicide, banned books, etc. These topics really test their search abilities—they have to research the topics while staying on appropriate sites. I'm very pleased that they are able to do that research from school.[34]

Liz, a library director at an independent school in Massachusetts, explains her school's decision not to filter.

> We decided long ago that education around Internet use is not only more effective than filtering, but also that it teaches information literacy skills that our students need in their lives outside our walls. We have an acceptable use policy that details what is and is not appropriate Internet use, we have a student-run iSafe club that develops activities and initiatives for use with the whole school, we offer parent education nights and the occasional speaker, we monitor student Internet use in the library and in computer labs, and there are consequences for flagrant inappropriate use (which, in a girls' school, is rare).[35]

Barbara, an upper school librarian in Texas, finds that her school's Internet use allows flexibility for faculty and students.

> Filtering is a necessity in a school where the ages range from 4 to 18, and technology is pervasive. Our solution has been to create a tiered filtering system with increasing options within every division [lower school, pre-K-4; middle school, 5 through 8; and upper school, 9–12]. Teachers in the divisions are periodically asked to review what is blocked and make recommendations for changes. Students can request permission to have sites unblocked, and it is often routinely done if the change is clearly necessary for academic work. It is a very effective approach though there are times when the Upper School faculty objects; however, since they are part of the review process, usually their concerns are answered.[36]

Internet use in private schools appears to be different from what is experienced in the majority of public schools. Fewer private schools filter online content; and the emphasis is on *educating students* to search the Internet effectively and safely, giving them freedom plus responsibility for their decisions. Teachers, at least in Barbara's school, have an opportunity to give input into which sites are blocked and may request changes; and students may request that sites be unblocked for academic purposes. The inclusion of the school librarian, faculty, and students in decisions about Internet use is a marked difference from many public schools where the technology staff, many of whom are not librarians and have no grounding in the principles of intellectual freedom, decide what adult and minor users may access with little recourse.

Turnabout—Filter This Site!

Ironically, some public school educators request that additional websites be blocked. With the battles in many schools to *unblock* filtered sites, care should also be taken when requests are made to *block a site* that is currently accessible. In an article for *American Libraries*, Doug Johnson, the director of

Media and Technology for Mankato [Minnesota] Area Public Schools, supported the idea that requests to block an accessible site should be treated like a material challenge.[37] Doug is correct in stating that this type of request is similar to a challenge of a library media center resource, which requires a process during which a committee considers whether the request should be carried out.

Doug Johnson is not alone in his thinking on this topic. Tom, director of Information Technology in a midwestern district, states,

> As a general rule, we only block sites as required by CIPA. We resist blocking other sites. We receive very few requests to have sites blocked. Most are a result of sites obviously misclassified by our filter provider or students doing unsupervised searches. Although we don't have a formal policy [for blocking of additional sites], we do have a documented process for staff to follow. In these cases, we gently remind teachers [or other complainants] of our Resource Selection Policy which says we promote intellectual freedom and provide a learning environment where we guide students as they acquire critical thinking and problem solving skills. We let staff know that we recognize the need to keep young students away from inappropriate material. We encourage them to guide student inquiries through online [subscription] resources like World Book or Galenet or by providing very specific links for students to use.[38] In other words, requesting a site be blocked should not automatically guarantee that result if the school district supports intellectual freedom.

In a time of extensive filtering, attempting to censor additional sites is another form of censorship and should be treated in that manner.

Equity Issues and Access to the Internet

According to the American Library Association (ALA), "Intellectual freedom is the right of every individual to both seek and receive information from all points of view without restriction."[39] Beyond filtering there are two other threats to students seeking electronic information using the Internet. First, not all students have physical access to sufficient computers and the Internet at school or at home. Second, the long-held principle of Network Neutrality is threatened. The school library professional must be aware of both the Digital Divide and Network Neutrality as threats to students' intellectual freedom.

The Digital Divide

Some minors' equity of access to the Internet is threatened by the Digital Divide. In many parts of the country, there is a "technology gap," and students living in poverty do not have sufficient access to computers and the

Internet in school and at home. According to the National Center for Education Statistics, the estimated ratio of students to computers in high-poverty schools is much higher than in more affluent schools. Socioeconomic factors affect home use of the Internet by students, with impoverished Black and Latino children having less access.[40] A U.S. government report states, "In general, those who are poor and live in rural areas are about 20 times more in danger of being left behind [in technology and Internet use] than wealthier residents of suburban areas."[41] The "Libraries Connect Communities: Public Library Funding and Technology Access Study 2006–2007" found that "more than 73 percent of [public] libraries report they are the only source for free public access to computers and the Internet in their communities."[42]

 The Digital Divide

"The Digital Divide is defined as the disparity between individuals with and those without access to a computer and the Internet. The divide is applicable to all population sectors encompassing both adults and children, but the focus of much attention has been on segments of the population seen as underserved—low income, [individuals from] rural and multicultural areas, and women."[43]

Students who lack ready access to computers and the Internet face handicaps in their education. When teachers assign homework, students without technology resources must rely on using a school computer, attempt to travel to a public library, or use a friend's computer and Internet connection. Teachers may not be allowed to assign homework that requires computers. In this case, everyone loses. Students who lack computer access also experience difficulty finding resources for personal information needs such as medical and social information.

The Digital Divide affects students' First Amendment right to receive information if they are unable to obtain the necessary access to computer technology and the Internet. These same students already face educational, economic, and social disadvantages. The school library professional must make every effort to advocate for equitable educational opportunities for *all* students. S/he can promote access for students on the wrong side of the technology gap by organizing support for such ideas as:

- Promote the idea of teachers providing time in class for students to work on assignments requiring the use of technology.
- Equip inexpensive library-owned laptop computers with word processing and other software for students to check out for home use.

- Extend before and after school hours for school library media centers and computer labs and provide transportation for students to return home.

- Expand public library youth programs assisting students with their homework to include evenings and weekends.

- Collaborate with local youth clubs or other organizations to provide technology training for students from disadvantaged families.

Just as the *Library Bill of Rights* directs that "a person's right to use a library should not be denied or abridged because of origin, age, background, or views,"[44] student patrons should also not have their access to electronic information marginalized because computers and the Internet are not readily available to them.

Net Neutrality

In addition to technology protection measures mandated under CIPA and state filtering legislation, there is another threat to access to the Internet for schools, libraries, and their patrons. Since the 1960s, the Federal Trade Commission (FCC) held that Title II of the Communications Act of 1934 prohibited telephone and network companies from discriminating in the provision of telecommunications services such as telephone service and dial-up access to the Internet. As data began to be transferred over telephone lines [dial-up access], the FCC protected that transmission like other communications services.[45] The FCC supported the principle of "Net Neutrality," which provides that "data packets [any content] on the Internet should be moved impartially, without regard to content, destination or source."[46]

Beginning in 2002 the FCC started attempts to reverse its Network Neutrality principle. Federal courts rejected the move to eliminate Network Neutrality protections. However, in 2005 the Supreme Court ruled in *NCTA v. Brand X* that the FCC could exercise its own discretion as to whether to retain Network Neutrality provisions for all *broadband or high-speed Internet users*.[47] These changes reduced protections provided to Internet users in schools and libraries for many years.

As a result of the FCC's actions, telecom and cable companies have been lobbying Congress to create a two-tiered Internet in which content providers would pay a higher price for faster, unrestricted connections. A tiered Internet would especially favor large businesses or those with relationships to broadband network providers. Critics of the two-tiered system fear it may result in discrimination in access and pricing, and it may also stifle the creativity and threaten the existence of independent sites operated on a shoestring. Save the Internet [http://www.savetheinternet.com] and other groups are lobbying Congress to pass legislation to protect Network Neutrality.

The American Civil Liberties Union (ACLU) states Net Neutrality has three guiding principles:

- **"No discrimination against lawful content.** Net Neutrality ensures that Internet users have the right to access lawful websites of their choice and to post lawful content, free of discrimination or degradation by network providers. In other words, network providers cannot block or slow down lawful content they dislike."

- **"Equal Internet access at an equal price.** Under Net Neutrality, network providers cannot give preferential treatment to their own services at the expense of competing sites consumers want to use. In many markets, Internet access is only available through one or two providers. Equal access at an equal price means that network providers cannot abuse their monopoly by barring access, providing slower access, or charging higher premiums to popular services competing with their own."

- **"Consumers choose network equipment.** Since 1968, Net Neutrality has allowed consumers to choose the equipment they want, or make it themselves, and attach it to any network. Net Neutrality prevents network providers from eliminating competing equipment by making it incompatible with their gateway. In the process, it ensures that equipment choice remains in the hands of Internet users, where it rightfully belongs."[48]

The school library professional has a stake in whether the principle of Network Neutrality prevails. If it is weakened or eliminated, the intellectual freedom of students who use the Internet to inform themselves is threatened. Network Neutrality is specifically important to schools and school library media programs because students and teachers no longer rely solely on the print and non-print resources held within the media center. They use the Internet to access subscription databases, online encyclopedias and other reference sources, and e-books. Patrons search the Internet for primary source information, the latest news, and information that is not available locally. The Internet is used in schools both to *obtain* information and to *exchange* ideas and communicate with others. If the principle of Net Neutrality is no longer honored, schools and libraries may find themselves experiencing slower connections and having less access to resources while paying higher costs.

The school library media specialist can take the following steps to advocate for Network Neutrality and preserve student patrons' First Amendment rights as they access information via the Internet:

- Establish up to three key messages for retaining Network Neutrality.
- Inform students and staff about the threat to Network Neutrality.
- Publicize the pro and con effects of Network Neutrality for the school, public library, and community.

- Create a display of materials and websites about Network Neutrality.

- Help students organize a local "Save the Internet" campaign.

- Use the Net Neutrality issue to help inform students about their First Amendment rights to receive information via the Internet.

- Cooperate with public library staff to organize a local letter-writing or petition campaign directed at your federal legislators.

- Participate in the advocacy campaign for Net Neutrality mounted by state and national library associations and other groups.

Educating in a Filtered Environment

The Internet is an ever-expanding resource that can be an educational bonanza if employed wisely. Unfortunately, the Internet's entertainment value and its unsavory aspects can distract students in their use of this global resource. Despite this, as noted in Chapter 2, students do have the right to receive information under the First Amendment. In *Board of Education v. Pico*, the Supreme Court stated that "the right to receive ideas is a necessary predicate to the recipient's meaningful exercise of his own rights of speech, press, and political freedom," *id.* at 867, and further stated that "students too are beneficiaries of this principle." *Id.* at 868[49] In contrast, filtering software, required under CIPA, NCIPA, and state filtering laws, has restricted minors' use of the Internet in schools, thereby limiting their access to information.

To protect minors' rights, the ALA has taken a strong position on access to information found on the Internet. "Access to Electronic Information, Services, and Networks: An Interpretation of the *Library Bill of Rights*" states that any information retrieved, used, or created, whether in print or in a digital format is "constitutionally protected unless determined otherwise by a court of law with appropriate jurisdiction. These rights extend to minors as well as adults."[50] The ALA also supports educating minors to use the Internet safely as opposed to relying on filters.

Filtering and Ethics

Filters are here to stay unless federal and state legislation requiring filters changes, or until the Internet no longer poses threats to young users. Financially and politically, many administrators have decided they must use filters. A school administrator in Virginia summed up the feelings of many, stating, "It would be politically disastrous for us not to filter. All [of] the good network infrastructure we've installed would come down with the first instance of an elementary school student accessing some of the absolutely raunchy sites out there."[51]

Many school library media specialists face ethical dilemmas when they are compelled to work with filters required by law, while at the same time wanting to protect students' First Amendment right to receive legal information via the Internet. Veanna Baxter, a former school library media specialist in Pennsylvania and an ethicist, addresses their plight:

> "A dilemma occurs when we must make a decision, or be subjected to a decision made by another, that is in direct opposition to our set of core values. In our careers, we face choices daily, make decisions, and go on with our work. It becomes difficult, however, to reach a comfortable decision if there are two choices, both of which seem to be the right thing to do, thus creating *a 'right versus right' dilemma*. Library media professionals face this kind of dilemma when they are required to comply with CIPA. They see two choices in their situation:
>
> 1. It is right to filter because children and young adults must be protected from inappropriate information even if it means losing some valuable resources.
> 2. It is also right to provide minors in schools with available information from the Internet under the First Amendment."
>
> "In the *right versus right dilemma* above, library media specialists may conclude that this is a situation over which they had no control or choice and will simply accept the decision of the authorities to filter content on school computers."
>
> "However, for other school library media specialists, carrying out the requirements of CIPA is an affront to their personal code of ethics, as well as the *Code of Ethics of the ALA* which states, 'We uphold the principles of intellectual freedom and resist all efforts to censor library resources.'[52] The school library professional now has to find a way to deal with another dilemma:
>
> 1. It is right for me to respect those in authority and obey federal and state laws with which my school district must comply.
> 2. It is also right for me to be dedicated to the basic philosophies of my profession and to the right of minors to receive information."
>
> "These are dilemmas of monumental proportions. At first glance it would appear that one must either find another profession or ignore one's deeply imbedded core values. What options are available: quit your job, circumvent the law, or find another way? *Sometimes finding another way is the only way!* Ethicists call this a *trillema*, the third choice, another way."[53]

A Baker's Dozen: Strategies

Given current laws and the political climate in local communities around the issue of filtering, what can library media specialists do to advocate for use of the Internet in an educationally sound manner and to ensure students' access to legal information? According to Mary Ann Bell, "One way to keep abreast of what's going on and to speak out against policies you may disagree with is by joining a technology committee. This is the single most important step a librarian can take."[54] Bell's advice is just the beginning. Critics of filters believe that educating students to make wise choices when using the Internet will have a more lasting benefit to students than use of filters within schools. Here are a "baker's dozen" of strategies or *trillemas* that do not involve filtering but can produce powerful results.

- Review the district's current board-adopted acceptable use policy (AUP) for inclusion of such topics as *access to legal information based on students' First Amendment rights*, student and staff responsible use, student instruction on safe and effective Internet use, protecting personal privacy, parental consent for Internet use, and recognition of the educational uses of new Web 2.0 social technologies. Advocate for revisions of the AUP to make it comprehensive, legal, and proactive.

- Provide administrators and faculty with information about the filters and their over-blocking and under-blocking failures. Begin a dialogue within the school about faculty and minors' rights to legal information under the First Amendment.

- Volunteer to provide ongoing staff development, including topics such as minors' First Amendment rights, Internet safety, high-quality online curricular resources, evaluation of online resources, and the effective use of the Internet by students.

 Teaching about Intellectual Freedom

School Library professionals can protect students' First Amendment rights to use the Internet by organizing a systematic schoolwide program focusing on safe and responsible use. Internet safety resources for educators and parents abound, including:

- **iSAFE**   http://www.isafe.org
- **NetSmartz**   http://www.netsmartz.org
- **GetNetWise**   http://getnetwise.org
- **Kidsmart**   http://www.kidsmart.org.uk
- **CyberSmart!**   http://cybersmart.org/home
- **Center for Safe & Responsible Internet Use**   http://cyberbully.org

- Work collaboratively with teachers to plan units incorporating *all* types of library media center resources including those found on the Internet.

- Assist teachers in developing pathfinders or webquests with clickable links to carefully selected online resources for use during curricular units.

- Introduce staff and administrators to the educational uses of Web 2.0 social, collaborative, and interactive technologies such as blogs, wikis, podcasts, and others as they are developed. [Note: Information on Web 2.0 technologies will be more fully developed later in the chapter.]

- Develop a K-12 information and technology literacy curriculum that includes teaching how to use the Internet safely and ethically.

- Share expectations for how students may use the Internet and email, and hold them accountable for violations of improper behavior.

- Encourage *student-directed* Internet safety and Web 2.0 social and collaborative technology activities.

- Develop a library media program website with links to educational resources as well as the school's subscription-based online databases.

- Work to dispel the erroneous idea that filters replace the need for student supervision by school staff to ensure responsible student decisions about Internet use.

- Advocate among administrators and technology staff for filters to be set at the least restrictive setting, and create a workable decision-making process under which teachers may request erroneously blocked websites be unblocked *on a timely basis* for use in classroom and library research. Determine criteria for staff requests to override the filter.

- Request that library media specialists become part of the "authorized school staff" in the district with the ability to unblock websites for legal research in the library media center.

- Seek advice from the ALA Office for Intellectual Freedom on concerns and questions about filtering and its impact on students' intellectual freedom.

- Reach out to parents by providing varied educational opportunities and resources, including short classes, newsletter articles, safety brochures, and books in the library media center about safe and beneficial Internet use by children and young adults.

Some states have realized that mandated filtering is not enough. Virginia has passed legislation to promote Internet safety and responsible use by minors for both public and private schools. In 2006 the General Assembly of Virginia enacted legislation requiring acceptable Internet use policies.[55] Virginia's law also mandates that Internet safety be taught.[56] As a result, the Virginia Department of Education, Division of Technology has an impressive set of online guidelines and resources. Betsy, a library media specialist in Virginia, is enthusiastic about the mandated Internet safety program, "I am thrilled that our legislature recognizes that *knowledge* is the greatest protector of our students. As we provide young people with the skills necessary to evaluate websites, and share the pitfalls of certain types of Internet sites, we are preparing them not only for their academic life, but also for becoming well-informed, discerning citizens in what is often an overwhelming world of information."[57]

Mandated local and state Internet safety programs and the "baker's dozen" of nonfiltering strategies provide many options for ensuring Internet use as an integral resource in the K-12 curriculum. They also will protect minors' rights and bring about more productive results than the "one-size fits all" filtering solutions currently used in many schools.

The Internet and Elementary Students

Educators have a special concern for protecting very young students as they begin to use the Internet in school. Filtering software companies tout their ability to allow different settings at the elementary, middle school, and high school levels, and some districts take advantage of that feature. If there is differentiated filtering, more restrictive settings are frequently used at the elementary level.

As with any instruction, teachers and library media specialists must pay attention to the development and maturation of students. Children under the age of 10 may lack the cognitive maturity to be able to understand the hierarchical nature of the search process. According to Lynne A. Jacobsen,

> Children in second grade and above are expected to find information using electronic means. Children at this stage are just beginning to learn to read. As a result, they tend to rely more on visual and auditory information than on textual information. Young children (5 to 10 years old) are being forced to negotiate digital library interfaces that require complex typing and proper spelling and reading skills, or that necessitate an understanding of abstract concepts or content knowledge beyond young children's still-developing abilities. They are just beginning to enter the developmental stage where they can classify objects and understand hierarchical structure, so it is difficult for children to come up with subject headings and synonyms to use in constructing searches.[58]

As a result, even with filters, educators are concerned that younger students do not have the reading, spelling, and typing skills necessary for successful searching. Therefore, they require significant adult assistance and coaching.

Filtering is only one means of protecting elementary students as they begin to use the Internet. Judy, an elementary library media specialist in Pennsylvania, states,

> At our elementary school we follow the rule of "close supervision." Our students are not using the Internet in K through 6 unless they are "over the shoulder"

monitored. The assignment is guided, or even the student who just has a question is guided. "Guided," for me, means that the student does not have carte blanche access to the Internet, but must discuss their information need with me before they can search. I try to influence the teachers to consider: the level of searching; how many resources students should use; and to decide whether students will visit pre-selected Web sites, use kids' directories (like Kids Click), or use selected search engines.[59]

Jenanne, an elementary library media specialist in Wisconsin, describes Internet use by students in her school.

We have one filter for all schools. Students are not allowed to use the lab without a teacher present, so we have not seen a need for more filtering at any level. I teach an Internet course to all 4th graders during the first semester. I put a lot of emphasis on safety. I make sure that the parents are made aware of safety issues involving the Internet through articles in the district newsletter. All of our teachers are encouraged to use a personal Web page to make links for their students to use. We host the faculty websites internally [using an Intranet], and some of our teachers have posted student projects on their Web pages.[60]

Lisa, a school library media specialist in a preschool–eighth grade independent school in New York, shares her school's philosophy on filtering and use of the Internet by young students.

We do not filter. We do have an acceptable use policy that all students in grades five through eight must sign. No student is permitted on the Internet without adult supervision. *Ever.* Students under six are not permitted on the Internet but can be with a teacher one-on-one to look up information. I teach classes cooperatively about Internet safety, plagiarism and website evaluation. We try to be proactive. We make a presentation to parents at the beginning of the school year on Internet safety and also why we do not filter. We are not immune to challenges to this policy, and not a year goes by that a parent isn't outraged about something a student accidentally saw. We have as many meetings as needed to explain our policy clearly and rationally: Filters don't work, that filtering is biased, and that filters can deny access to essential resources.[61]

Elementary student Internet use as described by these three school library professionals includes much guiding, monitoring, and teaching. They use pathfinders and webquests, and visit websites designed for younger children. Where filters are used to protect against children viewing inappropriate images, the emphasis is on *education* and developing the skills students need to successfully navigate the Web. Consideration must also be given to students' cognitive maturation.

Social Technologies in Schools

Many educators, law enforcement officials, parents, and legislators have voiced concerns over the use of Web 2.0 technologies, such as adult social networking sites especially by preteens and teens. In December 2007 the Pew Internet & American Life Project (PIAL) announced findings in its "Teens and Social Media" report. Researchers conducted telephone interviews with 935 teens, ages 12–17, living in the continental United States; interviewees were selected from previous PIAL project contacts in 2004, 2005, and 2006. The report revealed the following about those youth interviewed:

- 93 percent use the Internet.
- 64 percent participate in content-creating activities, such as sharing personal artistic creations, creating/working on blogs, and/or maintain personal Web page.
- 55 percent have created a profile on a social networking site.[62]

Researchers concluded that "use of social media [a.k.a. social technologies]—from blogging to online social networking to creation of all kinds of digital material—is central to many teenagers' lives."[63]

These findings were substantiated by a study published by the National School Board Association (NSBA) in 2007. The study included three data sources: an online survey of over 1,200 students, an online survey with over 1,000 parents, and telephone interviews with 250 school district leaders who make decisions on Internet policy. The NSBA's "Creating & Connecting: Research and Guidelines on Online Social—and Educational—Networking," reported 9–17 year olds spend 9 hours a week on social networking activities.[64] Other findings of the study include:

- 59 percent of students use social networking to communicate with their peers about education topics, including college planning, careers, and politics; and 50 percent discuss schoolwork.
- Other popular social networking activities by minors include posting messages (41 percent), downloading music (32 percent), downloading videos (30 percent), updating personal websites or profiles (25 percent), posting photos (24 percent), and blogging (17 percent).
- Some officially approved, educationally focused social networking is occurring in schools, including student website programs (69 percent) [undefined in the report], online collaborative projects (46 percent), online pen pal programs (46 percent), and classroom wikis (22 percent).
- 27 percent of districts reported having a structured teacher/principal online community.
- 36 percent of district leaders hope that social networking will teach students to work together to solve academic problems.

- A minority of students report negative experiences online, including cyberbullying (7 percent), unwelcome attention (3 percent), or an unknown person trying to meet them in person (2 percent).[65]

Despite the percentages of students engaged in the use of Web 2.0 social technologies, library media specialists and other educators must recognize that there are students without easy access to computers and the Internet. This "silent minority" is caught in the Digital Divide, and school library professionals must be their "voice" advocating for equity in the use of technology and access to information in electronic formats.

Current students are "digital natives," using a term for those who have grown up with technologies such as computers, cell phones, video games, and digital music players.[66] Therefore, educators, including the library media specialist, must make an effort to balance their concerns about the possible dangers of using *adult* social networking sites with the exciting opportunities for students to use other types of Web 2.0 social technologies, such as blogs, wikis, podcasting, chat, forums, and photo-, audio-, and video-sharing *in collaborative school projects*. Not only will these social technologies engage students' interests, but their use will also help teens and preteens develop the skills needed to collaborate effectively in an adult workplace.

 What is . . .?

Web 2.0: The term refers not to hardware or software but rather "practices such as sharing thoughts and information through self-publishing and harnessing the collective intelligence of all users to generate information and solve problems . . . Web 2.0 is full of established tools such as blogs (personal publishing), wikis (collaborative publishing), real simple syndication (RSS), content aggregators, streaming video (YouTube), file sharing, podcasting, and social networking (MySpace)."[67]

Social technology: "Refers to the connection of people for cooperation, collaboration, and information sharing through computer-mediated communication environments. Social technology connections can be synchronous (live interaction) or asynchronous (delayed). They may involve one-to-one (email, instant messaging), or one-to-many (blogs, Web postings), or many-to-many (wiki) communication."[68]

Social networking sites: "A social networking site is an online place where a user can create a profile and build a personal network that connects him or her to other users."[69]

Blog AKA Web log or weblog: "A website that contains an online personal journal with reflections, comments, and often hyperlinks provided by the writer."[70]

Wiki: A website set up to allow users to edit and add content in a collaborative manner.[71]

Using Social Networking in Schools and Public Libraries

The Young Adult Library Services Association (YALSA) of the American Library Association has developed online resources on social networking directed toward school and public library professionals and teenage Internet users. Check the YALSA website [http://www.ala.org/yalsa/yalsa.cfm] for the most recent materials.

Digital collaborative and creative technologies are simply *another format in which to access and receive information,* and as such, school library professionals must protect students' First Amendment right to use them.

Media coverage of preteen and teen use of social networks plus fears of online predators has caused Congress to introduce overly protective legislation such as the Deleting Online Predators Act (DOPA). Depending on the definitions, such legislation could block many of the Web 2.0 tools. National organizations, educators, and others have been working to help lawmakers understand that education for safe Internet use is more productive than restrictive laws limiting access to social technologies in an instructional setting. Recently, some federal legislators have begun to support "Internet education" as a way to protect students online.

Sara's Story: Social Networking as a Reference Tool

School library media specialists can be catalysts for change by proactively demonstrating to teachers and administrators the educational values of the social technologies. This can be accomplished by starting a library blog or asking the IT staff to set up a wiki for staff use during curriculum revision or another collaborative task. Ideas for effective use of social technologies abound on library association professional websites, in personal blogs, and library and technology professional literature.

An independent college prep boarding school in Massachusetts set up a library account on Facebook. According to Sara, an instructional librarian at the school,

> We wanted to try **social networking reference** because it seemed to be pretty successful at other libraries around the country, and we thought that it would work well with our user group: teenagers who are between 13 and 18 (the Millennial Generation). These students like to receive content digitally, want instant gratification, and already spend huge amounts of time on social networking sites. After consulting with our Student [Library] Advisory Committee, we were told that the vast majority of students at the school prefer Facebook to MySpace. We talked to them about Facebook, why they use it, and how we should develop and market our profile. After that, we set up our account and added each one of them as our first "friends."

Almost immediately, our account was shut down. Apparently, you cannot pose as an **entity** on Facebook. You must be a real person! Eventually, Facebook allowed us to reinstate our account, but the name had to change, so we became "Winston Booker" [pseudonym for account name].

One feature that I especially like is "status updates." Students will use this feature to let their friends know where they are or what they're doing. Ex: "Susie is studying in the library." I use the status feature to push information at the students. I'll often write something like "Winston is at the library until 9:15 tonight. Ask a reference question on my wall!" [a section of a Facebook profile where others can write messages][72] or "Winston is reminding you to return your library materials before you leave for break!" I also use Facebook to publicize events.

I am always encouraging students to ask reference questions by either writing on my wall or sending a private message. Many students do take advantage of this, especially on cold nights or at 2 A.M.! Last spring, I got a private message from a student who was upstairs in the library and wanted to let me know that the wireless Internet wasn't working. I thought it was pretty funny that he used Facebook to contact me instead of walking down a flight of stairs.

Student response to our account has been mixed. Some students are completely on board and understand why we're using Facebook as a reference tool. Other kids think that it's weird and worry that we're just on there to snoop for rules violations. I make it pretty clear to students that we have no interest in or time to read their profiles. We simply want to use Facebook to make the library more accessible to them![73]

Walking a Fine Line

Under CIPA, NCIPA, and state filtering legislation, districts have had their right to make a local decision about whether to filter Internet content taken away from them if they receive specified federal and state funding. With concerns about social networking and online predators, more federal and state legislation may be on the way. As a result, most school library media specialists are in the position of trying to work within a filtering system that is in direct opposition to the principles found in the *Library Bill of Rights* and the *Code of Ethics for the ALA*.

Betty, the school library professional in a public school district without filters but with strong support from the community, provided her thoughts on working in this environment.

It is crucial that school library media specialists be willing to be moral, ethical leaders in the community. If you are not willing to walk the talk, don't pretend. Passion and true belief, confidence in your staff and students comes through when you are pleading any case. Don't be afraid. Be willing to concede that all people make mistakes. How are students to learn if everything is carefully covered for them and there is no possibility of making a mistake? Handle incidents with professionalism and a sense of humor. When there is a problem, don't overreact, and solve it quickly and quietly. Be the information literacy and technology expert and lead![74]

School library professionals, whether in public or private schools, walk a fine line trying to uphold their ethical beliefs, provide access to information protected under the First Amendment, satisfy parents' concerns, and obey the law. When considering intellectual freedom and Internet use in schools, school library media specialists must keep in mind that students' right to receive *legal* information and ideas under the First Amendment is not limited by format.

✍ Key Ideas Summary

This chapter discussed federal and state filtering legislation, the effect of filtering on students' access to information, and strategies the school library media specialist may use to promote improved and safe use of the Internet for students. To review, here are some of the major ideas:

- CIPA requires that elementary and secondary schools that accept selected federal funding certify that they have installed filters on *all computers* used by minors and adults to protect against *visual depictions* of child pornography, obscenity, or material "harmful to minors" as defined under federal law. It also requires that schools certify the existence and implementation of an Internet safety policy and indicate how minors' Internet access will be monitored.

- NCIPA applies only to schools receiving E-rate discounted services and requires that schools create and implement an Internet safety policy with specific components.

- Although filters have become more sophisticated, they still result in over-blocking and under-blocking.

- Based on fear, many districts are also using filters to limit students' access to legal information on the Internet beyond CIPA requirements.

- Critics of filters believe that educating students to make wise choices when using the Internet has a more lasting benefit than use of filters within schools.

- The Digital Divide continues to be a serious issue for economically disadvantaged students, both in access to information on the Internet and access to computers.

- More than a dozen strategies, which do not involve filtering, support library media specialists' efforts to advocate for use of the Internet in an educationally sound manner and to ensure students' access to legal information.

- Educators, including the library media specialist, must make an effort to balance their concerns for the possible dangers of social networking with the opportunities offered by collaborative digital learning tools.

Library Bill of Rights Interpretations

- American Library Association. "Access to Electronic Information, Services, and Networks: An Interpretation of the *Library Bill of Rights*"

- American Library Association. "Free Access to Libraries for Minors: An Interpretation of the *Library Bill of Rights*"

- American Library Association. "Restricted Access to Library Materials: An Interpretation of the *Library Bill of Rights*"

All interpretations may be found at the ALA Office for Intellectual Freedom website: http://www.ala.org/oif.

Recommended Resources

- **American Library Association, Office for Intellectual Freedom website,** http://www.ala.org/oif

   The website includes a broad range of intellectual freedom resources relating to filtering and filtering legislation.

- **Center for Safe and Responsible Internet Use (CSRIU),** http://www.csriu.org/ and/or http://www.cyberbully.org

   Nancy Willard is the executive director of CSRIU and a former educator, lawyer, author, and consultant in the area of safe use of the Internet by youth, effective student Internet use management in schools, and cyberbullying and cyberthreats to schools. The website contains links to many of Willard's articles and presentations as well as her blog.

- **"Children and the Internet: Laws Relating to Filtering, Blocking and Usage Policies in Schools and Libraries," National Conference of State Legislatures,** http://www.ncsl.org/programs/lis/cip/filterlaws.htm

   The site includes summaries of and links to *state laws* on filtering in public schools and libraries.

- **Chmara, Theresa. "Minors' First Amendment Rights to Access Information," In** *Intellectual Freedom Manual,* **7th ed. Office for Intellectual Freedom, American Library Association, 384–393. Chicago: American Library Association, 2006.**

   This brief chapter centers on court cases and their impact on student patrons' rights to use materials in the library as well to access information via the Internet.

- **Crimes Against Children Research Center,** http://www.unh.edu/ccrc

   Created in 1998, the Center focuses on the incidence and impact of violence against children including youth Internet safety. The site provides links to articles on Internet safety and suggestions for making Internet safety education materials more consistent with current research.

- **Heins, Marjorie, Christina Cho, and Ariel Feldman.** *Internet Filters: A Public Policy Report.* **2nd ed. New York: Brennan Center for Justice at New York University School of Law, 2006.** Available in print and downloadable at http://www.fepproject.org/policyreports/filters2intro.html

A brief but compelling overview of the use of filters in libraries and schools, reports of research on over- and under-blocking of Internet content, and recommendations for working in a filtered environment.

- **Lamb, Annette. "Intellectual Freedom for Youth: Social Technology and Social Networks" 36 no. 2,** *Knowledge Quest* **(November/December 2007): 38–45.**
  The author provides eight ways for library media specialists to take action to promote social technologies in schools and their library media programs by describing the issue, the role of the school library professional, and first steps that may be taken.

- **"Minors' Rights to Receive Information Under the First Amendment," Memorandum, Jenner & Block, prepared by Theresa Chmara and Daniel Mach, February 2, 2004,** http://www.ala.org/ala/oif/ifissues/issuesrelatedlinks/minorsrights.htm
  A legal memorandum from Jenner & Block, lawyers to the Freedom to Read Foundation, on minors' First Amendment rights to receive information and a discussion of the use of Internet filtering software.

- **Rushworth M. Kidder,** *How Good People Make Tough Choices: Resolving the Dilemmas of Ethical Living.* **New York: Simon & Schuster, 1995.**
  The founder of the Institute for Global Ethics offers guidelines and principles the reader may apply to daily personal and workplace issues.

- **Save the Internet,** http://www.savetheinternet.com
  Information on Network Neutrality is available at this website created and maintained by a coalition of groups who believe the principle must be retained.

- **Virginia Department of Education, Division of Technology, "Guidelines and Resources for Internet Safety in Schools,"** http://www.doe.virginia.gov/VDOE/ Technology/OET/internet-safety-guidelines.shtml
  Virginia's state department of education has assembled an impressive set of resources to assist Virginia educators in teaching Internet safety to K–12 students, including detailed ideas for integrating Internet safety across the curriculum.

Notes

1. Harris, Christopher, "Dealing with DOPA," May 11, 2006, Infomancy Blog, http://schoolof.info/infomancy/?p=212.
2. Bocher, Bob, "FAQ on E-Rate Compliance with the Children's Internet Protection Act and the Neighborhood Children's Internet Protection Act," February 19, 2004, pp. 2, 3, 6, 11, http://dpi.wi.gov/pld/pdf/cipafaq.pdf.
3. Public Law 106-554, Subsection C. Neighborhood Children's Internet Protection Act, Section 1732 (1) (1) (A) (i)-(v), http://ifea.net/cipa.html.
4. Ibid, Sec. B (2).
5. National Conference of State Legislatures, "Children and the Internet: Laws Relating to Filtering, Blocking and Usage Policies in Schools and Libraries," http://www.ncsl.org/programs/lis/cip/filterlaws.htm.
6. National Center for Education Statistics, "Internet Access in U.S. Public Schools and Classrooms: 1994–2005," "Highlights," November 2006, pp. 9, 36–43. http://nces.ed.gov/pubs2007/2007020.pdf.
7. Ibid, 9.

8. Shontz, Marilyn L., and Lesley S. J. Farmer, "SLJ Spending Survey," *School Library Journal* 53, no. 1 (January 2007), 47.

9. Heins, Marjorie, Christina Cho, and Ariel Feldman, *Internet Filters: A Public Policy Report,* 2nd ed. (New York: Brennan Center for Justice at NYU School of Law, 2006), 3.

10. Heins, Cho, Feldman, *Internet Filters,* 73.

11. Haynes, Charles C., et al., *The First Amendment in Schools* (Alexandria, Virginia: Association for Supervision and Curriculum Development and the First Amendment Center, 2003), 84.

12. Bell, Mary Ann, "The Elephant in the Room," *School Library Journal* 53, no. 1 (January 2007), 41.

13. Sandra, email to author, February 16, 2007.

14. Ibid, March 23, 2007.

15. Ibid, April 2, 2007.

16. 20 USC § 6777 (c)

17. 47 USC § 254(H) (D) (A) (i)

18. Anita (pseudonym), email to author, October 7, 2007.

19. Terry, email to author, May 8, 2007.

20. Wolak, Janis, et al. "Online 'Predators' and Their Victims: Myths, Realities, and Implications for Prevention and Treatment," *American Psychologist,* 63 no. 2 (February–March 2008), 111.

21. "'Internet Predator' Stereotypes Debunked in New Story," American Psychological Association Press Release, February 18, 2008, http://www.apa.org/releases/sexoffender0208.html.

22. Wolak, Janis, 124–125.

23. Wilson, Josh, email to author, September 27, 2007.

24. Williard, Nancy, "Preventing Another Julie Amero Tragedy," Center for Safe and Responsible Use of the Internet, http://cyberbully.org/onlinedocs/preventingamero.pdf.

25. "Filter-Savvy Students Barred from Most of the Web," *American Libraries Online,* October 20, 2006, http://www.ala.org/ala/alonline/currentnews/newsarchive/2006abc/october2006a/matanuska.cfm.

26. Stoppa, Becky, "Students Lose Ability to Surf for Porn, Music," October 13, 2006, *Anchorage Daily News,* http://www.adn.com/news/education/story/8299283p-8195472c.html.

27. Stoppa, Becky, "INTERNET: The District Called its Policy Curtailing Access to Most Sites a Response to Abuse," October 13, 2006, *Anchorage Daily News,* http://www.adn.com.

28. Ibid.

29. Joel, email to author, February 26, 2007.

30. Terri, email to author, May 29, 2007.

31. "Firewall" definition, SearchSecurity.com, http://searchsecurity.techtarget.com/sDefinition/0,,sid14_gci212125,00.html.

32. Betty (pseudonym), email to author, September 12, 2007.

33. Code of Virginia, Chapter 52, § 22.1-70.2. "Acceptable Internet use policies for public and private schools," Section 1. D. http://leg1.state.va.us/cgi-bin/legp504.exe?000+cod+22.1-70.2.

34. Cathy, email to author, October 14, 2007.

35. Liz, email to author, November 12, 2007.

36. Barbara, email to author, November 7, 2007.

37. Johnson, Doug, "Lessons School Librarians Teach Others; Class: The Subject Is Integrity," *American Libraries*, December 2004, http://www.ala.org/ala/oif/iftoolkits/ifmanual/lessonsschoollibrariansteachothers.pdf.

38. Tom, email to author, February 9, 2007.

39. American Library Association, Office for Intellectual Freedom, "Intellectual Freedom and Censorship Q & A," http://www.ala.org/ala/oif/basics/intellectual.htm.

40. Valadez, James R., and Richard Duran, "Redefining the Digital Divide: Beyond Computers and Access to the Internet," *The High School Journal* 90, no. 3 (February/March 2007), 32.

41. Rogos, Amanda, and John Latta, "Digital Divide, 4th Wave," http://www.fourthwave.com/DigitalDivide.htm.

42. "Libraries Are Key Online Access Points," *American Libraries* 38, no. 10 (November 2007), 11.

43. Rogos and Latta.

44. American Library Association, Article V, *Library Bill of Rights*, http://www.ala.org/ala/oif/statementspols/statementsif/librarybillrights.htm

45. American Civil Liberties Union, "Internet Freedom and Innovation at Risk: Why Congress Must Restore Strong Net Neutrality Protection," April 5, 2007, http://www.aclu.org/freespeech/internet/26829res20070405.html

46. "Net Neutrality (definition)," SearchNetworking.com, http://searchnetworking.techtarget.com/sDefinition/0,sid7_gci1207194,00.html

47. ACLU, "Internet Freedom."

48. Ibid.

49. Chamara, Theresa, and Daniel Mach, "Memorandum: Minors' Right to Receive Information under the First Amendment," February 2, 2004, http://www.ala.org/ala/oif/ifissues/issuesrelatedlinks/minorsrights.htm.

50. American Library Association, "Access to Electronic Information, Services, and Networks: An Interpretation of the *Library Bill of Rights*," www.ala.org/ala/oif/statementspols/statementsif/interpretations/accesstoelectronic.pdf.

51. Heins, Cho, Feldman, *Internet Filters*, 6.

52. American Library Association, Article II, *Code of Ethics of the American Library Association*, http://www.ala.org/ala/oif/statementspols/codeofethics/codeethics.htm.

53. Baxter, Veanna, email to author, September 27, 2007.

54. Bell, Mary Ann, 42.

55. Virginia Acts of Assembly, chapter 52, § 22.1-70.2 of the Code of Virginia, http://leg1.state.va.us/cgi-bin/legp504.exe?061+ful+CHAP0052+pdf.

56. Ibid.

57. Betsy, email to author, September 21, 2007.

58. Jacobsen, Lynne A., "How Children Search," in *Cataloging Correctly for Kids: An Introduction to the Tools*, edited by Sheila S. Intner, Joanna F. Fountain, and Jane E. Gilchrist, 4th ed. (Chicago: American Library Association, 2006), 17.

59. Judy, email to author, October 13, 2007.

60. Jenanne, email to author, October 12, 2007.

61. Lisa, email to author, October 14, 2007.

62. Lenhart, Amanda, et al., "Teens and Social Media," Pew Internet & American Life Project, December 19, 2007, http://www.pewinternet.org/pdfs/PIP_Teens_Social_Media_Final.pdf.

63. Ibid.

64. National School Board Association, "Creating & Connecting: Research and Guidelines on Online Social—and Educational—Networking," July 2007, http://www.nsba.org/site/docs/41400/41340.pdf.

65. Ibid.

66. Prensky, Marc, "Digital Natives, Digital Immigrants," 2001, http://www.marcprensky.com/writing/Prensky%20%20Digital%20Natives,%20Digital%20Immigrants%20-%20Part1.pdf.

67. Mills, Lane B., "The Next Wave Now: Web 2.0.," *School Administrator* 64, no. 8 (September 2007), 8.

68. Lamb, Annette, and Larry Johnson, "Social Technology and Social Networks," *School Library Media Activities Monthly* XXIII, no. 5 (January 2007), 40.

69. Pew Internet and American Life Project, "Social Networking Websites and Teens: An Overview," January 7, 2007, http://www.pewinternet.org/PPF/r/198/report_display.asp.

70. Merriam-Webster's Online Dictionary, http://www.m-w.com/dictionary/blog.

71. "Wiki" definition, techterms.com, http://www.techterms.com/definition/wiki.

72. "Facebook wall," Webopedia, http://www.webopedia.com/TERM/F/Facebook_wall.html.

73. Sara, email to author, November 9, 2007.

74. Betty (pseudonym), email to author, September 12, 2007.

CHAPTER 8

Access to the Library Media Program for Students with Disabilities

> Accessibility is much more than being able to get through the door of a school building. It means being actively and meaningfully included in all facilities, services, and programs. It means being able to use materials and technology that are available to other students.... Whatever a person's abilities, the library media center is one location where a student can interact with and use all available sources of information to gain knowledge, achieve success and independence, and nurture a love for lifelong learning.[1]
>
> —John E. Cox and Debra M. Lynch

Introduction

School library professionals have both legal and ethical responsibilities to provide *access* to resources and services in the library media program for students with physical, cognitive, and learning disabilities, as well as chronic illnesses and disorders. For disabled students, access is an integral part of their intellectual freedom. Access in this context includes everything from physically entering the facility to obtaining resources and services that fit students' intellectual and physical abilities. The mandate for access comes from many sources. The First Amendment ensures the right to receive ideas and information to all citizens *regardless of age or ability,* and federal and state legislation described later in the chapter protects students with disabilities. The American Library Association *Library Bill of Rights* states in Article I, "Books and other library resources should be provided for the interest, information, and enlightenment of all people of the community the library serves."[2] For a library media specialist, "all the people ... the library serves" includes helping students with any special need.

The *Code of Ethics* of the American Library Association states in Article I, "We provide the highest level of service to all library users through appropriate and usefully organized resources; equitable service policies; equitable access; and accurate, unbiased, and courteous responses to all requests."[3] The library professional must consider the diverse needs of those with disabilities when selecting and organizing the collection. Providing access goes beyond collecting appropriate resources and the technologies to allow their use. It includes a library staff that is knowledgeable and dedicated to ensuring students can locate and use information to meet their needs. Access also involves teaching information and technology literacy skills to enable students with disabilities to be successful lifelong information seekers and consumers.

"Access to Resources and Services in the School Library Media Program: An Interpretation of the *Library Bill of Rights*" states, "School library media specialists assume a leadership role in promoting the principles of intellectual freedom within the school by providing resources and services that create and sustain an atmosphere of free inquiry."[4] Every student, regardless of ability, has a claim to intellectual freedom while using the library media center, and it is the responsibility of the school library professional to protect that right.

Legislation Supporting Students with Disabilities

At one time, few school library professionals considered how to accommodate students with disabilities in school library media programs. Over the years, education has become more *inclusive* because Congress passed three major laws that impact how students with disabilities are educated. Today, students meeting the various definitions of "disabled" are taught with their peers instead of being isolated, and they have the right to be active users of the school library media center. The relevant legislation includes:

- **The Rehabilitation Act of 1973:** This act and its reauthorizations are civil rights legislation that prohibit discrimination against individuals, including K–12 students, on the basis of a disability in programs conducted by federal agencies and in programs receiving federal financial assistance.[5] **Section 504** of the law has particular relevance to schools that accept federal funds, stating that "no otherwise qualified individual with a disability in the United States shall be excluded from, denied the benefits of, or be subjected to discrimination under any program or activity that either receives federal financial assistance or is conducted by any Executive agency ..."[6] School districts must implement procedures to ensure that students with disabilities have access to the full range of programs, activities, and services.[7] Under Section 504, schools must develop specific plans to meet the needs of individual students, including accommodations and modifications to ensure students receive a *free appropriate public education* [FAPE].[8] If an private school does not accept federal funds, it *may* be exempt from Section 504 regulations.[9]

- **The Individuals with Disabilities Education Act (IDEA):** Originally enacted in 1975 as the Education for All Handicapped Children Act, IDEA became law in 1990. In 2004 the law was reauthorized as the Individuals with Disabilities Education Improvement Act (IDEIA); however, it is still most frequently referred to as IDEA. The law, combined with No Child Left Behind (NCLB) legislation in 2002, requires that all schools and districts be held accountable for student achievement, including students with disabilities.[10]

  IDEA also requires "public schools to make available to all eligible children with disabilities a free appropriate public education (FAPE) in the least restrictive environment (LRE) appropriate for their individual needs."[11] Students with disabilities must be considered for assistive technology use if it is needed to meet the requirement for FAPE.[12]

  IDEA mandates that public schools find, evaluate, develop a service plan, and provide services for children and young adults with disabilities enrolled *by their parents* in private, including religious, elementary, and secondary schools in a school district.[13] However, under the law, children placed in private schools by their parents do not have the same rights as those attending public schools. 34 CFR 300.137 (a) states "No parentally-placed private school child with a disability has an individual right to receive some or all of the special education and related services that the child would receive if enrolled in a public school."[14] They may not get the same services, and not all children with disabilities will receive services.[15]

- **The Americans with Disabilities Act of 1990 (ADA):** This is also civil rights legislation that prohibits discrimination on the basis of a disability. Title II of the ADA requires state and local governments, which includes public schools, to provide those with a disability an equal opportunity to all programs, services, and activities including public education and requires them to follow specific architectural standards in new construction or renovation of older buildings. However, public entities are not required to make accommodations or modifications that would result in undue "financial and administrative burdens."[16] ADA regulations apply to "almost every entity in the United States, regardless of whether it receives federal funds; churches and private clubs are the only two entities that are exempt from the ADA."[17] Unless a private school is affiliated with a church, it is covered under Title III of the ADA and must comply with its provisions.[18]

There are also state laws that address the accessibility of instructional resources for those with disabilities. For example, in 2000 the Kentucky legislature passed the Kentucky Accessible Information Technology (AIT) Act, KRS 61.980-61.988. The law requires that all state-supported institutions use information technology that is accessible to disabled persons. School districts are required to provide students with disabilities with access "that is equivalent to the access provided individuals who are not disabled" (KRS 61.982).[19] Because state legislation in this area varies widely, check with local special education staff and district legal counsel to determine which laws may apply to school library media programs.

Creating an Accessible School Library Media Program

Section 504 of the Rehabilitation Act, the Individuals with Disabilities Education Act, and the Americans with Disabilities Act directly or indirectly require that students with disabilities receive a free appropriate public education (FAPE) and that students with disabilities be educated in the least restrictive environment with their nondisabled peers, to the maximum extent possible.[20] Equal access to the library—its facilities, programs, and services—is part of providing a free appropriate education. However, the accommodations or modifications needed to meet individual student needs shall not cause an "undue burden" on the library.[21] The actions school library professionals take to meet the legal requirements will depend on the individual educational needs of their students.

 Disability Statistics Snapshot

- 11 percent of youth ages 6–14 or about 4 million children have a disability (2007).[22]
- For youth under the age of 15, boys are more likely to have a disability (11 percent) than girls (6 percent) (2007).[23]
- 13.7 percent of students, or approximately 6.6 million children enrolled in public schools, are served under the Individuals with Disabilities Education Act (IDEA) (2005).[24]
- Approximately half of children served under IDEA have a specific learning disability (2002).[25]

There are many types of disabilities ranging from cognitive to physical to emotional to specific learning disabilities. Federal and state laws and their interpretations are very complex; therefore, the library media specialist should direct questions about local situations related to particular students with disabilities to a school district special education coordinator or disability officer.

To comply with the requirements of the three federal laws, the school library media specialist must consult with many persons—the disability officer, the Individual Education Plan Committee, special education staff, classroom teachers, disabled students, and their parents. Planning collaboratively will ensure that both identified and nonidentified disabled students will receive accommodations and modifications necessary to enable them to access the school library media center, its resources, and services. Barbara, an independent upper school librarian in Texas, states, "In our libraries, we coordinate with the classroom approach whenever possible."[26]

Barriers to access to the library media program and its resources may take many forms for students with disabilities, including:

- insufficient staff knowledge
- physical access barriers
- incomplete collection
- inaccessible library website and electronic resources
- inadequate technology.

Knowledge and Attitude

Library professional and support staff want to be welcoming and ensure access; however, their knowledge of the best way to create a beneficial environment for *all* students may be in direct proportion to their experiences with students with disabilities. To enable these students to be successful, the library media specialist needs to know "how the particular student learns best, in what environment the student will be needing information, what tasks are involved for the student, and what tools would be the most appropriate to use at a particular time."[27]

Rebecca, a library media specialist at an elementary school in Wisconsin, has worked with students of all abilities in preschool through graduate school. Her experiences with her son, who is deaf but fully mainstreamed, have led her to seek ways to address the special needs of students using the school library media center.

Don't wait for students with special needs to introduce themselves, advises Rebecca. Chances are you are already serving students with special needs, whether they are formally diagnosed or not. And even if you aren't, there are definitely students with different learning styles who would certainly benefit from information being presented in different ways. I look at this as a kind of continuum—students with specific disabilities and modification needs are at the edges, but there are many students who fall in the middle whose library access will also improve because of your attention.[28]

Collaboration between special education staff and the school library media specialist is key to ensuring that students with disabilities have the maximum possible access and that their First Amendment rights are protected. Special education staff have knowledge of the applicable laws and how they are applied in school settings, information on positive learning strategies, expertise with assistive technologies, and background about the needs of individual students using the media center. Mary Alice, a media specialist in a large district in Minnesota, states, "Special education teachers are natural partners for me because they know how to develop meaningful learning activities for diverse learners. I especially credit Carol, a special education instructor, who used technology to foster student motivation and learning. Her ideas and our partnership spread beyond special education;

they added new dimensions to mainstream classrooms and our growing middle school media program."[29]

Library staff can also gain information on characteristics of particular disabilities, recommended resources, and useful assistive technologies through other sources. These include local special education inservice programs, cooperative education agencies programming, professional literature, library association and government websites, conferences and workshops, postgraduate courses, and materials published by organizations associated with specific disabilities.

School library media specialists have knowledge about print and electronic resources and information and technology literacy skills to share with special education staff. The collaboration between the library media specialist and teachers will benefit students with disabilities both in their classrooms as well as in the library media center. Mary Alice explains, "I assisted a high school special education teacher with digital photo editing and printing. She took digital photos of food products at a local grocery store where she takes her students to apply their menu-planning and math skills. The photos were used to provide illustrations for a statewide test given to special education students. The photos helped the students think through their task as they completed word problems."[30]

In addition to gaining information from a wide range of sources, library staff should check their *personal attitudes* toward students with disabilities. Rebecca advises,

> Library media specialists need to be really honest about their attitudes toward serving students with special needs. Most of us would never dream of being overtly discriminatory, but do you feel uncomfortable around students with special needs? Do you feel sorry for them? Do you unconsciously avoid them? Those actions can be just as harmful.[31] It's not enough to simply be tolerant, you must be proactive.[32]

If library staff do not feel at ease with students with disabilities, those students' access to program resources and services, and therefore their intellectual freedom, will be affected.

School library professionals must emphasize to students and faculty that everyone has different strengths and weaknesses. To help engender empathy, Linda, a special education teacher and preservice school library professional in Utah, states,

> I tell my students that everyone has disabilities. Some disabilities are just more visible than others. For example, I wear contacts. Without my eyesight being corrected, I would not be able to drive or teach. I probably would not be able to do much because my eyesight is really bad! They just laugh at this, but I think it

helps them realize that we never know what individuals are dealing with. It helps my students be more tolerant and accepting of others and themselves.[33]

When a student with special needs enters the library media center, is s/he certain of a welcome from all library staff? Behaviors of some students with disabilities may be distracting and interfere with the work of other students. Strategies to help these students work independently include posting written rules, using visual cue cards, creating routines, and developing structured programming.[34]

Library staff should initiate frequent contact with students with disabilities, letting them know help is available. Yet, it is just as critical to not "hover" or to give the impression that the student is helpless. Linda notes,

> It is very important to follow the advice a master teacher gave to me years ago. She told me to treat each student FAIRLY. She said fairness did not mean equal; it meant giving the student what they needed. Her insight has been invaluable. Going out of our way to treat disabled students differently only spotlights their disability. On the other hand, supplying disabled students with what they need (even if one student needs more help than another) allows the student to see he or she is valued, not pitied.[35]

The goal for the library media program is to encourage the student with a disability to be as independent as possible, yet provide support when it is requested or needed.

Katherine, a preservice library media specialist and experienced special education teacher in Washington, states,

> The most significant learning that I have gained from my work with these students is that each one of these students is a completely unique individual. I have had flashes of understanding and communication with even the most severely delayed and disabled students. There are a host of labels, diagnoses, and categorizations that are used to assign these students to groups and to qualify them for eligibility for various services. However, I believe the most effective way to serve these students is to simply get to know them as individuals and to never, ever close the door of possibility about what they can do. I admit that I sometimes think, "He/she will never be able to do that," but over and over the student I would least expect will come up with some absolutely stunning demonstration of a capability that I had no idea the student possessed.[36]

After acknowledging that each student has different needs and capabilities, the school library media specialist must provide individualized assistance and differentiated instruction to the degree possible. Special education teachers will be able to share examples of instructional adaptations for the school library professional. When teaching the information and technology literacy curriculum, the school library professional can apply instructional strategies such as using graphic organizers, supplying materials at different reading levels, and presenting instruction to smaller groups.[37] Rebecca states,

> My background is in teaching. When I became a library media specialist, I found that making modifications and presenting information in different ways was important in my library, too, especially because the atmosphere is not as structured or controlled as a classroom. I was interested in trying to create an environment where *all* students could be as independent as possible in fulfilling their information needs. This especially struck home when my own son lost his hearing due to an illness. He now wears a hearing aid and cochlear implant and is fully mainstreamed. I've seen firsthand how very subtle changes can make a world of difference to him. It's only logical that this is true for other students with different types of special needs.[38]
>
> You don't need to learn about every modification right away. Present information in multiple ways to help students with a variety of learning styles. Break tasks into small steps for students. These suggestions are just good teaching strategies for all students, but they're also easy to forget. Some of the things that help my son are simple, such as having steps written on the board to accompany verbal directions, turning on the closed captioning for videos, and using a visual signal, like flicking the lights, for transition times. These all help him fill in the gaps for things he's missed because of his hearing. It turns out that other kids in his class benefit from those little changes, too.[39]

Becky, a former kindergarten teacher and now a middle school/high school librarian in the state of New York, asserts, "Even after working with many disabled students in a variety of settings and holding a degree in Special Education, I feel much of meeting the needs of students with disabilities is a journey of getting to know the individual and his/her strengths and weaknesses. It is hard to be totally prepared for every student ahead of time."[40] The important point for library staff is to make an effort and reach out to students.

Liz's Story

Liz is a New Jersey K-3 elementary library media specialist with some teaching responsibilities. Her experiences from grade school to the present illustrate how attitudes toward people with disabilities have changed.

> My first experience with "a person who is disabled" was in 4th grade. Kenny, a boy in my class, used a wheelchair and always ran over my feet. I didn't see him as being different from anyone else so I yelled at him and told the teacher. Much to my surprise, I got in big trouble. My teacher called my parents and asked that they meet to discuss my insensitivity. From that moment on I was supposed to treat Kenny differently, and I did as I was told.

Fast forward twelve years later when I finally learned that I was the one who was right about the way Kenny should be treated. My first job was as a Community Education Specialist. I traveled all over the state educating students about developmental disabilities (learning disabilities, epilepsy, cerebral palsy, blindness, deafness, autism). During this time the ADA was passed, and it was very exciting. I even went to the celebration at the Capitol. The most interesting part of this job was the training I received to teach about each disability. I interviewed many people with disabilities, coached for the Special Olympics, and experienced firsthand what it would be like to be blind and in a wheelchair. I was assigned to patch my eyes, wear sunglasses, use a white cane, and spend the day at the mall. Another time, I had to use a wheelchair for a day at a mall. We needed this training to see what it would be like to live as someone with a disability. This was the most educational experience of my life. You wouldn't believe how people reacted to me. When I was blind people felt they needed to shout at me. They also treated me as if I were five years old. When I was in the wheelchair, people wouldn't look at me or talk to me.

I learned a lot during that job. People with disabilities want to be treated like everyone else. It is very difficult to live in a world that is created for sighted people with legs that work. Put the person before the disability when naming it. For instance, it is preferred by some that we say "person who is disabled" instead of "disabled person." When talking to someone who uses a wheelchair, crouch down to be eye-level instead of them looking them looking up at you. Always face someone who is deaf when you talk to them so they can read your lips. So, my classmate Kenny would have benefited from all of us treating him like everyone else, instead of *being* treated differently.[41]

As Liz points out, there is a need to be sensitive to the language used in communication with and about persons with disabilities. Despite frequent changes in terminology, common sense rules apply.

- Refer to the individual first, not his/her disability. Example: the person who uses a wheelchair, not the wheelchair person.
- Be aware of current terminology about persons with disabilities.[42]

♿ Disability versus Handicapped

- **Disability:** "a word for a condition that might affect someone's mobility, hearing, vision, speech, or thinking ability."[43] Examples include blindness and paraplegia.
- **Handicap**: "a barrier that is environmental or attitudinal (such as no ramps or elevator, information not available in Braille, negative stereotypes)."[44]

Deborah's Disabilities Etiquette

Deborah Kenrick is a disabilities columnist in Cincinnati, Ohio, who writes the online column "In My View." Deborah is blind and writes extensively about persons with disabilities. While her columns are written for a general audience, library media specialists can gain many insights from Deborah's advice.

"No Need to Avoid People with Disabilities"
By Deborah Kendrick

It's an amazing phenomenon that many people with disabilities experience. You go to a room that will soon be filled with people. You settle in and wait for others to arrive. But when they do, no one sits in your row or at your table.

All too often, people who (as yet) have no disability ignore the ones who do. The reason is almost always borne of uncertainty, wondering if there are "rules." Here, then, are my own 10 elements of etiquette for easing interactions with people with disabilities.

1. **Is it OK to offer help?**

   People with disabilities are just people. Sometimes they use crutches or canes or guide dogs or wheelchairs or look different in other ways. But everyone needs help sometimes. If you think a person with a disability needs your help, offer it. Sometimes the answer to your offer will be yes and sometimes no, but it will almost always be appreciated.

2. **Is it OK to talk about hearing and seeing when talking to someone who is deaf or blind?**

   Of course it is. People who are deaf or blind live in the same world with people who hear and see in the usual ways. They enjoy the same movies and plays and concerts and basketball games. It would make everyone feel uncomfortable and foolish to use different words for the same commonplace experiences. Blind people say, "I was watching TV last night" and "I'll see you later" to a friend. They say, "Let me see that" when they want to examine an object more closely. Deaf people say, "I heard a funny story" and "Yes, I am listening to you" for the same reasons. Even if you "see" with your hands or "hear" with your eyes, the words we use are the same.

3. **What should I do when I can't understand someone speaking?**

   People who have experienced a stroke, were born with cerebral palsy, or have other neurological disorders will sometimes have speech that is difficult to understand. Impaired speech, however, doesn't mean impaired thoughts or feelings.

   Please don't ignore what a person is saying because it is difficult to understand. Ask the person to repeat. If you understand part of the sentence, you might say something like, "I know you're asking me something about baseball, but I'm not sure what it is." Let comprehension and communication be a shared problem. It's frustrating, but not nearly as frustrating as never being understood.

4. **How do I let a blind or deaf person know I am speaking to them?**

   Use a person's name if you can: "Hey, John, that sweater's a great color for you" or "Do you want another beer, Mary?" If you don't know the name, tap him or her lightly on the arm. A blind person doesn't know he or she is being personally addressed without a name or some contact, and a deaf person has to see you to know you want conversation.

5. **Speaking of speaking**, always speak directly to the person with the disability. Ask me what I want to eat or do or look at, not the person I'm with. You learned in about the second grade that it was rude to talk about someone as though she or he weren't there, so why would you forget your manners just because a person is sitting in a wheelchair, has an unusual speech pattern, or difficulty making eye contact? If the person has an intellectual disability that requires slower speech or more patience, you'll figure it out.

6. **When you're speaking to a blind person, let them know if you are going to walk away.**

   A simple "I'm going to go talk to Sam for a minute" will suffice. It's embarrassing to be caught addressing the air or an empty chair because you don't realize your friend has gone.

7. **When speaking with someone in a wheelchair, make eye contact.**

   Squat down to be at the same level with the person in the chair or, if convenient, pull up another chair for yourself.

8. **Always ask permission to pet a guide dog or other assistance dog.**

   Guide dogs and other service animals are trained to guide or assist with physical tasks. The bond is essential. The dog depends on its human for food and affection. The human depends on the dog for safety and assistance. By petting without permission, you are endangering the safety of the person who uses the dog.

9. **It's OK to ask about a person's disability.**

   Ask questions that express interest in the person here and now, about techniques or equipment or approaches to problems, rather than the "Why are you defective?" variety. We humans are all curious about one another, and most of us like to talk about our own lives. Asking, "How do you make a phone call when you can't hear?" or "How do you use the hand controls on your car?" will usually launch a lively exchange. It's interesting and not as intrusive—or even disparaging—as "What happened to you?" might be.

10. **Afraid you'll forget all of the above in the anxiety of approaching a person with a disability?**

    The most important rule when encountering people with disabilities is to have the encounter. It's better to be asked to dance and get your feet stepped on than to be left at the table. It's better to be told a joke—even if you don't get it—than to be left out of the conversation. If simply treated as people first, most who have disabilities won't care as much if you get any of the other "rules" right."[45]

Reprinted with permission from Deborah Kendrick.

School library media specialists will find Deborah's "rules" for communicating with persons with disabilities practical. They incorporate common sense and compassion. Without any special training, library staff and volunteers can follow her guidelines for successful and sensitive interactions with students with disabilities.

Physical Access to the Library Media Center

School library media centers can have physical barriers that prevent student users from obtaining the resources and services they seek. The first barrier may come when trying to get into the library media center. A heavy door, one that does not open easily, or that is too narrow for a wheelchair can block patrons from entering. Inside the library media center, there can be other obstacles for students with disabilities, including tables and other furniture set too closely together for free movement across the facility, insufficient width between shelving units, lack of accessible computer workstations, and low lighting. Shelving may be too high for a small child, shorter person, or an individual in a wheelchair to reach a book. Library staff may not be aware of the physical shortcomings of the library media center and their effect on students with disabilities. Linda, a preservice school library media specialist in Utah, observed, "I had always thought the library at my school was handicap accessible until I viewed it in my mind's eye from the seat of a wheelchair. A student in a wheelchair could not even use the alternative door through the back of the library because the ramp is steep, and the door (which opens in) is heavy!"[46]

One of the best ways to check physical access to the library media center is through the eyes of the school's physically disabled students. Ask students about the ease of opening the door to the media center, navigating library furniture, obtaining magazines and books from library shelving, and using the computers and electronic resources, including the library's website. Pat, a middle school library media specialist in Washington, took the initiative, stating, "I spoke in depth with Crystal, an 8th grader at my school who suffers from spina bifida. We talked about the library and if she felt like she was able to get around in it comfortably. She helped me realize that, while she can maneuver through the floor stacks, she cannot turn around in between them."[47] After querying students, use their suggestions to improve the physical access to the facility and its resources.

In 2001 the ALA Council adopted the "Library Services for People with Disabilities Policy." It states, "Libraries play a catalytic role in the lives of people with disabilities by facilitating their full participation in society. Libraries should use strategies based upon the principles of universal design to ensure that library policy, resources and services meet the needs of all people."[48] Any alterations to enhance access to the media center should be rooted in the principles of *universal design*. Three of 11 principles include:

- "**Equitable Use:** The design is useful and marketable to people with diverse abilities."
- "**Flexibility in Use**: The design accommodates a wide range of individual preferences and abilities."

- "**Simple and Intuitive Use**: Use of the design is easy to understand, regardless of the user's experience, knowledge, language skills, or current concentration level."[49]

While the modifications may be made to meet the needs of persons with a broad range of temporary or permanent disabilities, the changes can also be beneficial to other users.

 Universal Design

Definition: "Universal design is the process of creating products (devices, environments, systems, and processes) which are usable by people with the widest possible range of abilities, operating within the widest possible range of situations (environments, conditions, and circumstances)."[50]

All "public areas" of the library media center should be accessible to students with disabilities. Laying out the media center in a logical arrangement and posting a floor plan near the entrance will assist students, staff, and visitors. Students using wheelchairs should be able to move easily throughout the media center and have sufficient space to navigate through the stacks. Barbara, an independent upper school librarian in Texas, states, "For those with physical disabilities, we have 36″ aisles for easy wheelchair maneuvering with counters and desks being at a lower level to provide access to a flat work surface. Frankly, we have an active student body with the usual share of broken bones, sports injuries, etc., so our physical handicap adaptations are frequently necessary on a temporary basis, too."[51] Depending on the number of disabled students, sufficient tables and computer workstations should be adjusted for use by persons in wheelchairs.[52]

Many simple and inexpensive changes can be made to enhance the library experience and access of all students.

- Eliminate obstacles and clutter in high traffic areas.
- Replace door knobs with levered door openers.
- Adjust lighting to avoid dim areas and glare.
- Install multiple types of signage (pictograms, large print, Braille).[53]
- Modify circulation desks and book returns for accessibility.
- Create differentiated activity areas for different noise levels.
- Provide study carrels and noise-cancelling headphones for those who are distracted by noise and activity.[54]

These modifications make the media center more physically accessible to a wide range of students, and they also enable students with attention deficit disorder and others who are easily distracted to work more effectively. Physical access helps ensure access to information in whatever format is required to meet student needs.

Access to Library Media Program Resources

"Access to Resources and Services in the School Library Media Program: An Interpretation of the *Library Bill of Rights*" states that school library professionals collaborate with others to create a collection suited to the developmental and maturity levels of students served.[55] As noted in Chapter 3, it is the responsibility of the library media specialist to select resources for all students, and those choices affect student access to a broad range of ideas. For students with physical, cognitive, or learning disabilities, whether specifically identified or not, there are other considerations to be taken into account during the selection process. The media specialist may be selecting materials for students who are blind, deaf, autistic, cognitively impaired, or learning disabled.

There are three issues to keep in mind regarding resources for students with disabilities. The first is selecting appropriate fiction and nonfiction resources in a variety of formats as well as useful and accessible electronic resources. For example, the library media specialist may select paperbacks for students unable to physically hold heavy volumes; toys, audio, video, and multimedia format resources for students with cognitive disabilities; and large print books and magazines for those with visual disabilities.[56]

The second issue is ensuring that students can locate, retrieve, and use the selected resources successfully. Location of resources includes taking the diverse needs of students using the media center into consideration. For example, those with hearing impairments may require clear signage, adequate lighting, print instructions for using electronic and other resources, and possibly assistive technology such as audio amplification devices. For students with low vision, it is important to consider adequate lighting, type size, magnification devices, and text-to-voice software to make information accessible.[57] Retrieval and use may also involve providing the audiovisual equipment and computers needed to access the information. Lastly, because not all disabilities are visible, library staff must be knowledgeable about who is disabled and needs assistance and the best strategies for providing the help.

As an experienced library media specialist, Rebecca advises,

Any time students can acquire materials on their own is beneficial. That might mean anything from call numbers printed in bigger fonts on the spines of books for visually impaired students or using "reachers" and "grabbers" for students who don't have full mobility. Adding picture cues on the shelves can make students with learning disabilities who struggle with the Dewey decimal system more independent; but it also helps prereaders, English language learners, and even teachers who just want to "grab a quick book on insects" to take back to their classroom.[58]

Lastly, school library media specialists must make the collection reflect its users. It is essential to make available to students with special needs fiction and nonfiction resources that reflect accurate information about their disabilities. Reading biographies or fiction with realistic characters who have overcome problems in similar circumstances can be enlightening and liberating. In addition, having books in the collection can inform and engender empathy among nondisabled students.

 Schneider Family Book Award

Annually, the Schneider Family Book Award recognizes authors or illustrators in three age categories (ages 0–10, 11–13, and 13–18) "for a book that embodies an artistic expression of the disability experience for child and adolescent audiences. The book must portray some aspect of living with a disability or that of a friend or family member, whether the disability is physical, mental or emotional."[59] Recent award winners include a book about a musician who loses his hearing, a girl struggling with mixed feelings about life with her autistic brother, and a friendship between a young girl with cerebral palsy and a boy who has been in trouble with the law. The award is administered through the ALA Awards Program Office, and information on award criteria and past winners is available on the ALA website.

Not all resources are available commercially in a format needed by students. In 1997 Congress passed the Chaffee Amendment, which permits "copies of previously published, non-dramatic literary works to be translated into Braille, audio, or digital text and distributed to individuals with print disabilities."[60] The amendment allows only authorized entities, such as federal agencies and selected nonprofit organizations, to produce the work in a specialized format; teachers and school library media specialists may not adapt the materials.[61] The primary nonprofit organizations that provide access to print materials under the Chaffee Amendment are the National Library Service for the Blind and Physically Handicapped, Recording for the Blind and Dyslexic, and the American Printing House for the Blind.[62]

The school library professional can also borrow materials in formats to meet students' needs. The National Library Service for the Blind and Physically Handicapped, administered by the Library of Congress, is a network of regional libraries that distributes free Braille and audio books and magazines to eligible users via postage-free mail. Equipment is also loaned at no cost to users.[63] The Described and Captioned Media Program is funded by the U.S. Department of Education and supplies on free loan orally described and captioned educational media such as videotapes, CD-ROMs, and DVDs for students who are blind, visually impaired, deaf, hard of hearing, or deaf-blind. The program also provides a clearinghouse for information related to accessibility, deafness, blindness, and related topics.[64]

Providing an accessible collection ensures that all students can take advantage of their legal right to read and receive information. It is worthwhile for the school media professional to inquire whether the library's resources meet the needs of students with disabilities. Soliciting ideas from students about their favorite magazines, the kinds of books they enjoy, and if current electronic resources meet their needs can help a library media specialist engage students in dialogue to inform future resource selection.

Access to Resources through Technology

Technology is an integral part of the way that students access information for assignments and recreation. Beyond the usual types of technologies present in a school library facility, *accessible technology* can be used by people with a wide range of abilities and disabilities.[65] It incorporates the principles of universal design and may be used directly or with "assistive technology." Accessible technology includes:

- **Accessible software applications**—"give users more than one way of accomplishing a task ... allow users to use the mouse alone, the keyboard alone, or a combination of the two."[66]

- **Accessible multimedia products**—in videotape, CD, DVD, or Internet format "include synchronized text captions for spoken information and other audio content and provide synchronized audio descriptions for visual content. They offer more than one way to input commands or respond to prompts."[67]

- **Accessible websites**—allow those with a broad range of abilities and disabilities to "navigate the site, access content, and participate in interactive web activities. Accessible websites provide a text equivalent (typically a description) for all non-text elements, such as audio, video, graphics, animation, graphical buttons, and image maps."[68]

Rebecca suggests,

Much of your existing technology may have accessibility features already built in. Microsoft Office includes a narrator to read text, a magnifier, and ways to slow down the mouse or keyboard actions. (http://www.microsoft.com/enable) by turning on some of Firefox's accessibility features, not only does it improve access for students with disabilities it may help others as well. (http://www.mozilla.org/access/features) For example, I slow the mouse clicks down when I'm first teaching the kindergarteners to log on to the computers, and it makes them much less frustrated.[69]

 Assistive Technology

Assistive technology, as defined by the Individuals with Disabilities Education Act (IDEA), is "any item, piece of equipment, or product system, whether acquired commercially off the shelf, modified, or customized, that is used to increase, maintain, or improve the functional capabilities of a child with a disability."[70]

Accessible technology may require the addition of *assistive technology*. There are numerous assistive technologies available to allow those with special needs to work *independently*. Familiar assistive technologies range from wheelchairs to keyboards with large keys to text-to-speech software that reads text in a computer-generated voice.[71] Assistive technology is available in low-tech versions such as large print books, audio books, and the use of signage and symbols for visual cues.[72] There is also high-tech assistive technology that is more costly and may include products such as a voice output communication aid, designed for use by individuals with communication or speech disabilities. It provides synthesized speech, from simple messages to complex sentences, using symbols, text, or both.[73] Library staff should be trained to use a school's assistive technology and software to provide or enhance access to resources for disabled students.

The number of assistive technologies is large and increasing annually. Websites such as ABLEDATA (http://www.abledata.com), maintained for the National Institute on Disability and Rehabilitation Research of the U.S. Department of Education, provides objective information about assistive technology products. The site also contains a bibliography of books, articles, and electronic publications relating to assistive technology.

There are numerous benefits to using accessible and assistive technologies in a library media center. They allow students with a wide range of abilities *barrier-free* access to information with as much independence as personally possible. Technology allows students with disabilities greater opportunities to complete assignments and interact with their peers, thereby reducing isolation and promoting self-esteem. The skills developed through use of the accessible and assistive technologies will allow students to develop lifelong learning skills.[74]

According to Mary Alice, a media specialist in Minnesota, not all students require accessible software or assistive technology and can use computer hardware and software used regularly by other students.

> One of our senior high special education teachers teaches Organizational Skills to older special education students. Collaboratively, we've worked to provide Microsoft Publisher, which students use to publish Zines. Their collections of creative writing are a source of pride. One of the students, Alex, is very interested in writing and wanted to be published. According to his teacher, he "discovered his voice" in writing. He took photos of things that he cared about and included them with his poetry and other creative writing in the Zine he created. I made sure that the software was purchased (out of the media center budget) and installed; previously, it was available only in our business education lab. It's rewarding to support this creative teacher who encourages those students to "stretch" and to see how the students flourish using technology.[75]

Access to the Library Website and Electronic Resources

A large part of information-seeking in today's library media center focuses on use of resources found on the Internet or through subscription-based resources—online databases, electronic encyclopedias or other reference books, and e-books. It is necessary to evaluate the accessibility of each electronic product to ensure its use by students with disabilities, including the blind or those with low vision, the deaf or hard of hearing, those with fine motor disabilities, and those with cognitive disabilities. Ask electronic product vendors to demonstrate accessibility features. Check the company's website for certification of meeting or exceeding the technical specifications and performance-based requirements for electronic and information technology access that are required under the Electronic and Information Technology Accessibility Standards of Section 508 of the Rehabilitation Act (http://www.access-board.gov/sec508/standards.htm#Subpart_a). While Section 508 applies to federal agencies, it provides a standard for accessibility for many types of products and applications that can be used by schools. Assistive technology, such as screen reader software, may also be needed to enable some students with disabilities to access the information.

Many library media programs have Web pages that provide links to useful resources such as interactive Web tools to create citations. Locating information using the Internet can be difficult for students with disabilities, and the school library professional must take care to ensure that the library media program's website is accessible. This involves learning about accessible design concepts and standards, browser accessibility features, and assistive technology. Two entities, the Web Accessibility Initiative of the World Wide Web Consortium, also known as WC3 (http://www.w3.org.wai), and Web Accessibility in Mind (http://www.webaim.org), provide guidelines and a vast number of resources that library media specialists can use for ensuring Web page accessibility for the disabled. The Trace Center, College of Engineering, at the University of Wisconsin–Madison (http://trace.wisc.edu) also offers many resources aimed at improving Web page use for disabled persons. Once the Web pages are completed, the library professional can use free online accessibility tools, such as WebXAct and others, to perform automated checks of Web pages for accessibility issues. The online tools each differ a bit and are not infallible, so manual checks and the judgment of the creator are still vital.[76]

The library media professional must work with school technology personnel to ensure that the technical aspects of Web use do not limit or eliminate access to electronic resources for students with disabilities. The need to access information in an electronic format is crucial to students with disabilities, and the skills they develop will support their information seeking as adults. For disabled students, achieving access in its many forms is an integral part of their intellectual freedom.

Tina's Story

School library media professionals are responsible for offering services to the entire student population, including those with disabilities. Tina, a K-5 grade library media specialist in Pennsylvania, describes her students and the services she provides to those with significant cognitive disabilities.

There are two classes of "life skills" students with seven students in the intermediate class (Gr. 3–5) and six students in the primary (Gr. K-2). They have been included in our building for about 10 years. Each class has a special education teacher and two classroom aides. Some students can read aloud simple, primer type texts; and most can recognize numbers, letters, and colors. Some can also do simple math addition and subtraction especially when the problem is "hands-on." While they can follow the simple plot of most picture books they have difficulty understanding characterization, and have difficulty with more than two or three step sequencing. Most attend speech therapy, and one student has a device that speaks for him [voice output communication device]. The students are usually well mannered, polite, and want to do their best; but some need lots of reminders. Depending on what has been placed in each student's IEP [Independent Education Plan], some come to the library on a weekly basis in the regular education setting [with those students without cognitive disabilities]. They also visit the library as a class by themselves on a weekly basis.

When the life skills students first came to the library I was very apprehensive because I had never had any training on instructing students with severe cognitive disabilities. I felt even more anxious after being informed that I was not expected to instruct them, but rather to allow them to acquire social skills. It was suggested that this meant that they were to use their library period as a time to meet and mingle with their regular education peers. In my mind, this presented a conflict. The regular education students were not in the library to spend time being a "buddy" and socializing; they had a curriculum to follow and assignments to complete. There were some moments that allowed regular education and life skills students to acquire their individual skills together. However, most of the time, the regular education students had information and activities to complete relating to their library lessons. The life skills students, under the direction of their individual aides, practiced sitting quietly, writing their names and numbers, and writing just one response to the lesson. Most of the time, however, I felt the life skills aides were learning the lesson and showing me what they could do.

Where I feel the life skills students achieved success in understanding and using the library was when they came as a class. I tailor the story time and activities to allow them to practice basic skills. Since the class is small—usually only about seven or eight students—they all get a chance to participate and practice their speaking skills. In selecting the story to be read aloud, I choose books with large, bright illustrations with a simple plot involving a few strong characters. Some of the activities I incorporate into the story involve counting and identifying colors and letters. When I ask them to respond about the story, I usually give them a choice of two answers to keep them on topic. To accompany the stories, I draw simple pictures for them to color and practice using their fine motor skills.[77]

As Tina stated, she had initial fears about providing instruction and services to students with severe cognitive disabilities. However, over time she has incorporated differentiated instruction techniques when working with these students. Like Tina, library media specialists must overcome their concerns, seek assistance for modifications and adaptations from students' instructors, and see each student as an individual who can "grow" as a result of his/her library experiences. When the school library professional follows that course of action, the intellectual freedom of students with even the most severe cognitive disabilities is recognized and supported.

Access for ALL

School library media specialists are legally and ethically responsible to provide a physically accessible library media center facility with resources in varying formats to meet the needs of all students. Library staff also are an integral part of the "library experience" for students by providing a welcoming atmosphere, instruction in library media and technology skills, and assistance as needed. When the school library media professional makes a serious effort to ensure access to information for students with disabilities, the intellectual freedom of *all* students is reinforced. In one final thought Rebecca stated,

Instead of worrying about what [disabled] students can't do, I think about their parents and families and how they are truly expecting us to do our best with their child at school. Intellectual freedom is a right for all students, but in the instance of children with special needs, it can be impeded by physical or other barriers to information. What I've found, is that the more I try to open things up for students with special needs, the more it actually improves access for everybody. And that's our goal, really, isn't it—for students to become independent learners and thinkers.[78]

✍ Key Ideas Summary

This chapter explored access to the library media center facility, and its resources and services for students with physical, cognitive, and learning disabilities in the context of their First Amendment rights and intellectual freedom. To review, here are some of the major ideas:

- Three federal laws—the Rehabilitation Act, the Individuals with Disabilities Education Act, and the Americans with Disabilities Act—provide the legal framework under which students with disabilities receive a free appropriate public education and are educated in the least restrictive environment with their nondisabled peers.

- For students with disabilities, access to the facility, its resources, and services is an integral part of their intellectual freedom.

- Barriers to accessing the library media center and its resources can take many forms: insufficient staff knowledge, physical access barriers, an incomplete collection, an inaccessible library website and catalog, and inadequate technology.

- Collaboration between special education staff and the school library media specialist is key to ensuring that students with disabilities have the maximum possible access to library facilities, resources, and services, and that their First Amendment rights are protected.

- The library media specialist must be proactive in reaching out to students with disabilities.

- The personal attitudes of library staff and volunteers toward disabled students and their level of knowledge about disabilities can affect students' access to the collection and services.

- Small changes can assist students with disabilities, and those accommodations may also improve learning for nondisabled students.

Library Bill of Rights Interpretations and Policies

- American Library Association. "Access to Resources and Services in the School Library Media Program: An Interpretation of the *Library Bill of Rights*," http://www.ala.org/oif.

- American Library Association, "Library Services for People with Disabilities Policy," (2001), http://www.ala.org/ala/ascla/asclaissues/libraryservices.cfm.

Recommended Resources

- **Bishop, Kay. *The Collection Program in Schools: Concepts, Practices, and Information Sources*. 4th ed. Westport, Connecticut: Libraries Unlimited, 2007.**

In its fourth edition, this reliable reference includes sources for materials for students with visual or hearing impairments, learning disabilities, those with attention deficit disorders, chronic illnesses, and others.

- **Hopkins, Janet.** *Assistive Technology: An Introductory Guide for K-12 Library Media Specialists.* **Worthington, Ohio: Linworth Publishing, 2004.**
  Hopkins provides comprehensive information on using assistive technology to make a school library media program accessible to students with a variety of disabilities.

- **University of Washington, DO-IT, "Universal Access: Making Library Resources Accessible to People with Disabilities,** http://www.washington.edu/doit/UA/PRESENT/libres.html#L3
  This website includes information on legal and access issues, communications recommendations, and a checklist of items to consider for creating an accessible library.

- **WrightsLaw**, http://wrightslaw.com
  This site offers hundreds of articles, cases, newsletters, and other information about special education law and advocacy.

Notes

1. Cox, John E., and Debra M. Lynch, "Library Media Centers: Accessibility Issues in Rural Missouri," *Intervention in School and Clinic* 42, no. 2 (November 2006), 106.

2. American Library Association, Article I, *Library Bill of Rights*, http://www.ala.org/ala/oif/statementspols/statementsif/librarybillrights.htm.

3. American Library Association, Article I, *Code of Ethics of the American Library Association*, http://www.ala.org/ala/oif/statementspols/codeofethics/codeethics.htm.

4. American Library Association, "Access to Resources and Services in the School Library Media Program: An Interpretation of the *Library Bill of Rights*," http://www.ala.org/ala/oif/statementspols/statementsif/interpretations/Default675.htm.

5. U.S. Department of Justice, Civil Rights Division, Disability Rights Section, "A Guide to Disability Rights Laws," September 2005, 16, http://www.ada.gov/cguide.pdf.

6. Ibid, 17.

7. "Civil Rights Legislation, The Rehabilitation Act of 1973, Section 504, (P.L. 93-112)," Assistive Technology Online Training Project, http://atto.buffalo.edu/registered/ATBasics/Foundation/Laws/civilrights.php#rehab2.

8. Torrans, Lee Ann, *Law for K-12 Libraries and Librarians* (Westport, Connecticut: Libraries Unlimited, 2003), 218.

9. Torrans, 215.

10. National Center for Technology Innovation, "Moving Toward Solutions: Assistive & Learning Technology for All Students," January 2006, www.nationaltechcenter.org/documents/MovingTowardSolutions-ExecSummary-Web.pdf.

11. "A Guide to Disability Rights Laws," September 2005, 15, http://www.ada.gov/cguide.pdf.

12. "Schools and AT," Assistive Technology Online Training Project, http://atto.buffalo.edu/registered/ATBasics/Foundation/Laws/schools.php.

13. U.S. Department of Education, Office of Special Education Programs, "Children Enrolled by Their Parents in Private Schools," 11-16-06, http://idea.ed.gov/explore/view/p/%2Croot%2Cdynamic%2CTopicalBrief%2C5%2C.

14. Ibid.

15. Friedman, Sheila, "Module 16, Children with Disabilities Enrolled by Their Parents in Private Schools," Building the Legacy: IDEA 2004 Training Curriculum, National Dissemination Center for Children with Disabilities, August 2007, 3, http://www.nichcy.org/training/16-discussionSlides1-15.pdf.

16. "A Guide to Disability Rights Laws," 3.

17. Torrans, 215.

18. Henderson, "Overview of ADA, IDEA, and Section 504, Americans with Disabilities Act of 1990."

19. Noble, Steve, "The Kentucky Accessible Information Technology in Schools Project," *Information Technology and Disabilities* XI, no. 1 (August 2005), http://www.rit.edu/~easi/itd/itdv11n1/noble.htm.

20. Smith, Tom E. C., "Section 504, the ADA, and Public Schools," 2001, LD Online, http://www.ldonline.org/article/6108.

21. Torrans, 217.

22. U.S. Census Bureau Disability Statistics, May 29, 2007, http://www.census.gov/Press-Release/www/releases/archives/facts_for_features_special_editions/010102.html.

23. Ibid.

24. Rothschuh, Jessica, April Kirk Hart, and Wendy Lazarus, "Helping Our Children with Disabilities Succeed: What's Broadband Got to Do with It?" Digital Opportunity for Youth Issue Brief, No. 2 (July 2007), The Children's Partnership, www.childrenspartnership.org/AM/Template.cfm?Section=Reports1&Template=/CM/ContentDisplay.cfm&ContentFileID=2284.

25. Ibid.

26. Barbara, email to author, November 7, 2007.

27. Neal, Jerry D., and Dennis Ehlert, "20 Ways to Add Technology for Students with Disabilities to the Library or Media Center," *Intervention in School or Clinic* 42, no. 2 (November 2006), 119.

28. Wojahn, Rebecca Hogue, email interview, May 19, 2007.

29. Mary Alice, email to author, January 26, 2008.

30. Ibid.

31. Wojahn, May 19, 2007.

32. Wojahn, Rebecca Hogue, "Everyone's Invited: Ways to Make Your Library More Welcoming to Children with Special Needs," *School Library Journal* (February 1, 2006), http://www.schoollibraryjournal.com/article/CA6302984.html.

33. Linda, email to author, April 20, 2007.

34. Downing, Joyce Anderson, "Media Centers and Special Education: Introduction to the Special Issue," *Intervention in School and Clinic* 42, no. 2 (November 2006), 72.

35. Linda, April 20, 2007.

36. Katherine, email to author, April 24, 2007.

37. Rock, Marcia L., et. al., "REACH: A Framework for Differentiating Classroom Instruction," *Preventing School Failure* 52, no. 2 (Winter 2008), 33.

38. Wojahn, May 19, 2008.

39. Ibid.

40. Becky, email to author, April 20, 2007.

41. Liz, email to author, April 22, 2007.

42. King County [Washington], Department of Executive Services, Office of Civil Rights, "Sticks and Stones," Kids Web (March 27, 2007), http://www.metrokc.gov/dias/ocre/stick.htm.

43. Ibid.

44. Ibid.

45. Kendrick, Deborah, "No Need to Avoid People with Disabilities" (March 15, 2005), http://www.citybeat.com/2005-03-16/inmyview.shtml.

46. Linda, April 20, 2007.

47. Pat, email to author, December 22, 2007.

48. American Library Association, "Library Services for People with Disabilities Policy" (2001), http://www.ala.org/ala/ascla/asclaissues/libraryservices.cfm.

49. Connell, Bettye Rose, et al., "Principles of Universal Design," The Center for Universal Design at North Carolina State University, Version 2 (April 1,1997), http://www.design.ncsu.edu/cud/about_ud/udprinciplestext.htm.

50. Vanderheiden, Gregg C., "Universal Design … What It Is and What It Isn't," Trace R & D Center, University of Wisconsin–Madison (revised May 6, 1996), http://trace.wisc.edu/docs/whats_ud/whats_ud.htm.

51. Barbara, email to author, November 7, 2007.

52. Irvall, Birgitta, and Gyda Skat Nielsen, "Access to Libraries for Persons with Disabilities – CHECKLIST," International Federation of Library Associations and Institutions IFLA Professional Reports, No. 89, International Federation of Library Associations and Institutions (2005), 6, http://www.ifla.org/VII/s9/nd1/iflapr-89e.pdf.

53. Wojahn, "Everyone's Invited."

54. University of Washington, "Universal Access: Making Library Resources Accessible to People with Disabilities," http://www.washington.edu/doit/UA/PRESENT/libres.html#L3.

55. American Library Association, "Access to Resources and Services in the School Library Media Program: An Interpretation of the *Library Bill of Rights*," http://www.ala.org/ala/oif/statementspols/statementsif/interpretations/Default675.htm.

56. Bishop, Kay. *The Collection Program in Schools: Concepts, Practices, and Information Sources*, 4th ed. (Westport, Connecticut: Libraries Unlimited, 2007), 193.

57. Downing, 72–73.

58. Wojahn, May 19, 2007.

59. Schneider Family Book Award, "About the Schneider Family Book Awards," http://www.ala.org/ala/awardsbucket/schneideraward/schneiderfamily.htm.

60. American Library Association, Office for Information Technology Policy and Lesley Harris & Associates, "Accessibility Basics for Librarians: Access to Print Materials," 2004, http://www.ala.org/ala/washoff/oitp/emailtutorials/accessibilitya/accessibility.cfm.

61. Ibid.

62. Accessibility Basics for Librarians: Chaffee Resources.

63. National Library Service, "That All May Read," http://www.loc.gov/nls/what.html.

64. Described and Captioned Media Program, "Services," http://www.dcmp.org/About/Default.aspx?A=2.

65. University of Washington, Access IT, "What is accessible electronic and information technology?" DO-IT Factsheet #1110, http://www.washington.edu/accessit/articles?1110.

66. Ibid.

67. Ibid.

68. Ibid.

69. Wojahn, May 19, 2007.

70. §300.5, Assistive technology device, IDEA, http://a257.g.akamaitech.net/7/257/2422/04nov20031500/edocket.access.gpo.gov/cfr_2001/julqtr/pdf/34cfr300.5.pdf.

71. University of Washington, Access IT, "What is assistive technology."

72. Hopkins, Janet, "School Library Accessibility: The Role of Assistive Technology," *Teacher Librarian* 31, no. 3 (February 2004), 16.

73. AbleData, "Cameleon," http://www.abledata.com/abledata.cfm?pageid=113583&top=22&productid=187425&trail=0&discontinued=0.

74. Hopkins, "School Library Accessibility ..."

75. Mary Alice, January 27, 2008.

76. WebAIM, "A Review of Free Online Accessibility Tools," http://www.webaim.org/articles/freetools.

77. Tina, email to author, December 7, 2007.

78. Ibid.

CHAPTER 9

Advocacy for Intellectual Freedom: Building Common Ground

Protection of access to information occurs school by school, incident by incident, when each school librarian applies the principles of the profession without compromise.[1]
> —Frances Beck McDonald, Ph.D., Mankato State University

Defining Advocacy in Terms of Intellectual Freedom

The American Association of School Librarians (AASL) has defined advocacy as the "On-going process of building partnerships so that others will act for and with you, turning passive support into educated action for the library media program."[2] Advocating for intellectual freedom is not effective if confined to celebrating Banned Books Week. School library media professionals' belief in the principles of intellectual freedom must be reflected in their year-round, day-to-day actions. For example, by actively protecting minors' library records, library media specialists are following state law and adhering to the *Code of Ethics of the American Library Association.* Aligning routine behaviors with professional ethics impacts students' intellectual freedom and sends a strong message to the entire school community about the importance of those principles.

Advocacy Within the School Community

What makes some schools *intellectual freedom friendly* while others become contentious battlegrounds? The difference may be as simple as the resolute advocacy for intellectual freedom and access carried out by a dedicated school library media specialist over a period of time. While one person can achieve a great deal, having allies who support minors' access to information—administrators, teachers, and support staff—can change a school's climate. Parents, extended family, and the rest of the community also have a keen interest in what children and young adults read and view while at school. Informing them about selection practices and seeking their support for the family's right to guide their child(ren)'s reading moves advocacy into the broader community. The school board, as policy-making representatives of the community, also has a stake because it is responsible for setting district policy.

Advocacy Begins with the School Library Professional

The library media specialist is the most well-informed person in a school about intellectual freedom, access to information for students, and minors' First Amendment rights. No one knows how many school library media specialists actively advocate for intellectual freedom or access to library facilities, resources, and services for students. It is likely that many do so both consciously and unconsciously. Advocacy, from a school library professional's perspective, begins with staying informed and alert to the local, state, and national "climate" for intellectual freedom and minors' rights. Advocacy is a professional obligation. The American Library Association (ALA) suggests the following strategies that school library media specialists may undertake *before* reaching out to others about intellectual freedom:

- Read newspapers, magazines, and other publications as a "citizen," monitoring library patrons' civil rights.
- Study the current issues about intellectual freedom and First Amendment rights.
- Seek up-to-date information on censorship and other intellectual freedom issues in professional literature and through attendance at conferences and workshops.
- Subscribe to intellectual freedom-related electronic lists.
- Purchase a subscription to the ALA *Newsletter on Intellectual Freedom.*
- Become familiar with pro-First Amendment organizations.
- Scrutinize lawsuits dealing with student free speech rights at the state and federal levels.
- Join ALA's Intellectual Freedom Round Table.
- Serve as a member of a state school library media organization's intellectual freedom committee.[3]

The more knowledgeable and "connected" the school library professional is to the intellectual freedom community locally, statewide, and nationally, the more effective s/he will be in advocating for minors' First Amendment right to receive information.

Educating Administrators, Teachers, and the School Board

School library media specialists receive instruction in intellectual freedom principles and promoting access to resources for students in their preservice library school or certification classes, and the learning continues throughout their careers. In contrast, principals and teachers usually do not learn about the principles of "intellectual freedom" or "access to information" in their education classes, nor is it likely that they learn about First Amendment court decisions that have produced case law affirming minors' rights to receive ideas and information in school library media programs. If minors' intellectual freedom rights are to be protected, the library media specialist must educate administrators and teachers about these topics. The library professional has the background knowledge and the responsibility under the *Code of Ethics of the ALA* to "uphold the principles of intellectual freedom and resist all efforts to censor library resources."[4]

Advocating with Administrators

Some administrators realize the valuable role that their school library media specialists play. Jeffrey Gibson, a former principal, states,

> School administrators want to believe that they are champions for the students they serve. However, at times school administrators find themselves in situations where student rights and/or parental prerogative come into conflict with what the administrator believes to be in the best interest of the student. Censorship and access to print and electronic resources are areas where the choices for the administrator do not always lead to clear-cut decisions. In these areas it is easy for administrators to find that they are *not* champions for student rights. If not adequately prepared, administrators can also find themselves in situations that are, at a minimum, embarrassing and, perhaps, illegal—subjecting themselves and their schools to lawsuits....
>
> To whom can administrators turn for help? The answer is to team with the school's library media specialist. Library media specialists have specific training in censorship and other intellectual freedom issues. Just as library media specialists are valuable resources to students and teachers, they can serve the same role for school administrators. The library media specialist can assist with questions of materials selection, the process for handling book challenges, and a variety of other intellectual freedom issues.... A school administrator needs to be up to speed on district policies related to these issues as well as state and federal laws and legal opinions. The time to do this is *before* the irate staff member or assertive parent calls. There is no substitute for being prepared.[5]

Besides educating principals about materials selection, censorship attempts, and district reconsideration procedures, the school library professional must also help the principal make the connections between intellectual freedom and "growing" future citizens. Principals spend much time working toward improvement of their schools' standardized test scores, but they also have a desire to see their students travel successfully on the path to adult citizenship. Today's students are being educated for citizenship in a global society.

Students need access to materials about an array of subjects: social studies, art, science, reading, math, literature, music, health, and others. If students experience free access to information in print and electronic formats, their intellectual curiosity is aroused. When the library media center collection reflects information presenting all points of view, students have an opportunity to use the resources to study the many facets of current issues, evaluate information sources, and make informed decisions. Students who are trusted to seek information about real problems from diverse sources are more engaged in their own learning. Free access to information in the school library media center creates an academic atmosphere in which students learn democratic principles and begin to apply them.

The principal also needs to be aware of the connection between intellectual freedom and the curriculum. Threats to intellectual freedom are not isolated to library media center resources. For years, there have been conflicts in communities about specific books or ideas taught as part of a school's curriculum. English teachers have had both "classics" and contemporary literature attacked as obscene, un-Christian, too violent, and for realistically portraying drug use, premarital sex, alcoholism, and racism. Science teachers have found themselves in the middle of controversy over teaching evolution. In social studies classes, teachers address complicated societal issues and must take great care in dealing with controversy in the classroom. In reality, the continuation of our democratic way of life depends on free and open examination of ideas by students during their education. When literature is scrutinized, condemned, and removed from language arts classes, students' intellectual freedom and their right to receive (and examine) ideas is affected. When scientific theory is attacked and unproven ideas are forced upon instructors, students' right to receive accurate information is impaired. When free inquiry is stifled in the study of contemporary issues, students do not have the opportunity to sort out the diverse ideas, a critical skill for citizens. Therefore, on behalf of his/her students and faculty, the principal must also become a defender of the intellectual freedom principle—unconstrained access to information.

The school library professional can use these strategies to inform administrators about intellectual freedom, and the time to begin is *before a challenge occurs.*

- Connect students' free access to legal information in the school library media center collection to the education of "future" citizens. Maintaining a strong democracy is yet another rationale for administrative support of intellectual freedom.

- Meet with the principal to review the materials selection policy and procedures for acquisition. Follow-up activities could include sending the principal lists of new materials and inviting him/her to the media center to view new resource displays.

- Review the district's reconsideration procedures annually with the principal. Clarify any steps or responsibilities in the reconsideration process that are in question.

- Gain the respect of the principal by providing a brief written memo and initiate oral discussion on an aspect of intellectual freedom as issues arise.

- Avoid library jargon, and include examples to make the concepts of intellectual freedom more concrete.[6]

- Provide the principal with short articles and brochures about intellectual freedom and access to information for students.

- Inform the principal about court case decisions related to minors rights in school library media programs.

- Arrange with administrators for opportunities to educate teachers, students, and parents about the selection and reconsideration of materials in the media program collection.

- Plan with administrators for regular inservice training devoted to intellectual freedom as it applies to the school library media center and the classroom.

Gaining the principal as an ally in advocating for and protecting students' First Amendment rights is crucial. If the principal does not support a collection with materials reflecting a broad range of ideas on controversial issues, believe that students' library records should be confidential, or accept that minors' have the right to research a variety of topics, it is more difficult for the school library professional to ensure students' access to information and protect their intellectual freedom.

Advocating with Teachers

Most teachers and other staff lack grounding in the principles of intellectual freedom. They may not have a clear understanding of the difference between (1) the broad administrative control public school principals and boards of education have on the removal of curricular materials required in courses and (2) the narrow control administrators and boards have when it comes to removing library resources intended for free inquiry by students.[7] As noted in Chapter 2, case law on student First Amendment rights from *Virgil v. School Board of Columbia County*, 862 F.2d 1517 (11th Cir. 1989) and the *Right to Read Defense Committee v. School Committee of the City of Chelsea*, 454 F. Supp. 703 (D. Mass. 1978) differentiates between curricular and library resources. For additional information, refer to Figure 2.3, "Court Cases on Intellectual Freedom Involving Minors' First Amendment Rights," located in Chapter 2.

The school library professional can advocate with teachers for minors' access to information by using a number of strategies. Marcia, the sole library media specialist in a small rural district in Wisconsin, used food to entice faculty into the media center for a display and discussion on banned books and censorship. She states,

To get the message about Banned Books out to the teachers and support staff in our school, we hosted a "party" for them in the study room in the LMC. We served *Subversive Soda, Challenged Chips, Censored Salsa, and Banned Brownies.* To provide information for staff, our library assistant made a banner with facts about why, how, and who bans/challenges books. She also created a collage of book titles and the reasons why they have been banned. The response from teachers and staff was very positive.[8]

Catherine, an elementary library media specialist in the Midwest, actively solicits assistance from the faculty to provide a wide range of materials for the media center.

Our district has an up-to-date materials selection policy with reconsideration procedures. I helped create the policy, and it endorses the *Library Bill of Rights* and "Access to Resources and Services in the School Library Media Program: An Interpretation of the *Library Bill of Rights.*" Our district supports an unbiased collection that reflects a variety of points of view.

I encourage individual teachers to help select materials for the library media center and provide them with a brief *lesson in selection.* I distribute a flyer to faculty and staff requesting suggestions of individual titles or topics for addition to the collection. Prior to ordering, I check reviews to be sure we are making a good selection. When the item arrives, I contact the staff member and let them know the item they wanted is now part of the collection. If teachers request materials on a particular topic, I prepare a list of recommended materials and ask them to prioritize their choices. This has worked very well, and my principal has been told repeatedly by reading specialists, the language arts coordinator, and the faculty that our library collection is outstanding.[9]

Besides developing an unbiased collection, Catherine's outreach to faculty secondarily develops, among teachers, positive feelings toward the library media program and its collection. The principal also has independent reports on the quality of the collection engendering confidence in Catherine's selection choices. The principal's knowledge of the collection's value to staff and students will be crucial if a challenge occurs.

Other strategies to educate teachers and support staff about the importance of access to information in the library media program collection and intellectual freedom principles include:

- Meet with new teaching staff to explain library policies related to materials selection, reconsideration of a resource, privacy of library records, interlibrary loan, and Internet use.
- Plan and collaboratively work with teachers and students on learning experiences incorporating First Amendment speech rights.

- Integrate a different facet of intellectual freedom into each staff inservice program.

- Select professional materials related to censorship and make them available to staff.

- Distribute posters and other First Amendment promotional materials for class-room use.

The support of teachers in advocating for and protecting students' First Amendment rights is essential. When a challenge occurs, the "education" of faculty on the topic of intellectual freedom may pay off with colleagues opposing attempts to censor library media center collection resources. Equally important, faculty who understand students' First Amendment rights can incorporate information about those rights into their instruction.

Advocating with the School Board

As discussed in Chapter 2, the well-known court case *Board of Education, Island Trees Union Free School District v. Pico* (1982) and other more recent cases, including *Counts v. Cedarville School District* (2003), demonstrated that school board members did not understand or support the concepts of intellectual freedom or access to information as applied to minors. Educating principals and teachers is requisite to developing allies for minors' right to access infor-mation, but it is also *essential* to extend the efforts to inform the school board or other governing body.

Cultivating the ideals of intellectual freedom for minors among school board members is more difficult than doing so within the school itself because most library media specialists have little direct contact with mem-bers of the board of education. In addition, school board members are elected, may come from diverse backgrounds, and likely hold dissimilar opinions. Still, while opportunities to present and nurture the ideas are less frequent and are dependent on the size of the district and its hierarchal structure, there are ways to spread the message.

The support of the district administrator is essential for granting access to a place on the agenda of a board meeting. But, even if a school library media specialist cannot get agenda time for a special presentation to the board, s/he can take advantage of other opportunities, such as when a mate-rials selection policy is being considered for adoption or revision. The library media professional involved in the policy development or revision process can explain why ALA documents, such as the *Library Bill of Rights* or *The Right to Read* statement, are part of the policy or appended to it. An ex-planation of the reconsideration process and the rationale for it can also contribute to board members' understanding, as can knowing the selection criteria and the process. Insight into the reasons behind each significant component of the policy helps educate board members about the need to build a collection that provides a wide range of topics with varying points of view. It is vital to establish and reinforce the connection between access to information for children and young adults and their ability to make informed decisions as adult citizens. Having a strong collection accessible to students supports our democratic process.

There are other ways, both intentional and incidental, that school library professionals and the school library media program itself can inform board members about the program's goals and activities. The school library media specialist can write an article or column about library resources for a school or district newsletter, copies of which may be distributed to board members. The board may read a report or see photos of reading promotion activities related to the school library media program, including those for Banned Books Week. Board members may also be parents of children attending district schools, perhaps even a parent volunteer in the library media center. All these points of connection may begin to shape individual board members' views on the school library media program.

Krystal, the president of a school board in Wisconsin, states, "In my opinion, intellectual freedom is a shared responsibility—the school library in providing resources that are well balanced and culturally diverse and the students in the mature, responsible use of these resources."[10]

By promoting the principles of intellectual freedom and the school library media program with school administrators, teachers, and school board members, the school library media specialist is proactively developing potential advocates. These advocates may serve as allies during a challenge and also help promote minors' First Amendment rights. Using Gwen's analogy from Chapter 6, the school library professional is putting "coins" in the bank.

Teaching Students about Intellectual Freedom

Today's students are tomorrow's adult citizens. In Chapter 1, the connection between intellectual freedom and democracy was introduced. *The Freedom to Read* statement pronounces: "The freedom to read is essential to our democracy."[11] The school library professional builds the collection of resources to support the curriculum that is producing future citizens. S/he defends those resources against attempts at censorship, thereby allowing future citizens' unfettered freedom to information from all points of view. The media specialist teaches students the library and information skills they will apply to their information seeking throughout their adult lives. As a result, the school library media specialist is a key component in student learning related to citizenship and ensuring democracy.

The AASL "Standards for the 21st-Century Learner," are framed on these *common beliefs*:

- "Reading is a window to the world.
- Equitable access is a key component for education.
- The continuing expansion of information demands that all individuals acquire the thinking skills that will enable them to learn on their own."[12]

Any of these beliefs can be connected to instruction about intellectual freedom. The new Standards require learners to "Share knowledge and participate ethically and productively as members of our democratic society," and lists as one student responsibility to "Respect the principles of intellectual freedom."[13] While students may not be familiar with the term *intellectual freedom*, they can likely identify with the term *access*. In this context, "access" means having a library media program that strives to provide them with information reflecting many points of view and in a variety of formats.

The library media specialist can also find ways to incorporate intellectual freedom and its antithesis—censorship—into information and technology skills instruction. Lisa, a preK-8th grade independent school library media specialist in New York, states,

> We do have a banned books curriculum for 3rd and 4th graders in which we discuss challenged titles, and the students get to vote which book should be removed from the library. They usually come to the conclusion that there are some books that first graders shouldn't have access to but they should. Then we talk about who should decide, and they always say me. Then I say I decide that no one under 11 can have those books. That's when they get outraged, and we talk about open access.[14]

Marcia, a K-12 library media specialist in Wisconsin, recognizes the value of teaching students early about their right to read information from varying points of view.

> Weekly I teach Library Media & Technology classes to K-5 students and lessons "as-needed" to grades 6–12. I insert intellectual freedom issues into my lessons throughout the year under the curriculum heading "Demonstrating Positive Social & Ethical Attitudes & Behaviors." I teach students to:
>
> - Recognize that media can reflect different viewpoints and diverse perspectives and be constructed to convey specific messages, viewpoints, and values.
> - Understand what is meant by freedom of speech under the First Amendment to the Constitution.

- Define the concept of Intellectual Freedom in libraries including shelving and circulating materials representing all points of view to all people regardless of race, religion, age, national origin or social and political views.

I connect these concepts with books, poetry, or essays, such as *The Butter Battle Book*, by Dr. Seuss, in which we discuss how media can convey specific messages, viewpoints, and values. I have used "First they came for the Jews ...," a poem usually attributed to Pastor Martin Niemöller, as an illustration of how media can reflect different viewpoints and diverse perspectives. This is a wonderful example since, besides being controversial in its very subject matter, the poem's origins are widely disputed. There are many different versions available because it has evolved from culture to culture and continues to do so today.

The use of electronic resources such as Wikipedia spurs lively discussions about the ownership of information, how global collaboration provides us with higher quality information, and how we no longer have topic experts. We delve into personal options for accessing news and information on the Internet and how these may be biased, misleading, incomplete, and/or inconclusive. This leads into the issue of evaluating information for accuracy, relevance, appropriateness, comprehensiveness, timeliness and overall validity.

At the opening of the year, for all grade levels, I go through my "freedom to read" information and use our library policy as an example, assuring them the library staff are required [under state library records law] to protect their reading choices. I let them know that I will do my best to never give out the information about what they are reading to any teacher and that our relationship with our readers is absolutely confidential. [Note: Currently Wisconsin state library records law allows custodial parents and/or guardians to access the library records of their minor children up to age 16.] I extend that [confidentiality] to questions and searches for information. I assure them that they may always request a private time with me to check out books or to look for information. At the same time, I put the responsibility for making good choices back on them; they should keep their parents' wishes and guidelines in mind, since they are the ones ultimately responsible.[15]

Cheryl Youse, a high school library media specialist in Georgia, offered teachers in her school the opportunity to have her speak to their classes about banned books. Because of enthusiastic responses to her presentations, Cheryl spoke to 35 classes. She states,

When I visited the classes, I showed students a presentation on Banned Books. I also described a few of my experiences as a Media Specialist when people have had objections to books in my school library.... For example, I had one parent who asked me to remove a book about the human body from the library at a K-8 school. Her objection was that it had pictures in it. She was one of my favorite parent volunteers, and I asked if her sixth grade son possessed some of the parts shown in the illustrations. She said he did. I asked if she would prefer that her son first see pictures of those parts he did not possess, but was very curious about, in a book from the school library or in a magazine his buddy got from the gas station and keeps under his mattress. It took about five seconds for the mother to decide we should just leave that book right there on the shelf.[16]

While it was time-consuming for Youse to make a significant number of presentations, her message reached many students and teachers in an entertaining, yet intellectually stimulating way.

A collaborative model can be a productive way to teach students about intellectual freedom. For example, the library media specialist may team with social studies colleagues to plan units and provide resources for study of the First Amendment as it applies to *free speech*. As noted in Chapter 2, courts have interpreted "freedom of speech" more broadly than solely verbal communication. Under the umbrella of First Amendment "free speech," courts have also recognized a minor's right to *receive information*. In addition, the school library professional may consider teaming with language arts teachers, perhaps in conjunction with a unit in which the class is reading a banned book.

There are other ways to teach students about intellectual freedom and censorship. During Banned Book Week, a high school librarian at a Catholic high school in Wisconsin shares her ideas,

Using a banned books list from ALA, I gathered all the banned or once challenged books that we had on our shelves, wrapped a red BANNED label around each individual book (being sure that the title was still clearly visible), placed the books on display near the circ desk, and printed a sign which invited the students to read a banned book. The display brought much interest and many questions from students about why the books had been banned, who'd banned them, why did we own the books, and—of course—could they really check out a banned book.

Since this is an all-girls Catholic high school, the display was a real attention-getter, and the books flew off the display. When the girls check out their banned books, I have a mini ceremony and have them break the "BANNED" label so I can open the book to stamp the date due. The pile of broken labels is kept in a basket next to the books still on display as a further indication that the books on display are meant to be read. Fortunately I had enough to keep the display for the whole week—just a bit sparse toward the end. The school principal made a quick trip to the library to see the display and realized that she'd read most of the titles when she was in high school or college. The social studies classes studying the Constitutional amendments found the display particularly timely, useful, and thought-provoking. For those really interested in the topic, I also had gathered books about banning and why specific titles were selected.[17]

 Teaching about Intellectual Freedom

Three detailed lesson plans designed for middle and high school students by school library media specialists in Kansas, Wyoming, and Wisconsin appear in Appendix D. The lesson plans range from one day to several weeks and revolve around minors' First Amendment right to read and censorship. First Amendment teaching resources also are located at the end of the chapter.

Not everyone supports Banned Books Week and other anticensorship activities in schools and school library media centers. Some school administrators prefer that school library professionals not have a banned books display or organize any related activities. The reasons are unclear; however, the rationale may be that some words have little or no meaning to those outside the library community (*intellectual freedom*) while others appear to cause an inflammatory reaction (*banned books*).

An anonymous middle school library media specialist stated,

> Some librarians in my district are fearful of too much emphasis on Banned Books Week and don't do anything. The things I do in my library to teach about censorship are unique to my library, and sometimes I pay a heavy price for doing them. I have taken some major heat in the past. One year I had a mom in the library pulling books off the shelf!! Two years ago I had multiple conferences with my principal and parents about different activities we were doing, i.e., book talking Chris Crutcher and Robert Cormier books, giving students the ALA OIF website (for shame!), giving kids free choice of books, and probably the most ugly—our district's policy of not letting parents know what their kids have checked out![18]

Considering the unfriendly or even hostile situations some school library media specialists face, it may be possible to accomplish more by being sensitive to that fact that the phrase "banned books" triggers much emotion and seems to promote a more "in your face" approach. In some cases, it may be wise to advance the topic in a slightly different manner. For example, promote *the right to read*. Create a display using the Freedom to Read Foundation's tag line "Free People Read Freely." Centering displays and activities around positive reading messages and activities still allows for a display of books with controversial histories but gives the message a different focus.

Teaching students about their rights to receive information in a library may have a profound impact on their lives; however, they do not need to be passive learners. KidsSPEAK, a website sponsored by nine national groups, including the American Booksellers Foundation for Free Expression, offers ideas on how students can use their First Amendment rights to protest attempts at censoring of library and curricular materials. KidsSPEAK suggestions include:

- Request permission to speak at an open school board hearing if the school board is considering restrictions on reading materials or Internet use.
- Write a letter to the editor of your local newspaper explaining your opposition to potential censorship in the school.
- Circulate a petition protesting the censorship action and stating your position.
- Form an informal group to increase your "voice."
- Contact adults and organizations who support First Amendment rights for minors, and ask for their assistance.[19]

In Chapter 6, library media specialist Cassandra Barnett discussed the support given by students during attempts to censor materials in the library media center collection at the school where she works. Cassandra adds, "The students were outraged that someone would deign to tell them what they could or couldn't read. They asked for the parent's [complainant's] list and checked out as many of the titles as they could. They organized a petition drive and gathered signatures, which they presented to the school board. They spoke passionately at the town meeting about the freedom to read."[20] As Cassandra learned, students can be enthusiastic allies and willing to support efforts to protect their First Amendment rights.

Advocacy Outside the School Community

Gaining the principal, teachers, and members of the school board as allies in advocating for students' First Amendment rights is vital, but there is another constituency whose support is also essential—parents and other members of the community.

Gaining Support from Parents and the Community

A community is composed of parents, extended families, and persons of all ages with widely varying points of view. Some may support the school's efforts to offer access to information in the school library media program collection, while others may feel all minors, and especially younger children, should be protected. Efforts by the school library media specialist to make the materials selection process a transparent one, and to educate parents, guardians, and other community members about the collection and the library media program, may engender latent support that will become active should a challenge occur. However, some individuals will always retain their protective attitudes toward children and young adults.

Catherine, an elementary school library media specialist in Wisconsin, works with the faculty, principal, and parents to promote access to information for her young students. Catherine reaches out to parents throughout the year and states,

> Our library Web page explains our selection policy to parents and community members. I produce a quarterly newsletter that includes information for families on the new materials in the LMC and how they are selected.... We open the library for family browsing and checkout during parent-teacher conferences. Last year we began Summer Book Checkout for students in grades one through four. Girls and boys could check out up to 20 books for the summer with parent permission. Almost 1,000 books went home with students, and most came back well read. Each child who returned their books received a free paperback of their choice.[21]

Catherine's outreach to parents provides benefits to the children, the school, and the library media program. The parents appreciate knowing how materials are selected and the new titles now available for circulation. The *openness* of the selection process instills confidence in Catherine's work as a school library media specialist. Catherine is also adding "coins" to the bank.

While there are frequent media accounts of parents who oppose and want to remove books from curricular reading lists and school library media program collections, there are also parents who support the right of their children to read widely. Sharon, the parent of a teenager in New York, stated,

> Growing up I was a voracious reader with parents who supported my love of reading and never questioned my reading material. As the mother of a high school student I have tried to give my daughter that same freedom; albeit it is a much different world from the one I grew up in. When thinking about intellectual freedom, the bookless world portrayed in Ray Bradbury's novel *Fahrenheit 451* always comes to my mind. I never want my daughter to be brainwashed by others to believe that evil lurks in books or to have her reading choices limited by individuals that endorse that idea. It is a scary thought that a handful of individuals can have a book removed from the school library. This suppression of information promotes the theme of *Fahrenheit 451*—that books contain bad and disturbing ideas.[22]

It is not only parents who are concerned with children's access to books and information in the school library media center. More children are being raised by grandparents, for example. With the greater generational gap, older relatives may have difficulty accepting the availability of *edgier* books such as those that use more contemporary language or include sex or sexuality. Being straightforward in the selection process and acknowledging that parents, grandparents, or guardians have the right to determine the reading of their children will go a long way toward allaying any concerns.

Larra Clark, former manager of media relations for the ALA, has a suggestion for preparing a message that will be understood by a wide audience, from those who may know the term *intellectual freedom* to those who do not. She states,

> I've found that talking about "choice" is more understandable than "intellectual freedom" for many people. How would you talk to parents about "intellectual freedom" and its importance? I would speak about the importance of providing a wide range of reading materials because everyone's interests are different and readers mature at different rates. Using examples and stories make the discussion real. For instance, when my mom told me I couldn't read *The Shining*, I started reading every other Stephen King book I could find. Many people—including parents—can remember moments like this. If you can talk about gay and lesbian parents in your community, or about the fact that Chris Crutcher often relates

stories similar to the stories he hears as a child and family therapist, this can make intellectual freedom more concrete. Of course, you also encourage parents to be involved in their children's reading. If they or their child end up with a book they don't think is appropriate, you're [school library media specialist] happy to help them find an alternative.[23]

The school library professional must devise strategies to reach out and educate parents, guardians, and the wider community about the importance of access to information in the library media program collection. Effective ideas include:

- Create a "Parent's Page" on the library media program website and post tips on how parents can help their children with homework.
- Write a regular column about the library media program in the school or district newsletter.
- Host tours or short programs in the library media center during parent/teacher conferences.
- Offer workshops on topics such as "Good Books for Young Readers" or safe use of the Internet.
- Develop a special collection of parenting resources.
- Make presentations to local organizations about the changing library media program.
- Solicit volunteers to assist in the library media program.[24]

These are ways to inform the community about the library media program and its importance in the education of children and young adults, including preparing them to take a role in the democratic process. Library media specialists should look at every contact with a parent or community member as an *opportunity to advocate* in some way for minors' right to read and access information.

The Public Library as Partner

In addition to the school library media center, students usually have another library that they may use during the summer, evenings, and weekends—the public library. Trained youth services and other staff at the public library provide reference assistance and programming for young children through teens. Collaboration between public and school libraries is well documented in library professional literature and often includes summer reading activities, homework centers, print and electronic resource sharing, a reserve system for easy access to materials used for school assignments, and access to expanded subscription databases.[25] In a time of uncertain funding for all types of libraries, sharing resources and collaborating makes practical sense.

There are a number of ways to collaborate with the public library to improve access and promote intellectual freedom for minors, such as:

- Get to know your professional staff counterparts—those youth and general librarians who work with students.

- Set up a method for regular communication including alerts about homework assignment topics.

- Schedule regular meetings to discuss events, opportunities for collaboration, and other topics.

- Place links on the school library media program's Web page to the public library catalog, databases, and youth blog or the public library's social networking site for young adults.

- Create virtual pathfinders to help students locate materials in each library.

- Provide summer reading lists from the school.

- Visit each other's libraries at least annually.[26]

School library media specialists and their youth services counterparts can work together on Freedom to Read or Banned Books Week activities. School library professionals may request that youth services librarians visit their schools for book talks, to promote the public library's summer reading program and to help students apply for public library cards. Sheila, a K-12 rural library media specialist in the Midwest, states, "We do activities in September to obtain cards from the public library for all our students. This year's promotion was 'Get Carded @ your library.' I also have staff sign up for 'School' cards [to borrow public library materials] that they can use for supplemental materials that are insufficient in our library. These cards don't accrue any late fees. The teachers love it."[27] Judy, a middle school library media specialist, states, "Our middle school does a large volume of interlibrary loans with our public library. We also take our students on a tour of the public library, and they do a fun activity like a scavenger hunt with the public library staff. This helps the students feel comfortable with that staff also."[28]

Other public and school library professionals cosponsor author visits, and plan whole community reading activities. Marcia, the sole school library media professional in a rural district in Wisconsin, states,

> Our high school is performing the play "Charlotte's Web" this spring. The public librarian and I have decided to do a community "READ" project together. We have purchased promotional posters, books, audiotapes, and Playaways [battery-operated audio content with player in a single unit], as well as multiples copies of

Charlotte's Web in English and Spanish. She also bought it on Overdrive [Web-based digital audiobooks and e-books] for download by public library patrons. We plan to immerse the community in CW [Charlotte's Web].

I will supply books for all K-8 classrooms to read aloud and will promote the story in all of its forms at the schools, as will the public librarian. I have two high school students designing "READ" logos in "webs," and our middle school art teacher will have her students make table tents promoting reading CW and the play. These will be distributed to all restaurants in town, as well as be displayed on all of the tables in the libraries. We'll also advertise in sports programs and church bulletins and will have posters throughout the town.

We have an event planned at the public library on a Tuesday from 5 to 6 PM the week before the play. Costumed student actors will act out a skit from the play, the public library will sell copies of the book, and actors will "autograph" them in character. At the event, we'll hand out web-shaped cookies made by the middle school family living students. We hope that this will be an annual event, each year immersing the community in a wonderful reading experience that is multicultural and multigenerational.[29]

The collaborative efforts of Sheila, Judy, and Marcia demonstrate advocacy both inside the school and within the community. They are sure to bring more families to the public library and promote greater awareness of the school library media program. *Every* collaborative activity is a step toward promoting more access to *each* library, and therefore greater access to information for their *shared* youthful patrons.

School and public library cooperation aimed at greater access for children and young adults is a worthy goal; however, there are staff and economic considerations. Kris Adams Wendt, a public library director in northern Wisconsin, states,

The two worlds of the public and school library are interdependent as well as symbiotic. When school libraries are operating without benefit of sufficient certified personnel and/or adequate resources to support curriculum, those students whose parents are willing to transport them to the nearest public library cannot help but place additional stress on that institution's staff and materials budget. Equally unfortunate is a situation where school library media specialists are compelled to fill gaps created by lack of local government support for public library services. In a troubled, competitive atmosphere where one or the other might be viewed as somewhat parasitic, school and public library colleagues may easily find themselves losing sight of mutual interests such as *intellectual freedom*.[30]

Unfortunately, not *every* child, preteen, or teen has access to a public library. As noted in Chapter 4, some families must drive many miles to use a library, often one that is open a limited number of hours per week and has a small collection. Even if public libraries are viable in a large urban setting, minors may not have transportation to the library. These situations make advocacy for *access* to the resources of school library media centers and public libraries even more important. Despite the obstacles, school library media specialists and their public library counterparts can improve access to information through collaboration, support each other during challenges, and be a part of encouraging lifelong learning for their youthful patrons.

Professional Support

There are national, state, and local groups that oppose censorship and support intellectual freedom in libraries. They include the ALA, the American Civil Liberties Union (ACLU), and the National Coalition Against Censorship (NCAC), among others. (An annotated list of national pro–First Amendment organizations is located in Appendix B.) School library professionals, who have a vested interest in intellectual freedom and First Amendment issues, will benefit greatly by becoming a member of one or more of these organizations, especially the American Library Association (ALA). It is a step that will pay dividends in numerous ways. The funds from association dues are used to fight censorship; and as school library professionals are well aware, K-12 curricular reading lists and resources in library media collections are the most frequently challenged.

Former AASL President Sara Kelly Johns said, "As a new school librarian, it didn't take very long for me to realize that, if I ever became involved in a serious book challenge, one of the first places I would call for assistance would be the ALA Office for Intellectual Freedom. That connection led me to not even question becoming a member of ALA when Jim Bennett, a long-time ALA Councilor, put a membership form in my hand and said, 'Fill it out, and send it in. It's your professional duty.'"[31] Sara's voice, and that of the thousands of other ALA members, help keep advocacy for intellectual freedom strong for all library patrons.

The American Library Association (ALA)

The ALA is the oldest and largest library association in the world, and it has supported the principles of intellectual freedom for patrons using libraries, including youth in schools and public libraries, for over a hundred years. Its organizational efforts have striven to defend First Amendment rights, privacy, and the right to read for library patrons of all ages; and they have been largely successful. ALA's best-known pro-intellectual freedom documents include the *Library Bill of Rights*, the *Code of Ethics of the American Library Association*, and the *Freedom to Read*; and access, intellectual freedom, and privacy are three of the Association's core values. Within the association, the Intellectual Freedom Round Table offers members an opportunity to be part of the intellectual freedom community's discussion and education process. The library community owes much to the staff and member volunteers who continue to advocate for intellectual freedom at the national level year after year.

The ALA Office for Intellectual Freedom

The Association's advocacy and protection efforts center in the ALA's Office for Intellectual Freedom (OIF), which is charged with "implementing ALA policies concerning the concept of intellectual freedom ..."[32] For over 40 years, one of its priorities has been to support both members and non-members of the Association facing challenges. OIF staff provide assistance with actual and potential challenges to books, magazines, and other library resources.

The OIF website has a wealth of information ranging from developing a material selection policy to dealing with the media to intellectual freedom toolkits on such topics as privacy, the Internet, and dealing with challenges to gay, lesbian, bisexual, and transgender resources. With assistance from the ALA Intellectual Freedom Committee, OIF staff publish *The Intellectual Freedom Manual*, the definitive guide to intellectual freedom for all types of libraries. In terms of electronic communications, the OIF staff publishes a blog; maintains the Intellectual Freedom Action News (IFACTION), a news-only electronic list with media reports relating to intellectual freedom; and manages IFFORUM, an unmoderated discussion list.

For over 25 years, the Office for Intellectual Freedom (OIF) has led annual efforts to celebrate Banned Books Week in the fourth week of September. The OIF supports Banned Books Week by such actions as:

- Selecting an annual theme and making posters and other promotional materials available,
- Providing an annual list of the top 10 most challenged books,
- Contributing to new editions of *The Banned Books Resource Guide*, and
- Maintaining a lengthy list of suggested activities on its website.

The ALA Washington Office

The ALA Washington Office was established in 1945 and is charged with "tracking and influencing policy issues, legislation, and regulations of importance to the library field and the public."[33] This office monitors current federal legislation that impacts school library media programs and minors' access to information, seeking to influence, for example, overly restrictive legislation related to use of the Internet. Its website contains information related to current legislative issues. The staff produces the "District Dispatch" blog and maintains the ALA Washington Office Newsline (ALAWON), an email publication to keep members up-to-date on legislation affecting libraries. The office is another part of ALA's strategy to protect the intellectual freedom rights of library patrons, including youth.

The American Association of School Librarians

The American Association of School Librarians (AASL) is a division of the ALA. AASL staff do not provide individual support in case of censorship; instead, requests for assistance with challenges are forwarded to the ALA Office for Intellectual Freedom. AASL does, however, provide intellectual freedom resources such as downloadable brochures and electronic Resource Guides on the topics of censorship, filtering, ethics, and privacy.

The AASL Intellectual Freedom Committee has the following responsibilities:

- "Gather, prepare and make available materials advising school library media specialists of available services and support (1) in formulating Intellectual Freedom policies and (2) for resisting local pressure and community action designed to impair the rights of others.
- Work with the ALA Intellectual Freedom Office and with the Freedom to Read Foundation in gathering information as requested and responding to issues and concerns."[34]

AASL's Intellectual Freedom Committee collaborates with the intellectual freedom committees of the Association for Library Service to Children (ALSC) and the Young Adult Library Services Association (YALSA) to plan a program for the ALA Annual Conference focusing on those issues affecting the intellectual freedom of children and youth. Sessions and workshops on topics related to intellectual freedom are also held at the biennial AASL national conferences.

While not developed for this purpose, a school library professional may use AASL's "Advocacy Toolkit" to develop an Intellectual Freedom Advocacy Plan. A formal, written advocacy plan should: (1) identify the "target audience" and its agenda, (2) link the library media program's intellectual freedom message to the targeted group's agenda, and (3) determine how the message can be delivered effectively. Creating an advocacy plan is one of the first steps in promoting intellectual freedom and access to resources, services, and library media center facilities.[35]

The Freedom to Read Foundation

The Freedom to Read Foundation (FTRF) was established in 1969 and serves as the "First Amendment legal defense arm of the American Library Association."[36] Throughout its history, the FTRF has joined legal battles to protect the First Amendment rights of library patrons including those of minors in *Board of Education, Island Trees Union Free School District v. Pico* (1982) and *Counts v. Cedarville School District* (2003).[37] The FTRF publishes the quarterly *Freedom to Read Foundation News.* Membership in the FTRF supports the legal fight against censorship and advocates for maintaining the rights of citizens of all ages to use a library freely.

John W. Berry, former president of the Freedom to Read Foundation Board of Trustees, 2005–2007, states,

> The Freedom to Read Foundation's mantra is "free people read freely." FTRF is carefully watching the status of several cases affecting young people, many dealing with state legislation seeking to ban "violent video games." To date, several states have passed such legislation, and in each case, the laws have been challenged by First Amendment and industry groups. In every case, district courts have found the legislation unconstitutional. Groups like the Youth Free Expression Network, consisting of teens and adults, are raising awareness of free speech issues involving young people. It is our hope that they will join with us in protecting speech and thought.[38]

Walking the Talk

Becky, a middle school/high school librarian in the state of New York, described how she sees advocacy for students' intellectual freedom in the library media program, "It is a balancing act. We must provide our students with the information they need, educate administrators about access and intellectual freedom, and acknowledge parents concerns/rights in regard to their children."[39] Becky recognizes that there is no easy path to gathering allies to support minors' rights in school library media programs. She rightly characterizes the actions of school library professionals as "a balancing act." Yet there is no choice for the school library professional except to step forward as a leader. There is work to be done. A wide range of materials must be selected, the rights of children and young adults to read must be protected, library records must be kept confidential, access to legal resources on the Internet must be defended, and the rights of students with disabilities to use the school library media center and its resources must be championed. The First Amendment speech rights of minors to use all types of library materials must be secured. If not you—the school library media professional—then who? Our nation's students are counting on you.

✍ Key Ideas Summary

This chapter described a range of advocacy strategies and activities that can be used by school library professionals to promote access to information and intellectual freedom for minors in school library media programs. Some of the major ideas include the following:

- The school library media specialist needs to be informed and stay alert to the "climate" of intellectual freedom issues at the local, state, and national levels.

Continued

- The school library professional will use many different strategies to help inform administrators, teachers, and school board members about intellectual freedom and minors' First Amendment rights to access information in the school library media center.

- As tomorrow's adult citizens, K-12 students must be taught about their First Amendment rights and the antithesis to intellectual freedom—censorship.

- The library media specialist must reach out to parents, guardians, grandparents, and community members to inform them about the cause-and-effect relationship between access to information in school library media program collections and developing informed citizens.

- School library professionals and public library staff can collaborate to promote intellectual freedom and access to information for minors.

- The American Library Association and its Office for Intellectual Freedom and Washington Office have consistently protected and advocated for intellectual freedom and access to information for minors.

- Banned Books Week celebrations are a very visible way to bring attention to the hundreds of books that have been challenged or banned and to promote the right to read.

- The American Association of School Librarians provides resources and professional development opportunities to support the continuing education of school library media specialists.

- The Freedom to Read Foundation protects the First Amendment rights of library patrons through the U.S. legal system.

- Pro–First Amendment organizations, such as the ACLU, support the efforts of all types of libraries to combat censorship.

Library Bill of Rights Interpretations

- American Library Association. "Access to Resources and Services in the School Library Media Program: An Interpretation of the *Library Bill of Rights*"

- American Library Association. "Free Access to Libraries for Minors: An Interpretation of the *Library Bill of Rights*"

- American Library Association. "Restricted Access to Library Materials: An Interpretation of the *Library Bill of Rights*"

All ALA *Library Bill of Rights* Interpretations are available on the ALA Office for Intellectual Freedom website: http://www.ala.org/oif.

Recommended Resources

- **American Association of School Librarians, "AASL Advocacy Toolkit"** http://www.ala.org/ala/aasl/aaslproftools/toolkits/aasladvocacy.htm

In addition to the lengthy list of advocacy websites, the Advocacy Action Plan template can be adapted to prepare a local plan for promoting intellectual freedom.

- **"Banned Books Week," American Library Association,** http://www.ala.org/ala/oif/bannedbooksweek/bannedbooksweek.htm

    Includes information for the annual celebration, top challenged books and authors, dealing with challenges, and more.

- **First Amendment Center**, http://www.firstamendmentcenter.org

    This comprehensive website includes information on the five freedoms protected under the First Amendment: speech, press, religious liberty, assembly, and petition. Its content will be useful for high school library media specialists, teachers, and students.

- **First Amendment Schools**, http://www.firstamendmentschools.org

    The website supports the national school reform initiative designed to help schools teach and practice the civic principles and virtues vital to democracy, freedom, and the common good. Website resources include detailed lesson plans on the First Amendment right of free speech and summaries of court cases relating to the First Amendment.

- **Illinois First Amendment Center**, http://www.illinoisfirstamendmentcenter.com

    Teachers and school library media specialists will benefit from the resources designed to support instruction on First Amendment free speech including lesson plans, resources for school projects, curriculum guides, and other promotional materials

- **Intellectual Freedom Committee of the New York Library Association, "Intellectual Freedom Checklist"** from the New York Library Association's Intellectual Freedom Manual, 2002, revised 2003. http://www.nyla.org/index.php?page_id=443

    This checklist will assist library media specialists in determining their level of preparedness to protect the First Amendment rights of minors.

- **"Real Ideas from the Trenches," New York Library Association, School Library Media Section**, http://www.nyla.org/content/user_19/real%20ideas.pdf

    This short booklet describes successful advocacy ideas practiced by New York school library media specialists that can be adapted for educating others about intellectual freedom.

Notes

1. McDonald, Frances Beck, *Censorship and Intellectual Freedom: A Survey of School Librarians' Attitudes and Moral Reasoning* (Metuchen, NJ: Scarecrow Press, Inc., 1993), xv.

2. "Advocacy," American Association of School Librarians, http://www.ala.org/ala/aasl/aaslissues/aasladvocacy/definitions.htm.

3. American Library Association, Office for Intellectual Freedom, "What You Can Do to Oppose Censorship," http://www.ala.org/ala/oif/basics/whatcandooposecensorship.htm.

4. American Library Association, Article II, *Code of Ethics of the American Library Association*, http://www.ala.org/ala/oif/statementspols/codeofethics/codeethics.htm.

5. Gibson, Jeffrey, "Championing Intellectual Freedom," *Knowledge Quest* 36, no. 2 (November/December 2007), 47.

6. Fran, Roscello, interview by author, Washington, D.C., June 23, 2007.

7. Doyle, Robert P., *Banned Books: 2007 Resource Guide* (Chicago: American Library Association, 2007), 182–186.

8. Marcia, email to author, January 25, 2008.

9. Catherine, email to author, April 4, 2007.

10. Krystal, email to author, February 19, 2007.

11. American Library Association and the Association of American Publishers. *The Right to Read,* http://www.ala.org/ala/oif/statementspols/ftrstatement/freedom-readstatement.htm.

12. American Association of School Librarians, "Standards for the 21st-Century Learner, Common Beliefs" (Chicago: American Library Association, 2007), 2–3.

13. Ibid, 5.

14. Lisa, email to author, October 14, 2007.

15. Marcia, January 25, 2008.

16. Youse, Cheryl, "Banned Books: Engaging Students and Teachers," *KQWeb* (November/December 2007), http://www.ala.org/ala/aasl/aaslpubsandjournals/kqweb/kqarchives/volume36/362/362_Youse.cfm.

17. "Banned Books Week in Wisconsin," compiled by Ginny Moore Kruse, September 17, 2006.

18. Anonymous, email message to author, January 24, 2008.

19. kidsSPEAK!, "What Can I Do?," http://www.kidspeakonline.org/whatcanido.html.

20. Adams, Helen R., "What I Learned: An Interview with Cassandra Barnett," *Knowledge Quest* 36, no. 2 (November/December 2007), 19.

21. Catherine, April 7, 2007.

22. Sharon, email to author, February 8, 2007.

23. Clark, Larra, email interview with author, April 13, 2007.

24. American Association of School Librarians, *Toolkit for School Library Media Programs.* "Reaching Out: Parents & Caregivers and Community" (Chicago: American Library Association, 2003), 13.

25. Rowland, Martha, "Partnerships Means Active Participation," *CSLA Journal* 30, no. 2 (Spring 2007), 4.

26. MacDonald, Cynthia, "Public Libraries + School Libraries = Smart Partnerships," *CSLA Journal* 30, no. 2 (Spring 2007), 11–12.

27. Sheila, WEMTA list: Cooperation with Your Public Library? February 8, 2008.

28. Judy, email to author, March 10, 2008.

29. Marcia, email to author, February 8, 2008.

30. Wendt, Kris Adams, email to author, February 8, 2008.

31. Johns, Sara Kelly, February 18, 2007.

32. American Library Association, *ALA Handbook of Organization 2007–2008* (Chicago: American Library Association, 2007), 5.

33. American Library Association, *ALA Handbook of Organization 2007–2008,* 6.

34. American Association of School Librarians, "Intellectual Freedom Committee," http://www.ala.org/ala/aasl/aboutaasl/aaslgovernance/aaslcommittees/intelfreedom.cfm.

35. American Association of School Librarians, "AASL Advocacy Toolkit, Advocacy Action Plan," http://www.ala.org/ala/aasl/aaslproftools/toolkits/aasladvocacy.cfm.

36. Freedom to Read Foundation, "Free People Read Freely" [brochure], http://www.ala.org/ala/ourassociation/othergroups/ftrf/ftrforg/joinftrf/ftrforgmemberbrochure.pdf.

37. Ibid.

38. Berry, John W., email to author, February 21, 2007.

39. Becky, email to author, April 20, 2007.

Core Intellectual Freedom Documents from the American Library Association

Library Bill of Rights

The American Library Association affirms that all libraries are forums for information and ideas, and that the following basic policies should guide their services.

I. Books and other library resources should be provided for the interest, information, and enlightenment of all people of the community the library serves. Materials should not be excluded because of the origin, background, or views of those contributing to their creation.

II. Libraries should provide materials and information presenting all points of view on current and historical issues. Materials should not be proscribed or removed because of partisan or doctrinal disapproval.

III. Libraries should challenge censorship in the fulfillment of their responsibility to provide information and enlightenment.

IV. Libraries should cooperate with all persons and groups concerned with resisting abridgment of free expression and free access to ideas.

V. A person's right to use a library should not be denied or abridged because of origin, age, background, or views.

VI. Libraries which make exhibit spaces and meeting rooms available to the public they serve should make such facilities available on an equitable basis, regardless of the beliefs or affiliations of individuals or groups requesting their use.

Adopted June 18, 1948, by the ALA Council; amended February 2, 1961; amended June 27, 1967; amended January 23, 1980; inclusion of "age" reaffirmed January 24, 1996.

Reprinted with permission from the Office for Intellectual Freedom, the American Library Association.

Code of Ethics of the American Library Association

As members of the American Library Association, we recognize the importance of codifying and making known to the profession and to the general public the ethical principles that guide the work of librarians, other professionals providing information services, library trustees and library staffs.

Ethical dilemmas occur when values are in conflict. The American Library Association Code of Ethics states the values to which we are committed, and embodies the ethical responsibilities of the profession in this changing information environment.

We significantly influence or control the selection, organization, preservation, and dissemination of information. In a political system grounded in an informed citizenry, we are members of a profession explicitly committed to intellectual freedom and the freedom of access to information. We have a special obligation to ensure the free flow of information and ideas to present and future generations.

The principles of this Code are expressed in broad statements to guide ethical decision making. These statements provide a framework; they cannot and do not dictate conduct to cover particular situations.

I. We provide the highest level of service to all library users through appropriate and usefully organized resources; equitable service policies; equitable access; and accurate, unbiased, and courteous responses to all requests.

II. We uphold the principles of intellectual freedom and resist all efforts to censor library resources.

III. We protect each library user's right to privacy and confidentiality with respect to information sought or received and resources consulted, borrowed, acquired or transmitted.

IV. We respect intellectual property rights and advocate balance between the interests of information users and rights holders.

V. We treat co-workers and other colleagues with respect, fairness and good faith, and advocate conditions of employment that safeguard the rights and welfare of all employees of our institutions.

VI. We do not advance private interests at the expense of library users, colleagues, or our employing institutions.

VII. We distinguish between our personal convictions and professional duties and do not allow our personal beliefs to interfere with fair representation of the aims of our institutions or the provision of access to their information resources.

VIII. We strive for excellence in the profession by maintaining and enhancing our own knowledge and skills, by encouraging the professional development of co-workers, and by fostering the aspirations of potential members of the profession.

Adopted June 28, 1995, by the ALA Council; Amended January 22, 2008.

Reprinted with permission from the Office for Intellectual Freedom, the American Library Association.

APPENDIX B

Pro–First Amendment Organizations

American Library Association Office of Intellectual Freedom (OIF)
http://www.ala.org/oif
800-545-2433, ext. 4223

The ALA Office for Intellectual Freedom (OIF) staff provides assistance with actual and possible challenges to books, magazines, other library resources, and Internet access. The OIF website also has a wealth of information ranging from developing a material selection policy to dealing with the media to intellectual freedom toolkits on such topics as privacy, the Internet, and dealing with challenges to gay, lesbian, bisexual, and transgendered resources.

American Booksellers Foundation for Freedom of Expression (ABFFE)
www.abffe.com and www.kidspeakonline.org
212-587-4025

ABFFE was founded by the American Booksellers Association to be the booksellers' voice in fighting censorship. The association opposes restrictions on free speech, collaborates with other organizations to promote intellectual freedom concepts, supports Banned Books Week activities, and participates in legal challenges involving First Amendment rights. ABFFE supports KidsSPEAK, an effort to give minors an opportunity to participate in efforts against censorship.

American Civil Liberties Union (ACLU)
www.aclu.org
212-549-2500

The ACLU is a nonprofit and nonpartisan organization with more than 500,000 members and supporters.[1] One aspect of the ACLU's mission is to preserve First Amendment rights including freedom of speech. While involved in battles to protect all types of civil liberties, the ACLU brings legal challenges in cases curtailing First Amendment protected speech in the nation's libraries, including cases relating to book challenges. The ACLU has affiliate organizations in all 50 states, and they provide legal assistance and lobby state legislatures.

Freedom to Read Foundation (FTRF)

http://www.ftrf.org

800-545-2433, ext. 4226

Using the tag line, "Free People Read Freely," the FTRF serves as the "First Amendment legal defense arm of the American Library Association."[2] Throughout its history, the FTRF has joined legal battles to protect the First Amendment rights of library patrons including those of minors in such cases as *Board of Education, Island Trees Union Free School District v. Pico* (1982) and *Counts v. Cedarville School District* (2003).[3] The FTRF offers "legal and financial help in cases involving libraries and librarians ..."[4]

International Reading Association (IRA)

www.reading.org

800-336-7323 or 302-731-1600

The IRA is a professional association for those who teach reading, and it supports developing a lifelong reading habit. The association has approved "Providing Books and Other Print Materials for Classroom and School Libraries," a position statement supporting the funding of school library media center collections and calling for research into access for children to books at home.[5]

National Coalition Against Censorship (NCAC)

www.ncac.org

212-807-6222

The NCAC is "an alliance of 50 national non-profit organizations, including literary, artistic, religious, educational, professional, labor, and civil liberties groups"[6] who promote and support the First Amendment by educating the public about censorship and how to oppose it. It provides an online "Book Censorship Toolkit" to obtain assistance with book challenges in schools and contact information for speaking to NCAC about a challenge.

National Council of Teachers of English (NCTE)

www.ncte.org

800-369-6238 (Ext. 3634) or 217-278-3634

The NCTE is a professional organization for those who teach English and language arts at all levels, elementary through college. Its Anti-Censorship Center provides useful resources online, including "Students Right to Read," which gives procedures for responding to challenges. The Center also "offers advice ... and other support at no cost to teachers faced with challenges to literary works, films and videos, drama productions, or teaching methods."[7]

Notes

1. American Civil Liberties Union, "About Us," http://aclu.org/about/index.html.

2. Freedom to Read Foundation, "Free People Read Freely" [brochure], http://www.ala.org/ala/ourassociation/othergroups/ftrf/ftrforg/joinftrf/ftrforgmember brochure.pdf.

3. Ibid.

4. Ibid.

5. International Reading Association, "Providing Books and Other Print Materials for Classrooms and School Libraries" (September 1999), http://www.reading.org/resources/issues/positions_libraries.html.

6. National Coalition Against Censorship, "About NCAC," http://www.ncac.org/about/about.cfm.

7. National Council of Teachers of English, "Censorship Challenges—What to Do?", http://www.ncte.org/about/issues/censorship?source=gs.

Three Authors Speak about Censorship

Authors Katherine Paterson, Suzanne Fisher Staples, and Harry Mazer provide a glimpse into the creative process involved in writing fiction published for children and teenagers. No doubt many authors and artists of books for young readers have had to think about censorship, whether or not it is an awareness of self-censorship, limitations imposed by one's editor or publisher, or later responses to published works. In addition, some authors and artists have had reason to comment on the topic of *censorship*.

Harry Mazer, author of many young adult novels, including *I Love You, Stupid!* and a recent trilogy of World War II young adult novels: *A Boy at War: A Novel of Pearl Harbor, A Boy No More,* and *Heroes Don't Run,* shares, "I struggle each day not to let the fear of the censor poison my writing."[1] Mazer is also concerned with "closet censorship," wondering "Where have my books been quietly removed from school shelves without any voices raised in protest? Where has a librarian or teacher chosen not to order my books rather than risk arousing the censor?"[2]

Suzanne Fisher Staples, author of the Newbery Honor Book *Shabanu: Daughter of the Wind,* says,

> I have always been careful that what I write reflects as closely as possible the realities of life for people in Pakistan. That people take offense at those realities reflects their limited views. People in Pakistan who don't like the fact that I've chosen to write about camel herders can't possibly deny that these people exist, or that their lives are as I portray them. People in this country who don't like that I've written about those who afford women limited choices also can't deny that what I've written reflects reality.
>
> I would never leave out a scene because someone might object to it. I am a careful researcher and writer, and if a scene is necessary to the story I will include it. That's not to say I'm unaffected by these comments, which are made publicly.

They sting. Most often I have no way to respond to them. But I believe it's very important for people to know truths to which they might not otherwise have access.[3]

Katherine Paterson, Newbery Medal author of *Bridge to Terabithia* and *Jacob Have I Loved,* spoke about misconceptions about her characters' language and actions and why she cannot write "nicer" books in a speech delivered at an AASL President's Program on intellectual freedom in June 2002:

"One Sunday, an elderly friend approached me at coffee hour after church service. 'I'm so sorry,' she said, 'to hear about your troubles.' I racked my brain. My memory is bad and getting worse all the time, but surely I wouldn't have forgotten if my husband had lost his job or if there'd been a death in the family. She came to my rescue. 'I read the article in the newspaper last week,' she said."

"In anticipation of Banned Books Week, someone had called me from the local newspaper and said they were planning an article about the efforts all over the country to ban books and would I consent to be interviewed? I agreed. In the meantime, I did a book signing for my new book at a bookstore in Montpelier. So when the article appeared, it was topped with a full color picture of me four columns wide and 7 and $\frac{1}{2}$ inches high with large headlines which read: LOCAL AUTHOR'S ACCLAIMED CHILDREN'S BOOKS FACE PARENTAL PRESSURE, SCHOOL CHALLENGES. Then the paper in a neighboring town picked up the article, changing the headline. Now over the large picture of me in my bright red suit was the headline: 'DOES THIS WOMAN TEACH SATANISM?' And me a mild-mannered minister's wife!"

"I tried to explain to my dear friend at church that it was not I who was in so much trouble but the brave people who were defending my books. *'But couldn't you just make the books nicer so they wouldn't offend anybody?'* she asked earnestly...." [emphasis added]

"One day when I was speaking in a school in Vermont an earnest little boy raised his hand. 'When are you going to write a Christian book?' he asked."

"'Well,' I said. 'I am a Christian and I hope that all my books are Christian, but I don't think that's what you're asking me. I think you want to know when I'm going to write a book in which no one cusses and everyone behaves themselves.'"

"He nodded solemnly."

"'I'm sorry,' I said. 'But it probably won't happen. I think my job is to tell a story as truthfully as I can, and one person's truth is always going to offend somebody.'"

"'Couldn't you just make it nicer so that it wouldn't offend anybody?' my friend at church had asked? 'No,' I answer, not without a bit of sadness. Not if I am seeking to be true to my characters, true to the story I am trying to tell. [In *Bridge to Terabithia*] Jesse Aaron punctuates his speech with the word 'Lord,' and other words that I do not personally use or approve of because he is a little boy growing up in that part of the world who speaks as the people he lives among speak. If I made him into an example of appropriate speech and exemplary behavior, readers would not believe in him the way they obviously do."[4]

It is apparent from the comments of Harry Mazer, Suzanne Fisher Staples, and Katherine Paterson that authors recognize the possibility of censorship of their books whatever the context. Just like school library professionals striving to uphold the principles of intellectual freedom, writers can only be true to their characters and do their best.

Notes

1. Blume, Judy, ed. *Places I Never Meant to Be: Original Stories by Censored Writers* (New York: Simon & Schuster, 1999), 96.

2. Ibid, 97.

3. Staples, Suzanne Fisher, email interview with author, August 17, 2007.

4. Paterson, Katherine, "Tales of a Reluctant Dragon" (speech, AASL President's Program, Atlanta, Georgia, June 15, 2002).

APPENDIX D

Right to Read Lesson Plans

Ronda Hassig, a middle school library media specialist in the Blue Valley School District in Kansas, annually plans and cooperatively teaches a unit with social studies and language arts teachers about the right to read. Her lesson plan, tailored for 6th, 7th, and 8th grade students, requires two days during Communication Arts or Social Studies classes.

Patty Kearnes, a high school English teacher and preservice library media specialist in Wyoming, designed a one-day lesson to teach students about the many books that have been challenged or banned in the United States. It is generally taught during Banned Books Week in September and can be used with 8th through 12th graders.

Kristine Brown, a high school library media specialist, and Elizabeth Kara Glaaser, an English 11 instructor, team up annually to provide their students in Madison, Wisconsin, with an opportunity to research and then portray a mock school board hearing on whether a book should be banned. This lesson, taught at any time during the school year, includes a variety of activities for 11th grade students and can take up to 20 days.

The Right to Read Week Lesson Plan

Title of Unit: "The Right to Read"

Curriculum (Subject Area) Objectives:

To instill in 6th to 8th grade students the importance of their First Amendment rights of free speech and their freedom of choice when choosing a book from the library.

AASL Standards for the 21st Century Learner (2007)

Learners Use Skills, Resources and Tools to:

STANDARD 1: Inquire, Think Critically, and Gain Knowledge

(Skills: 1.1.2, 1.1.6, 1.1.7, 1.1.9)

STANDARD 2: Draw Conclusions, Make Informed Decisions, Apply Knowledge to New Situations, and Create New Knowledge

(Skills: 2.1.1, 2.1.3, 2.1.4, 2.1.5, 2.1.6)

STANDARD 3: Share Knowledge and Participate Ethically and Productively as Members of Our Democratic Society

(Skills: 3.1.1, 3.1.2, 3.1.3, 3.1.5)

STANDARD 4: Pursue Personal and Aesthetic Growth

(Skills: 4.1.1, 4.1.3, 4.1.5, 4.1.7)

Source: American Association of School Librarians, "Standards for the 21st Century Learner, 2007." The standards are available for download at the AASL website.

Grade Level for Activity: 6th, 7th, and 8th grades

Time Required for Activities: One week, most activities completed in two days

Resources:

The Giving Tree by Shel Silverstein

In the Night Kitchen by Maurice Sendak

Where the Sidewalk Ends by Shel Silverstein

Sylvester and the Magic Pebble by William Steig

The Amazing Bone by William Steig

Father Christmas by Raymond Briggs

Captain Underpants and the Invasion of the Incredibly Naughty Cafeteria Ladies from Outer Space by Dav Pilkey

The Lorax by Dr. Seuss

The Story of Ferdinand by Munro Leaf

Websites:

ALA 10 Most Challenged Books annual list (http://www.ala.org/oif)

KidsSpeak, "What's Your Censorship IQ?" (http://www.kidspeakonline.org/iq.html)

Videos:

The Day They Came to Arrest the Book, a 45-minute video based on the novel by Nat Hentoff

Fahrenheit 451, a 113-minute video based on the novel by Ray Bradbury.

Document: The First Amendment

Posters: First Amendment posters depicting freedom of speech, press, assembly and religion

Instructional Roles: The activities listed are done in conjunction with the core social studies and communications arts teachers with content presented by the library media specialist and invited guests.

Activities: 6th Grade

Communication Arts—Day 1

- Discuss the terms *challenge, censor, ban,* and *retain* and three reasons books get challenged, i.e., profanity, sex, and racism.
- Read *The Giving Tree* by Shel Silverstein. Ask students to guess why it was challenged.

Social Studies—Day 2

- Display and analyze the First Amendment using a graphic organizer (Fig. D-1).
- Students take the "What's Your Censorship IQ?" online quiz with discussion to follow. (http://www.kidspeakonline.org/iq.html)

Activities: 7th Grade

Communication Arts—Day 1

- Review the First Amendment and the terms *challenge, censor, ban,* and *retain.* Discuss reasons for holding a local "Right to Read Week." Read aloud the ALA's list of "10 Most Challenged Books" for the past year.
- Divide students into seven small groups. Assign each group a children's book that has been challenged, censored, or banned. As a group, the students will skim the book and report back to the whole group the name of book, author, and their inferred reason for the complainant's concern. The library media specialist will read the official reason the book appears on the ALA 10 Most Challenged Books annual list. The books are listed above.

Communication Arts—Day 2

- Explain that yesterday students dealt with children's books that have been challenged, and today they are going to view a 45-minute video, *The Day They Came to Arrest the Book*, about a challenge to *Huckleberry Finn*, a book with more mature concepts for middle and high school students. It is important to introduce students to the film because of the word "nigger." Prepare students for hearing it and discussing the film without using the derogatory term. After viewing, students discuss the film with the teacher and the library media specialist.

Activities: 8th Grade

Social Studies and Communication Arts
(combined class for 2 hours)—Day 1

- The 8th grade activity lasts 2–4 hours depending on time available. Students are divided into two groups. One group will hear an attorney discuss the First Amendment. Note: Select a lawyer who will engage students and help them to focus on the true meaning of the First Amendment and its freedoms.

- The other group is divided into three small groups, and they rotate through three 15-minute activities.

  1. The public library's young adult librarian speaks about the *Library Bill of Rights* and how the public library handles challenges.

  2. The vice-principal or principal addresses difficult questions about the First Amendment, such as "Who should have First Amendment Rights?" and "How large can an antiwar sign be in your yard and not be protected under the First Amendment?"

  3. The library media specialist discusses the First Amendment—its intent, its denial, and its abuse. Use posters that show pictures of the intent, denial, and abuse of four of the five rights guaranteed under the First Amendment. Have students fill out a graphic organizer, "First Amendment Analysis" [located at end of lesson plan], and talk about freedom of speech, press, assembly and religion.

- After 45 minutes, the two groups switch so when the 2 hours are over all students have attended the four sessions.

Social Studies and Communication Arts
(combined class for 2 hours)—Day 2

- Students view the film *Fahrenheit 451* with follow-up discussion led by the teachers and the school library media specialist.

Evaluation

Students complete a written reflection.

Follow-up

The "Right to Read" Week lessons are presented with varying activities for students in all three years annually for middle school students at Harmony Middle School. There are displays in the library media center that coincide with the national Banned Books Week theme.

Lesson Plan Created by

Ronda Hassig, National Board Certified Teacher and Kansas Master Teacher, 2008

Library Media Specialist, Harmony Middle School

Blue Valley School District

Overland Park, Kansas

First Amendment Analysis Graphic Organizer

<u>Vocabulary</u>

amendment – a change or revision

establishment – a settled arrangement or state of being

prohibiting – to stop or prevent

petition – a formal request or complaint

redress – to set right or make a wrong right again

grievance – a wrong or injustice

Analyze the document on the reverse side. Answer the questions directly on this sheet or on the document as asked.

What do you see on this document?

Are there words?   How many?
Is there a particular font used? Explain.
When this document was originally written how was it done?
By hand or by machine? Explain.

Are there any aspects of this document that are different or stick out at you like the words or letters? *Circle them.*

Are there any words you don't know? Put a square around the words you don't know. Then look left at the definitions.

Where do you think this document was written? Explain.

When do you think it was written? Explain.

Within the document there are five (5) rights guaranteed. <u>Underline them.</u>

Highlight the rights you think deal with the right to read.

Most important, why would this document have been written?

Figure D-1. First Amendment Analysis. (Reprinted with permission from Ronda Hassig.)

Banned Books Week Activity Lesson Plan

Title of Activity: "Stand Up for Books"

Curriculum (Subject Area) Objectives

To help students understand the complexities of censorship in terms of banned or challenged books and how their freedom to read needs to be protected.

AASL Standards for the 21st Century Learner (2007)

Learners Use Skills, Resources and Tools to:

STANDARD 1: Inquire, Think Critically, and Gain Knowledge

(Skills: 1.1.5, 1.1.7)

STANDARD 2: Draw Conclusions, Make Informed Decisions, Apply Knowledge to New Situations, and Create New Knowledge

(Skills: 2.1.3)

STANDARD 3: Share Knowledge and Participate Ethically and Productively As Members of Our Democratic Society

(Skills: 3.1.2, 3.1.5)

STANDARD 4: Pursue Personal and Aesthetic Growth

(Skills: 4.1.1, 4.1.2, 4.1.4, 4.1.5)

Source: American Association of School Librarians, "Standards for the 21st Century Learner, 2007." The standards are available for download at the AASL website.

Grade Level for Activity: 8th grade through high school, although modifications can be made for a younger audience

Time Required for Activity: One class period of 40–50 minutes

Instructional Role: May be presented in a classroom by a teacher or in the media center by a library media specialist

Resources:

Familiarize yourself with the current list of ALA banned books (http://www.ala.org/oif) and those authors and titles that have been challenged and/or banned in the past. You will also need to be familiar with the titles students have read or the authors that students enjoy in order to complete this activity. If you are not acquainted with young adult literature, seek advice from the school library media specialist. Display the poster "Censorship Causes Blindness," which is available from Random

House. Source: http://www.randomhouse.com/teens/firstamendment/ resources.html. The teacher may also have a prepared list of frequently banned/challenged titles that could be distributed to students at the conclusion of the lesson.

Activities:

1. On the first day of Banned Books Week, the teacher begins the class period by asking if anyone in the class has read *The Giver* by Lois Lowry or another title that the instructor knows many students have read. Students may not know authors' names, so it is always best to be prepared with specific titles for students. If students have read the title mentioned, have them stand up and continue to name titles/authors until all the students are standing.

2. Initiate a discussion with students on the common factor(s) that the titles/ authors share.

3. After some discussion, ask students how they would feel if they were not allowed to read a title because "somebody" decided it was not appropriate for them to read. This is a natural bridge to a discussion on censorship. This is also a perfect opportunity to discuss what to do if a student begins to read a book that is not appropriate for them or makes them feel uncomfortable: Return it to the library, and select another book.

4. Emphasize the importance of choice in selecting reading materials, and how it is everyone's duty in a democratic society to protect the right to read freely.

Follow-up:

After a discussion on banned books, it is fun to have students select a banned book that they have read and take their picture with their book (similar to the ALA READ posters). It works best to have students schedule a time within a specified time period for their photo, and it's important to do this while the discussion and the topic are fresh. These photographs can be displayed on a bulletin board with a catchy saying (e.g., GOT BOOKS?). A bulletin board with student photos is always a hit!

Lesson Plan Created by

Patricia Kearnes

High School English Teacher

Park County School District #1

Powell, Wyoming

Intellectual Freedom Advocacy Unit Lesson Plan

Title of Unit: "To Ban or Not to Ban–Censorship, Critical Reading, and Persuasive Speech"

AASL Standards for the 21st Century Learner (2007)

Learners Use Skills, Resources and Tools to:

STANDARD 1: Inquire, Think Critically, and Gain Knowledge

(Skills: 1.1.1, 1.1.3, 1.1.4, 1.1.5, 1.1.6, 1.1.7, 1.1.8, 1.1.9)

STANDARD 2: Draw Conclusions, Make Informed Decisions, Apply Knowledge to New Situations, and Create New Knowledge

(Skills: 2.1.1, 2.1.2, 2.1.4, 2.1.5)

STANDARD 3: Share Knowledge and Participate Ethically and Productively As Members of Our Democratic Society

(Skills: 3.1.1, 3.1.2, 3.1.3, 3.1.4, 3.1.5)

STANDARD 4: Pursue Personal and Aesthetic Growth

(Skills: 4.1.3, 4.1.4, 4.1.7)

Source: American Association of School Librarians, "Standards for the 21st Century Learner, 2007." The standards are available for download at the AASL website.

Grade Level for Activity: 11th Grade English

Student Novels:

I Know Why the Caged Bird Sings (Angelou)	*Black Boy* (Wright)
Go Tell It on the Mountain (Baldwin)	*Deliverance* (Dickey)
Snow Falling on Cedars (Guterson)	*The Bluest Eye* (Morrison)
The Things They Carried (O'Brien)	*The Bell Jar* (Plath)
One Flew over the Cuckoo's Nest (Kesey)	*The Color Purple* (Walker)
Catcher in the Rye (Salinger)	*Fahrenheit 451* (Bradbury)
The Adventures of Huckleberry Finn (Twain)	*Slaughterhouse Five* (Vonnegut)
The Grapes of Wrath (Steinbeck)	

Instructions to Students:

All of these novels have been banned or challenged in certain school districts and deal with potentially controversial topics. None of the books are banned in our school district. These books have been chosen because each one of them is a good choice for inclusion in the eleventh grade curriculum.

Student Journals: Students will read a book and complete five required journals on (1) plot, (2) theme, (3) characters, (4) the author, and (5) literary criticism. Each journal entry must be a minimum of one *full* page. Students also take notes while doing research.

The Presentation: All students will present the results of their reading and critical analysis of the book at a mock school board hearing explaining why the book should be banned and why the book should not be banned from the English curriculum. This presentation should have a serious tone and be in good taste. This unit requires not only literary maturity but also social maturity. Group members, along with the class, will cast a vote to include the novel in the eleventh-grade curriculum, include the novel in the school library, and/or ban the novel from either or both situations.

Library Resources:

Valued print reference sets include the four-volume Banned Books series published by Facts on File including book titles suppressed on political, religious, social, and sexual grounds and individual titles from the Harold Bloom series Modern Critical Interpretations published by Chelsea House. Students are introduced to Contemporary Literary Criticism published by Gale, Twayne's United States Author series, and Scribner's American Writers series. Students also use the Gale online literature databases Contemporary Literary Criticism Select and the Discovering Collection. The instructor and the library media specialist use the American Library Association Office for Intellectual Freedom resources on censorship as background information (http://www.ala.org/oif).

Activities:

1. After the library media specialist and the English teacher select the books, students are introduced to each novel, choose their books, and begin reading.

2. The library media specialist lectures for two days on the First Amendment, censorship, recent challenges, and reconsideration procedures.

3. The students spend four class periods in the library reading about the literary attributes of the novels, the authors, and the censorship histories. They take notes on their research and write five specific journals.

4. Every book is presented in a mock school board hearing lasting 20–30 minutes each where students explain why the novel is valued and why it is controversial, ending with a vote to include the novel in the eleventh-grade curriculum, include the novel in the school library, and/or ban the novel from either or both situations.

	English Teacher	Library Media Specialist
Advanced Preparation	Select and find copies of each of the novels that will be read.	Help select the books by checking on challenges and literary criticism for each book. Advise on reading level and availability.
Day 1	Sample Presentation Introduce and select novels Distribute unit handouts	
Day 2	Distribute novels/start reading Check reading levels/content	
Day 5	Discuss journal assignments Reinforce preparation for the presentation	
Day 6		**Lecture/discussion of censorship** a. First Amendment b. Terminology (censor, challenge, ban) c. ALA list of ten most challenged books of the year. Discuss reasons why books were challenged.
Day 7		**Lecture/discussion of censorship** a. Highlights of several important cases including *Board of Education v. Pico* and *Case v. Unified School District* involving *Annie on My Mind* b. Local school district policies for acquisitions and reconsiderations.
Day 9		**Author Information** Library media specialist highlights the major sources for author information including online and print resources. Discuss importance of currency and accuracy.
Day 10		**Literary Criticism** Library media specialist defines literary criticism and introduces the major online and print sources.
Day 11		**Censorship History** Library media specialist highlights the major print and online sources on censorship history of the novels. Also highlights the role of bias in many sources.
Day 12	Library Work Day	Assist students with finding materials
Days 13-15	Group preparation in library/ dress rehearsal	Assist students who are having difficulty
Day 16-20	Presentations/voting on each novel	Assist in evaluation of the unit

Figure D-2. Instructional Roles. (Created by Kristine Larson Brown and Elizabeth Kara Glaaser.)

Evaluation:

The teacher evaluates the groups on their school board presentations. Group members also evaluate each other. The teacher grades journals and research notes after the presentations. Behavior while researching, presenting, and listening is also included in the unit grade.

Follow-up:

Students will continue to develop expertise in literary criticism during their senior year when they must find, read, and critique literary criticism of novels and poems. They also learn to write literary criticism of their own. We believe that these skills are fundamental to success in college.

Lesson Plan Created by

Kristine Larson Brown   Elizabeth Kara Glaaser

Library Media Specialist   English 11 Teacher

Madison Metropolitan School District   Madison Metropolitan School District

Madison, Wisconsin   Madison, Wisconsin

Index

librarians. *See* library media specialists
library access, 175–76, 177–85, 188–90,
194, 195, 217–18. *See also* disabled students, physical access to libraries; students: access to information
library automation systems, 91–93
Library Bill of Rights (American Library
Association), 2–3, 10, 11, 43, 60, 101,
175, 227; interpretations, 55, 76, 103,
135, 169, 176, 195, 222
library materials, 37; access, 65 (*see also*
students, access to information);
administrative intervention, 51–52; disability orientation of, 189; policy communication, 44–45; rating of, 113;
restricted, 64–66; selection concerns,
52–54; selection objectives, 39–42, 66–
67; selection policy, 37–39, 40–41, 43–
45, 46–49, 54, 206; selection procedure, 42, 114, 131; selection resources,
55–56; selection responsibility, 39–40,
41–42; reconsideration process, 43–44,
114. *See also* budget; collection age
library media program goals, 66–67
library media specialists: absence of, 73–
74; administrative intervention, 51–52;
advice, 114; censorship and, 10, 109,
111 (*see also* censorship challenges;
censorship, self-); collaboration with
parents, 70–73, 213–15; confidentiality
policy, 97–99; disabled students and,
178–85; economic considerations, 68–
69, 73–75; intellectual freedom advocacy, 5–6, 7, 11, 134, 2–1, 202–206,
208–22; Internet and, 144–46, 149–53,
157–58, 159, 160–62, 163, 166–68; job
security, 132–34; library materials
selection, 39–40, 41–42 (*see also* library
materials); media relations, 130–31;
personal censorship stories, 111–14,
115, 125–26, 128, 129–30; personal stories and disabled students, 182–85,
193–94; policy implementation, 44–45,
46; principals and, 128–30, 145,
204–205; in private school, 18;
responsibility of privacy, 81–84, 84–87,
89, 91, 100–101; student reading,
60–64; teachers and, 205–207, 211.

See also censorship challenges; library
records; privacy; privacy advocacy
training; Radio Frequency
Identification (RFID) technology
library records, 79, 102; access to, 81;
disclosure of, 80–86; disclosure
penalties, 81; laws, 80–82, 82–84;
principal requests and, 84–86;
retention policy, 99–100. *See also*
privacy
library website access, 192–93
life skills students, 193–94
Livingston Organization for Values in
Education (LOVE), 121
Lynch, Debra M., 175

Mazer, Harry, 233
McDonald, Frances Beck, 61, 109
McMillan, Laura Smith, 47
McNichol, Sarah, 61
media, 113, 130–31, 135, 210
middle and high school student privacy,
88–91, 102
Minarcini v. Strongsville (Ohio), 34–35, 60
*Monteiro v. Tempe Union High School Dis-
trict*, 31
Morse v. Frederick, 29
MS magazine, 60
multicultural resources, 53
multilingual resources, 52–53
Muslim community, 9–10

National Association of the Advance-
ment of Colored People (NAACP),
8–9
National Coalition Against Censorship
(NCAC), 230
National Council for Social Studies
(NCSC), 5
National Council of Teachers of English
(NCTE), 230
National Library Service for the Blind
and Physically Handicapped, 189–90
National School Board Association
(NSBA), 164
Neighborhood Children's Internet
Protection Act (NCIPA), 22–23,
141–42, 144, 168

About the Author

HELEN R. ADAMS is a retired school library media specialist from Wisconsin. She is a past president of the American Association of School Librarians, has previously published books with Libraries Unlimited, and is currently teaching an online course on intellectual freedom issues for Mansfield University.

EDUCATIONAL RESOURCE CENTER
COLLEGE OF EDUCATION & HUMAN SERVICES
WRIGHT STATE UNIVERSITY